Divine ProVision™

Book One
of the Divine ProVision™ Series

Divine ProVision™

Positioning God's Kings *for* Financial Conquest

By Dan Stratton
with Rich Vermillion

Paradigm™
Seed Publishers, Inc.
www.pspublishers.com

If you purchased this book without a cover, you need to be aware that it is likely a copy that was fraudulently reported to the publisher as unsold or destroyed. Consequently, you may have purchased stolen property since neither the publisher, nor the authors, have received any payment for this stripped book.

This publication has been written with the intention of providing competent and reliable information concerning the subject matter covered. Nevertheless, it is sold with the express understanding that neither the authors nor the publisher are engaged in rendering specific legal, financial, or other profession advice regarding the reader's specific situation and circumstances. Laws and professional practices differ from state to state and country to country in most instances. If legal, professional, or expert assistance is required, the services of a qualified professional should be sought in your area. The authors and publisher specifically deny and disclaim any liability, loss, or risk that is incurred as a consequence, directly or indirectly, of the application and use of the contents of this book.

Actual accounts are used within this book, based on the authors' own recollection of the events that occurred. However, many names have been changed or omitted and some details excluded or altered, for both educational purposes, and to protect the anonymity of other people involved. Any similarities of events herein described to the stories or testimonies of others not personally known to the authors are purely coincidental.

The leaf logo, Paradigm Seed Publishers, Inc. logo, and the Divine ProVision text and logo, are all trademarks of Paradigm Seed Publishers, Inc. of Fort Worth, TX (www.pspublishers.com).

"ProVision Network" and logo are trademarks of the ProVision Network of New York, NY (www.provisionnetwork.org).

NEW INTERNATIONAL READER'S VERSION® and NIrV® are registered trademarks of International Bible Society. Use of either trademark for the offering of goods or services requires the prior written consent of International Bible Society.

Unless otherwise stated, all Scripture citations are taken from the King James Version of the Bible.

All Scripture citations marked "NKJV" are taken from the New King James Version. Copyright © 1982 by Thomas Nelson, Inc. Used by permission. All rights reserved.

All Scripture citations marked "NIV" are taken from the HOLY BIBLE, NEW INTERNATIONAL VERSION®. Copyright © 1973, 1978, 1984 International Bible Society. Used by permission of Zondervan. All rights reserved.

Scripture citations marked "AMP" are taken from the Amplified® Bible, Copyright © 1954, 1958, 1962, 1964, 1965, 1987 by The Lockman Foundation Used by permission. (www.Lockman.org)

All Scripture citations marked "NAS" are taken from the NEW AMERICAN STANDARD BIBLE®, Copyright © 1960,1962,1963,1968,1971,1972,1973,1975,1977,1995 by The Lockman Foundation. Used by permission.

All Scripture citations marked "Message" are taken from The Message. Copyright © 1993, 1994, 1995, 1996, 2000, 2001, 2002. Used by permission of NavPress Publishing Group.

All Scripture quotations marked (NLT) are taken from the Holy Bible, New Living Translation, copyright © 1996, and all Scripture citations marked "TLB" are taken from The Living Bible, Copyright ©1971. Both are used by permission of Tyndale House Publishers, Inc., Wheaton, Illinois 60189. All rights reserved.

Scriptures marked as "(CEV)" are taken from the Contemporary English Version Copyright © 1995 by American Bible Society. Used by permission.

Scriptures marked NIrV® taken from the Holy Bible, NEW INTERNATIONAL READER'S VERSION®. Copyright © 1996, 1998 International Bible Society. All rights reserved throughout the world. Used by permission of International Bible Society.

Weymouth's New Testament (J. Clarke, 1909) is part of the Public Domain.

International Standard Book Numbers:
1-933141-00-X (case bound)
1-933141-01-8 (perfect bound)
1-933141-02-6 (e-book edition)

Copyright ©2005 by Daniel J. Stratton and J. Richard Vermillion II

All rights reserved. Written permission must be secured from the publisher to use or reproduce any part of this book, in any form, except for brief quotations in critical reviews or articles.

Published by Paradigm Seed Publishers, Inc. of Fort Worth, Texas

Transcriptions by Donna Vermillion • Cover design by Neal Brown and Rich Vermillion • Back cover photo of Dan Stratton by Jeff Pearce (www.go2-solutions.com)

This book is dedicated to all of the people in the Body of Christ that feel disconnected and left out. Remember, in God's eyes, there are no second-class citizens.

ACKNOWLEDGMENTS

We are all products of teachers and mentors. My mentors have been highly influential in my life. Some I have had very close contact with, while others have mentored me from their writings and their lessons from the pulpit. Whether from near or far, I express my sincere appreciation to all of you for what you have invested into my life.

Ann Stratton has been the biggest influence and I acknowledge her as the person who rescued me—and then trained me in the ways of a disciplined Christian life. Her childlike faith and her bold tenacity for what she believes is a constant inspiration to me. She is my wife, my friend and my lover. I thank God daily for her.

—Dan

• • • • • • • •

First, I want to thank my wife, Donna, for the untold hours she labored in transcriptions and editing of the text, the support she gave me when I, myself, was writing, and for being the perfect "help meet" in every way. Thank you for all that you are, and all that you do. I love and appreciate you, my sweet, more than words can express.

I want to thank Neal Brown, not only for providing me a phenomenal cover concept to adapt for this project, but for going "above and beyond the call of duty" to provide these things through much personal sacrifice. Thanks, brother. You are a faithful friend.

To Julie Ramaine at the ProVision Network headquarters, a great big "Thanks, Sis!" for being such a "backbone" of support…and for putting up with my abundant emails and phone calls.

To Jeff Pearce, you are not only the best web developer I know, but a tremendous photographer to boot! Thanks for some great shots of Dan.

I must thank Ken and Susan Aldhizer, Michael and Phylissia Allmond, Randy and Jessica Jewell, Susan Dollery, and my most awesome mother, Vivian, for their prayers and support. Without our "A-Team" standing with us, this would not have been possible.

Many other people contributed in various ways—too many to name. For you all, I express my love and appreciation for everything you have done to help or bless us in some way.

Finally, I want to thank my business mentor, Dan Stratton, for entrusting to me the honor of being both his publisher and co-author. I greatly appreciate you.

—Rich

ABOUT THE AUTHOR

Daniel J. Stratton has been a member of the Wall Street community since 1981—*initially* as a Yale-educated businessman with exceptional financial acumen, and today as a pastor with a vision for the spiritual future of New York City. He is the founder and Senior Pastor of Faith Exchange Fellowship in New York City, and the founder and president of the ProVision Network.

During his career as one of New York's top traders, Dan worked on the New York Commodity Exchange and secured seats on the New York Mercantile Exchange. He was also a bold witness for Christ in a place where faith was not openly discussed. He led Bible studies, wrote and distributed a weekly faith newsletter to his fellow traders, and led monthly "Spirit of Revival" meetings. Then, in the mid 1990s, Dan and his wife, Ann, heard God's call and obeyed—Dan left his lucrative career on the Exchanges, and they founded a ministry, which has grown into four parts:

- Faith Exchange Fellowship
- ProVision Network
- ChristTown
- The Freedom Center

Dan and Ann Stratton have followed God's guidance, resulting in Faith Exchange Fellowship's becoming a lighthouse of hope to a community struggling in the aftermath of the 9-11 attacks. Their boldly-stated mission is to vanquish the root of all evil (the love of money), to stand triumphant against all fear, to declare victory over grief as the city heals, to proclaim the only peace that lasts, and to declare and demonstrate to New York City that *love never fails*. The church community and its ministries are growing rapidly, and Dan continues to believe that nothing is impossible in Christ.

Pastors Dan and Ann Stratton regularly appear as guest speakers around the nation. Their television show, *Only Believe*, airs in New York and New Jersey, and Dan's radio show, *Your Best Year Yet*, is heard throughout the Tri-State area.

More information about Pastor Dan and his ministry is shared throughout the remainder of this book. Additionally, you can find more information online at www.provisionnetwork.org.

ABOUT THE CO-AUTHOR

Richard Vermillion is an ordained minister, public speaker, author, businessman, and the president of Paradigm Seed Publishers, Inc. of Fort Worth, Texas. However, he is personally most delighted with his relationship with the Lord Jesus, his marriage of over fifteen years to his wife, Donna, and the two children they enjoy together.

Rich began his formal business education as far back as high school with numerous business courses, and subsequently continued at Virginia Commonwealth University in Richmond, Virginia. He studied real estate at the Mosley-Flint Schools of Real Estate. He also has a certificate in *Business Leadership Skills* from Cornell University, which encompasses the curriculum of three other certificate programs: *Financial Management for Making Business Decisions*, *Studies in Proactive Leadership*, and *Strategic Leadership: Preparing for an Uncertain Future*.

In the marketplace, Rich's "kingly anointing" has been primarily manifested in the fields of sales and marketing, management, and various publishing-related endeavors. He is an active member of the ProVision Network.

As a minister, Rev. Vermillion has been ordained for nearly fifteen years and has served his Lord and the Body of Christ as both a pastor and traveling minister. Known for a dynamic pulpit ministry, his prophetic teaching style is confronting—yet full of humor and simple to comprehend.

Rich was previously published with his own autobiography, *White Man in a Black Man's World*, which will be revised and republished through Paradigm Seed Publishers, Inc. in 2006. He is currently co-authoring the *Divine ProVision* Series with his business mentor, Dan Stratton. Rich also has several other provocative co-author and solo works in process that will be forthcoming in 2006 and beyond.

To learn more about these and any other new title releases by Paradigm Seed Publishers, Inc., visit us at **www.pspublishers.com**.
Be sure to also join our e-mail list for advanced news and updates.

ENDORSEMENTS

Publisher's Note: With his diverse background, Dan Stratton integrates comfortably into a broad spectrum of Christian, Jewish, academic, and business settings. Consequently, his growing list of endorsements for *Divine ProVision* continue to attract submissions from people representing a wide array of cultural, religious, and professional backgrounds. Since Dan's message is one of *unity* regarding the Body of Christ, these accolades bear tremendous testimony that Pastor Dan is one who truly practices the love of God that he proclaims.

Finally! Someone in the Kingdom of God has successfully connected the dots between the leadership of the church and the faithful professionals in the world who attend those churches. Daniel Stratton has brilliantly defined the roles of kings, and priests—and why the two groups of people can corporately enjoy great benefits when their collective efforts and callings work in transparent unity.

Dan has marvelously interpreted the respective roles of those leaders in the work place and how they can better relate to the leaders in ministry, and vice versa. Dan understands the simple fact that both groups of people want to see the Church built up and enhanced. This is a must read for every pastor or teacher—as well as for everyone who loves the Lord and has a calling in the workplace outside of the ministry.

—*Richard M. Johnson*
Managing Director
Stanfield Capital Partners, LLC
www.stanfieldcp.com

Dan Stratton serves a major need in the body of Christ: teaching kings to be kings in their full capacity. I would recommend *Divine ProVision* to any Christian whose true heart lies in the battlefield of the marketplace. In my opinion, this is the Christian businessperson's handbook.

—*Steven Thompson*
Diamond Executive, Cyberwize
www. plousiosgroup.com

Dan Stratton is truly a man of vision. While most people see things after they happen, Dan sees things and then *makes* them happen.

Billions of people around the world are facing death without Jesus as their Lord and Savior. That is an *unacceptable* casualty rate. However, without the financial provisions in hand—THE MONEY—we can't do much about it. It's high time for the Body of Christ to wake up to the victory the Lord Jesus has provided for us financially and walk in the light of its power. Dan Stratton is a God-anointed man that is thoroughly qualified to lead us into the manifestation of that victory—so that we *can* reap the harvest of souls.

Read *Divine ProVision*. Immerse yourself in the Word of God and find its message in the pages of your own Bible. Then take *your* place in the Lord's end-time army.

—Dr. Kenneth Copeland
Best-selling author, Minister of the Gospel for over thirty years
Kenneth Copeland Ministries
www.kcm.org

If you find cookie-cutter, "always-be-sweet" Christian messages to be woefully inadequate for helping you discover your ministry callings, then this book is for you. In *Divine ProVision*, Pastor Dan Stratton clearly delineates kingly business callings from priestly five-fold callings, and motivates you to discover—and step into—the ministry offices which have been uniquely prepared for you. *Divine ProVision* will help challenge you to begin the liberating walk of discovering, and fully flowing, in your callings.

—Carol S. Barnes
Computer services, Small-business owner
Optimum Yield, Inc.
www.optimumyield.com

Every so often, a book is written that is like a magnificent recipe—it has the perfect blend of ingredients that makes it delicious to devour! Dan's book *Divine ProVision* is such a book. It has the ingredients of natural wisdom, divine insight into godly truths, good common sense, and foresight into things to come. It will teach you, encourage you, and awaken you to God's moving in financial arenas. Finally, it will stir your faith and vision for things you have in your heart. It's a must read!

—*Tim Burt*
Inventor, Associate Pastor of Living Word Christian Center
Formerly the President of American Infant Care Products
www.lwcc.org

If you know you are called by God to do something great, this book is for you. Dan not only tells you that you can do it, but that there is a way to walk it out. It's time to hitch up your pants and get to work. This book will teach you how, while at the same time provoking you to finish the race set before you—and win!

—*Matthew Deutsch*
Certified Public Accountant
Principal, The Deutsch Group, LLC, Chicago, IL
Formerly with PriceWaterhouseCoopers, NY, New York

A must read for any Christian already in business or looking to start a business! Dan Stratton's bold and truthful delivery of the uncompromised Word of God releases to his audience an anointed recipe for success - spiritually, physically, mentally, financially, and socially.

—*Terri E. Stingley*
Writer and creator of paper management organizers
www.KnowWhatsWhere.com

I found my place in the Body of Christ through Pastor Dan Stratton's new book, *Divine ProVision*. This book gives deep insight through biblical principles to the king's role. The vision of the ProVision Network outlined in the book is one that I found myself being drawn into. Finally, a book that includes the king's position in the Body of Christ and a vision on how to fulfill our place in the Kingdom!

—*Darwin German*
Commercial real estate investor and entrepreneur
www.DarwinGerman.com

TABLE OF CONTENTS

Foreword by Doug Wead 1
Foreword by Jesse Duplantis 3
Searching...(An Opening Thought) 5

PART I: ORIGINS
Dan Stratton: A Biography by Rich Vermillion 9

PART II: KINGS AND PRIESTS
1   Kings and Priests I: Fundamentals 35
2   Kings and Priests II: Examining the Kingdom 47
3   Kings and Priests III: Divine Order 61

PART III: LAYING THE PROPER FOUNDATION
4   Running with the Pros 69
5   Where It All Begins 77
6   The Source of True Peace 85
7   Words Become Things 91
8   What Moves You? 97
9   Getting Deeper 101
10   Exchange 115

PART IV: CHANGING YOUR PARADIGM
11   Southern Hospitality? 125
12   Acorn, Baby! 133
13   Me, a Pastor? 139

14	*Copy Cat Fever*	145
15	*Study the Experts*	149
16	*Sending Out Your Ship*	155
17	*No Pain…No Money!*	159
18	*Broadway Blunder*	165
19	*Preparing for Divine Appointments*	171
20	*The Flip Side of Freedom*	175
21	*Women Warriors*	183

PART V: PRACTICAL WISDOM

22	*The Importance of Transparency*	201
23	*Capacity*	207
24	*Zeal Without Knowledge*	215
25	*Naiveté*	223
26	*The Safety of Godly Counsel*	239
27	*Has Anybody Seen My Money?*	245

CONCLUSION:

"It Isn't Done" 251

Paradigm Resources 257

FOREWORD

by Doug Wead

I can wholeheartedly recommend *Divine ProVision* to any Christian serious about his or her finances—and in advancing the Kingdom of God in this Earth. Why? Because not only is the book itself an outstanding resource for the Body of Christ to digest, but Dan Stratton himself is the only person I know with enough credentials and chutzpah to pull it off.

As one who has personally known Dan for a number of years, I can confidently say that the delightful, yet concise, biography about this Wall Street mogul included at the opening of the book does not even begin to tell the entire story of this unique man. As one begins to delve into the pages of teaching that follow, however, a clearer picture of Dan's inimitable perspective and calling comes to light.

I can confidently say that any reader of this powerful text will be compelled to more aggressively pursue God's unique plan for his or her own life. The simple reason for this bold assertion is the fact that Dan's message causes you to understand your calling better than you ever have before! Whether your destiny is to be a "perfecting priest" or "conquering king"—or both—by means of these pages you will more quickly be able to discern your "predominate anointing" and find your place in the Body of Christ as a part of God's great plan for these last days.

Without question, *Divine ProVision* is a book

that you will do well to read repeatedly—and encourage others to do so as well. Every journey into its pages will yield new and richer fruit as the words paint an ever-clearer picture in your heart of the valiant conqueror in Christ you already are.

Publisher's Biographical Note: Possessing an obvious "kingly anointing" (see Part II, *Kings and Priests*), Doug Wead is an author, humanitarian and philanthropist. He has written 27 books that have sold 5 million copies in 30 languages. His titles include the best-sellers, *All the President's Children* and *The Raising of a President*.

Mr. Wead also served in the White House under President Ronald Reagan, and as Special Assistant to President George H. W. Bush. As a corporate speaker, he has spoken to audiences in coliseums and soccer stadiums on four continents, as well as to smaller assemblies in other venues. Readers can learn more about this dynamic man by visiting www.dougwead.com.

FOREWORD

by Jesse Duplantis

I have known Dan Stratton for many years now, and I highly recommend his book, *Divine ProVision*. It's a book that contains more than just financial information, like how to operate from day to day or invest. It's filled with *spiritual* concepts that I believe every minister, and every Christian for that matter, needs to understand and then, apply.

I was thoroughly blessed as I read this book because it's motivating! I like that it asks me questions. One of my favorites is in Chapter Eight when the book asks, "What moves *you*?" Instead of just something I was reading, the book was *talking* directly to me, drawing me in, and inspiring me. Dan asked me questions I might not have asked myself, and then motivated me to think higher thoughts—divine thoughts!

I believe that Dan has done a wonderful job in allowing the Holy Spirit to flow through him with these great nuggets of truth, and I know that you will enjoy reading and applying them. Of course, this book is humorous in a lot of ways, but it is also point-blank *blunt*, and I like that! Bluntness means that there is no misunderstanding, and to me, when you are dealing with provision—whether it's spiritual, physical, or financial—you have *got* to understand what you're doing!

Dan Stratton is a man who is on both sides of the track: both a minister of the Gospel, and a Wall Street man of substance. I believe that when you are finished reading his wonderful book, you will have gained spiritual concepts that you need to be a success in this life.

So get ready! You're about to crack open some great truths that will reveal your kingship and propel you into a place of *Divine ProVision*!

> **Publisher's Biographical Note**: Dr. Jesse Duplantis is a dynamic evangelist who has traveled throughout the world for over twenty-five years preaching the Gospel of Jesus Christ. He is the founder of Jesse Duplantis Ministries (JDM), which has its International Headquarters in America and additional offices in the United Kingdom and Australia.
>
> A best-selling author, Dr. Duplantis' books have been translated into thirteen languages, including Braille, and are impacting millions of lives all over the world. In addition, his television broadcast is reaching millions through major television networks in the United States—including ABC, NBC, CBS, TBN, Daystar and World Harvest Television. His program is also broadcast internationally throughout Australia, Central America, South America, the Caribbean, Europe, the United Kingdom, Israel, and the Middle East.
>
> Dr. Jesse Duplantis is known throughout the world for his joy and his exuberant, evangelistic spirit. Possessing a tremendous "priestly anointing" (see Part II, *Kings and Priests*), this true evangelist/revivalist is impacting the world for Jesus Christ. For more information about this renowned man and his ministry, visit **www.jdm.org**.

SEARCHING...
(AN OPENING THOUGHT)

My throat was sore and I could feel that after the close of the market, I would be spitting blood once again because of all the screaming I had to do that day. Still, it was not time to take a break or even lose my focus. It was one of those rare occasions where I had "lifted a leg" on a quantity of oil, and having missed my opportunity to lock in my profit, I stood praying for direction. Out of my spirit came my measured and practiced mantra, "If the devil can't steal my joy, he can't steal my goods."

There it was. BANG!

"Buy 'em!" I yelled as I lifted 200 Crude Oil May Futures—before any sign of buying came into the pit from across the ring. I was down $10,000 and long...and riding the bull that I knew in my spirit was coming—and, of course, it did.

Jesus (in Hebrew, Yahshua) is Lord and He is alive! This is a truth that Christians and Messianic Jews everywhere embrace. Yet, there is also a mandate that He has laid down to every believer— we are to 'Go into all the world and declare the good news." Resources are required in order for His people to adequately fulfill this directive. Without money, this job is simply not going to get done.

He is the KING OF KINGS, and His Kingdom is one with rules and rewards. I have seen His anointing in the markets of New York as a trader and as a pastor. After many years of learning the world's system—and now His system in the

by Dan Stratton

world—I have come to know that there is a real contest being waged, and only the prepared man or woman will get the spoils. He who wields his faith with wisdom and with boldness will take his rightful place in God's plan. I have been called to find such men and women and help them to position themselves for the greatest move of God that the earth has ever seen. Are you one of them?

PART I
ORIGINS

"God has things in store for you that you cannot even imagine! All you have to do is expand your thinking to *see* the opportunities He has provided around you—and *seize* them when they come."

—Yahshua—

Jesus—The Way, The Truth, and The Life.

"I came that they may have and enjoy life, and have it in abundance (to the full, till it overflows)."

(John 10:10b, Amplified)

DAN STRATTON:
A BIOGRAPHY

Anyone who ponders the story of the humble origins of Dan Stratton will most certainly be amazed by his ability to achieve the goals that he has striven to reach. Against all odds, he was recruited by Yale University and later became an accomplished Wall Street businessman and millionaire who owned seats on various New York exchanges. Today, he is a Christian pastor in the heart of New York's Financial District, a traveling minister with invitations to speak around the world, and the founder of a growing Christian business network.

Who is this unique man? More importantly, what does he have to say to the rest of us? What wisdom can he share with the Church universal that will further prosper the business people, investors and aspiring entrepreneurs, while uniting these "kings" with the visions God has given His ministers to spread the Gospel around the world?

In this chapter we will continue to briefly explore the phenomenal life story of Dan Stratton to provide a foundation for the God-given wisdom contained in the subsequent chapters. We will take only a synoptic look at the events that shaped his character and world-view in order to introduce Dan to those who may not be familiar with his inspiring testimony. By first understanding his story, you will better appreciate both his revelation and its application to your own life.

by Rich Vermillion

MODEST BEGINNINGS

"In order for me to accept and ultimately live out what God had placed in my heart," said Dan, "I had to first overcome my small-town mentality. The firstborn of six children, I was born in a little town called Cottage Grove, Minnesota, which is a suburb of St. Paul. My parents were married when they were eighteen years old, and about twelve months later I was born. At nineteen my dad already had to work two jobs, and by the time he was twenty-five, my parents had five children. Because I was the oldest I did not get hand-me-downs, but all my siblings did. I grew up very, very modestly.

"Up until the time came for me to go to college, no one else in my family had ever progressed past the high school level of education. My dad was a silk-screen printer, and my mom was a homemaker and would also clean other people's homes for extra money—in the midst of raising five kids!"

When Dan was about fourteen years old, his father suffered a debilitating injury in an industrial accident that kept him out of work for the better part of two years. As a result, the Stratton family found themselves in a situation of having to live on food stamps just to survive. Dan's mother spent even more time out of the home, cleaning houses to supply some form of income.

About four years later, the time came for young Dan Stratton to go to college. He had managed to graduate high school as an accomplished student and stellar athlete, despite the hardships he and his family had endured at home. However, family funds were still quite tight, to say the least.

His father had only barely begun to work again. After about a two-year struggle to rehabilitate himself somewhat from the effects of the accident, Mr. Stratton had returned to work again. He had only scratched the surface in trying to reverse the financial effects of the catastrophe during the period in which Dan was graduating from high school. Consequently, when Dan was looking toward attending college, his parents did not have the financial resources in and of themselves to make it happen. But what seemed to be impossible began to unfold as an attainable reality in Dan's life.

Dan recalled, "In all my seventeen years, I had never ridden in an airplane, and I had only been in three states. I had gone to Illinois one time to play baseball, but other than that my travels only brought me to Wisconsin and Minnesota. The only people I knew who had ever been anywhere far away were my uncles who had been overseas on tours of duty in the armed services.

"There was not a lot of ethnic diversity where I lived. My town was made up of Lutherans and Catholics, and I had never even met a Jewish person. There was not anyone there who could not speak English. I can only remember knowing two African-American children who attended my high school. Needless to say, my experience was extremely limited. It was not that I was sheltered; it was just that there was not a great deal of cultural variety on my back doorstep."

"BIG BIRD" GOES TO YALE

Since Dan was an accomplished high school athlete, recruiters from several colleges came to interview him and to see if they could draft him to be a part of their school's football program. While being pursued by these scouts, he was also receiving literature from colleges and universities from around the nation soliciting him to join their campuses.

The cumulative input from these sources began to paint a picture on the inside of Dan—that of a larger life than what he had been accustomed to. The prospect of getting to travel, even just a little bit, was very exciting. Dreams began to form on the inside of him, and he began to take the limitations off of his mind and thinking, and to believe he could do something greater.

Princeton University had requested a film of one of his high school football games, and through yet unknown circumstances, the coach at Yale University was able to view this film as well. The Yale coach quickly called Dan and began to work with him to overcome all the obstacles that were facing the Stratton family in Dan's decision to attend college.

When the news spread that one of the coaches from Yale University had come to town to recruit him, everybody in Dan's family and social circle was just "hysterical" over the fact that one of the most expensive universities in the country had come to visit the poor Stratton family. There had never been any person in the Stratton family—or his mother's—who had ever gone to any college or university. He was not even aware of any other person from his high school ever even mentioning the Ivy League level of schools…much less attend one. And yet there, in the kitchen of their little home, was the defensive line coach, Dave Kelly, from Yale University telling his parents that it was possible for their son to attend one of the finest schools in the world.

"It was above and beyond my comprehension," Dan recollected. "He started talking about the different ways that we could finance my schooling, and it really opened up my eyes. I could have allowed the enormity of the situation to have scared and choked me because of all the possibilities for failure. In fact, my friends had been immediately disqualifying themselves at the thought of attending such a school because they did not think they could afford it. But I didn't let that deter me, and I took courage in what he shared with us...and something good happened! And you know what? Something good could happen to you, too—if you do not ever disqualify yourself from an opportunity or blessing."

Accordingly, Dan took courage and applied to these schools—despite the fact that everybody around him was telling him not to. Concerning this Dan commented, "But my philosophy was, 'You know, I *could* get in. Something good *could* happen. What do I have to lose? Why do I have to take the negative approach? Something good could happen to me. Other kids do it and succeed; why can't I?'"

Throughout all of his adventures and challenges, there was something on the inside of Dan that pulled on him—a calling toward something greater than what anyone in his family and hometown could comprehend. It was an inward conviction that would simply not let him quit, despite the obstacles and adversity.

As a result, Dan was accepted to Yale University and began to make preparations to attend. He recalled, "I remember graduating from high school in 1977, and heading off to Yale with only $500 in my pocket. My dad gave me the $500—which to him was a huge amount of money. Since we were used to surviving off of very little, we both actually thought that $500 was enough money to go to college on! I had no idea of the expenses such as the tuition, books, and room and board. Boy, did I get a shock later on!

"My not-so-wealthy economic status was not the only thing that made me 'stand out' in the crowd I was about to be a part of. I went to Yale University in the 1970's—the days of platform shoes. I wore my blond hair halfway down my back," Dan recalled with a smile. "It was the days of John Travolta. Where I had attended high school in Minnesota, everyone on our basketball team was at least six foot, two, and yet they would wear these platform shoes that would make them stand about seven feet tall! I was about six feet, three inches barefooted, so with my shoes on I was about six feet, seven. Everybody was wearing those shoes *back home*! But then...I went to Yale."

Dan Stratton: A Biography

On his first day of school at this prestigious university, there was a gathering scheduled for all the incoming freshmen in one of the majestic Yale buildings. "This place had oak walls and twenty-foot ceilings," Dan recalled. "They had fireplaces so large that I could stand in them (as long as I was not wearing my platform shoes). This place was so nice that I truly wanted to wear my best. So as I was flipping through my clothes, I settled on my light blue 'John Travolta' suit, my dark blue polyester shirt (it was 'in' back then), and my burgundy five-inch heels." No doubt, Dan's long blond hair was the perfect complement!

Dan continued, "I had been recruited by the school to come out and play quarterback for the team. Here I was walking across campus toward this meeting. Now, keep in mind, I had grown up in public schools and had come from nothing. It was only my first day at Yale, and I had about $375 left in my pocket. I still had not come into culture shock yet. I was thinking, 'Oh, this is going to be great. I'm dressed up.' I was feeling like John Travolta walking through Time Square, except I was walking through the campus of Yale up in New Haven! I was feeling so good about myself that I wasn't really paying attention to my surroundings. I failed to notice how everyone I walked past was dressed. I did not even notice all the clean-cut students who were walking around looking like they 'had it together.'

"So I got to the door. (I was a little bit late because my flight had been delayed.) I opened the door and stepped into this room full of blue blazers, wool pants, and short haircuts. Every eye in the place turned and looked at me, and in my mind I could hear everybody saying, 'It's Big Bird!' I knew what everybody was thinking, 'You shouldn't be here. You must be the quarterback on the football team!' Right away, they judged me and tried to categorize me into a box.

"Maybe you have tried to put other people in a box in the opposite way by giving excuses about why they were successful and you, seemingly, were not. Some have said, 'Oh that Dan, he was born on third base; he was born with a silver spoon in his mouth. That's why he was able to do so well on Wall Street.' That is not the case at all. If you want to be successful, you have to do like I did. Develop a mind-set of, 'I don't care if you call me 'Big Bird.' I don't care if I never took an advanced placement course. I am going to succeed anyway!'

"To this day, I don't even know what my SAT scores were! The other students at Yale would frequently ask me about my SAT scores. I didn't know what they were because where I grew up, we didn't even know we were supposed to take them! It might be funny now, but it sure wasn't back then. However, I became determined that no one was going to tell me what I could NOT do. Say this out loud, 'Nobody is going to tell me what I can't do!'"

BEEN THERE, DONE THAT

Despite the common misconceptions people have had about Dan's background, he really does know what it is like to have nothing. Yet, Dan persevered to the point of having nearly everything he ever wanted and overcame those adversities. However, the financial prosperity he would later achieve did not happen during his time attending Yale.

On the contrary, nearly the entire time he attended the Ivy League institution, Dan was on the verge of running out of money. He never knew from month to month whether he would come short of tuition and end up having to drop out of school. Every day, when he went to the school cafeteria to get a meal, he would go with fear and trepidation as to whether he would be on the "list" of students that could eat that day…or not.

Dan did everything he knew to do to keep the bills paid so that he could stay in school (and eat)! He worked at the nearby hospital doing some bookkeeping; he did some work at another cafeteria down the street to earn some additional money—all this, while attending school full time and playing quarterback for the football team. Since these were the days before ATM machines and internet banking, Dan had no way of knowing if the money he had earned working these jobs was being properly transferred to the school or not.

Every single day this went on. For Dan, the daily fear of being rejected at the door of the school cafeteria for being behind in tuition payments was worse than being actually turned away! "In fact, the real heart of this constant terror was the anxiety of whether somebody would find out how poor I really was," Dan confided.

Do you know what that is like? Do you live in a constant fear of being "discovered" as the broke person your finances tell you that you are? If so, take comfort. As Dan can attest, "I have 'been there, done that, got the T-shirt'—only I then burned the lousy thing so that I would not have it hanging on me all my life! If I overcame my fears and the barriers to my success, you can too!"

TWO SUITS

Although he did not yet know the saving grace of God, Dan Stratton was no doubt greatly helped by his Creator. Miraculously, he managed to make it through all four years at Yale. After the commencement ceremony in 1981, he moved to New York City—without anything to his name to speak of. There he began applying for jobs in the Financial District of this great city—on Wall Street itself. However, there were still a few complications for Dan to overcome...

"I didn't even have any business clothes!" said Dan. "I had no money and no job—and you need a suit to get a job on Wall Street! It was ridiculous that I was even down there at all. However, I did not let that stop me from going to Yale, and I certainly was not going to let it keep me from getting a good job either!" It was simply another obstacle that would soon be overcome.

Someone who took an interest in his courageous audacity was compelled to purchase for Dan two suits. Armed with the fruit of their generosity, Dan "attacked" Wall Street looking for his new employer. This provides us with another great lesson we can all learn from Pastor Dan's personal experience: *When you are willing to believe that you can accomplish something, somebody else will decide to invest in you and see if you can get it done!*

Two suits may not sound like much, but it was enough! All he needed was some decent business attire to afford him the opportunity to land a well-paying Wall Street career—and the Lord faithfully provided not only the suits, but also the job. Similar things on a much larger scale were in store for Dan later in life—especially once he became intimately acquainted with the One Who had been sustaining him throughout his journey.

WALL STREET INVASION

On August 3, 1981, he began working for J. Aron and Company—which is now both a Fortune 500 and a Global 500 company, as a part of Goldman Sachs. Transacting business around the world with precious metal commodities—primarily gold and platinum—J. Aron and Company is the primary supplier of these two metals to the U.S. Mint, as well as to many others internationally.

To anyone who truly considers the magnitude of gaining such first-time employment, the very thought that someone with his meager beginnings could get a job as a commodities trader for such a prestigious firm is nothing short of ridiculous. Yet it happened! "Big Bird" not only went to Yale, he miraculously landed a job working for one of the most esteemed commodity trading companies in the world! (Howbeit, no longer sporting his "John Travolta" suits.)

From within this commodities conglomerate, Dan's financial affluence—and knowledge—really began to accelerate. While learning from inside the world's most powerful financial center—Wall Street—businessman Dan was well on his way to success.

In 1982, J. Aron and Company was acquired by Goldman Sachs and became a wholly-owned subsidiary of one of the leading (and largest) financial firms in the world, specializing in the areas of investment banking, securities, and investment management. As is so common when one company is swallowed up into another, policies changed, promises were broken, and the contributions Dan had made to the overall organization became almost forgotten—lost in the shuffle. The transitions and changes that occurred in being absorbed into Goldman Sachs increasingly resulted in Dan's receiving what he considered a "raw deal." However, what would ultimately be the catalyst for his departure from the world's most highly respected financial institution would also eventually become the "opportunity of a lifetime" for this young American capitalist—still only in his twenties.

"During the process of the company reorganization, I eventually found myself having to part with Goldman Sachs—although I was not happy about how it took place. We cannot always control what situations happen to us, but we can certainly control how we *react* to them. Will we turn them to our advantage, or simply get mad and sulk for the next six months? I was certainly quite ticked off, but I was also contemplating my next move. I was turning my negative into a positive."

In those days, Dan was playing semi-pro football in addition to working on Wall Street. That night after he left Goldman Sachs, he was taking out his frustrations on other players at practice:

"I was a pretty big guy...a good athlete...so I was having a good time just beating up on everybody I could on the field."

The owner of the team called him over to the bench and said, "Okay Dan, you're done for the night."

"Why? What did I do?"

The owner replied, "Well, you are definitely in some mood tonight! With all that anger, I don't want you to hurt someone out there."

"Yeah," Dan said, "I felt like that deal today was pretty unfair. I made the company a lot of money, and they didn't give me the bonus I wanted. Some other things happened as well…so we parted ways."

He replied, "So, what do you want to do?"

Dan answered, "Man, I am going to build an operation to compete with them!"

"Oh yeah?" the team owner said, "So how much money are you going to need?"

"All I need is about a million bucks." (Dan was just answering his questions thinking this was just a simple conversation between two guys.)

The owner said, "Really? About a million bucks…how are you going to set it up?"

"Well, I'm going to hire a firm in Chicago; I'll set myself up here in New York since it is only a three- or four-person operation. All we need is a million dollars sitting there in the bank (it would only be at risk for a certain length of time). We made a lot of money for the company last year; so I figure that without their assets, and only a million bucks, I could probably give about a fifty-percent return to anybody who gave me that money to start with."

"Oh, really? You would give a fifty-percent return on that money?" The team owner inquired.

"Yeah, the way I've got this thing figured out I should be able to do that and still make payroll and get a decent income the first year to build on," Dan answered.

He said, "You can start Monday—I'll back you!"

You see, even though Dan had no idea the team's owner was seriously inquiring when he asked him those questions, Dan had enough confidence in himself to answer the questions rather than simply brushing them off. Furthermore, "Dan the Money Man" (as he would later be nicknamed by a close friend) had actually thought through those questions already—so he had bona fide answers to give the guy when he asked.

When he left Goldman Sachs, he did not go off somewhere to simply "lick his sores" like some wounded animal, but rather contemplated what he wanted to do next, and constructed a basic strategy to get it accomplished. So, when the right person asked the right questions—Dan had the right answers!

As Dan put it, "I thought we were just talking! But, as a result of that conversation, I found myself at twenty-four years old...on Wall Street...in business for myself!"

> "Whatever your hand finds to do, do it with all your might, for in the grave, where you are going, there is neither working nor planning nor knowledge nor wisdom. I have seen something else under the sun: **The race is not to the swift or the battle to the strong, nor does food come to the wise or wealth to the brilliant or favor to the learned; but time and chance happen to them all. Moreover, no man knows when his hour will come...**"
>
> (Ecclesiastes 9:10-12a, NIV, emphasis added)

From this passage of Scripture above, and Dan's personal testimony as recounted in these pages, one truth can be clearly discerned: God has things in store for you that you cannot even imagine! All you have to do is expand your thinking to see the opportunities He has provided around you—and *seize* them when they come.

Someone might complain, "Sure! It would be easy to start a company with a million dollars handed to you like that! But, I live in the real world! Things are not so easy for the rest of us!"

My friend, you can be assured that even with such a "golden egg" laid in Dan Stratton's lap that day, making a success with his new Wall Street investment firm was no "cakewalk." The million-dollar "bankroll" was not for investment funds to be spent—rather it was primarily needed to provide the capital required to meet the Exchange's minimum criteria for a company to get access to the trading pits. That money, as Dan told the team's owner it would, literally "sat in the bank" as Dan built his company's financial foundation. In fact, during those early days as an arbitrageur, Dan often had to find creative ways to come up with additional funds to use for investment capital in the trading pits of the Exchange.

Consequently, even with a "million bucks" dropped on him as he sat on the sidelines of a football field, Dan still had to apply himself with great perseverance in order to see his goals and dreams fulfilled. The same confidence and diligence that earned Dan Stratton favor with this new financial backer were also the same character traits that allowed him to follow through with that windfall, and become a successful businessman.

PREACHER IN THE PIT

By 1984 Dan had advanced in his Wall Street career to the point that he was now experiencing some of the "fruits" of his labor. He started to think about expanding his firm's investment exposure and began to look around the Financial District for other prospects. One day, Dan took a walk down Wall Street to the New York Futures Exchange looking for that new trading opportunity. As a result of what he found there, he purchased a seat on the Futures Exchange and began investing in those markets as well.

Established now in both the Commodities and Futures Exchanges, Dan's growing enterprise was reaping from the confidence and hard work that it had been established upon. However, the One who had given Dan the grace to accomplish all these things—despite Dan's ignorance of Him—was about to claim His rightful place in this young man's life.

A few weeks later, on October 21, 1984, Dan Stratton gave his life to the Lord Jesus Christ at Redeeming Love Christian Center in Teaneck, New Jersey—which had been the church home of his fiancée, Ann Difiore, for the previous three years. Dan began to attend faithfully and regularly with his lovely future bride, and he grew rapidly in the things of the Lord and in the knowledge of His Word.

After experiencing the New Birth of salvation through Jesus Christ, Dan began to take his newfound faith and growing understanding of God's Word down to the trading floors of the Exchange—with the same boldness that he had used to become a successful arbitrageur. The commitment he had made to the Lordship of Jesus Christ in his life was, to Dan, also a commitment to be a witness for Him wherever he went. However, there in the heart of New York City's Financial District, those who were so grossly immersed in the "love of money" did not take kindly to his new message.

"Preacher Dan" in the Financial District of New York City (Circa 1995)

"The persecution I experienced at Yale was nothing compared to the battles I endured there in New York as a Christian commodities trader," Dan recalls. "Although most of my preaching now takes place in my home church, where I am the pastor, and in churches across the country, my ministry did not start off in such a preacher-friendly environment.

"I did not learn to preach in a nice little church, where the congregation kindly looked at me and cheered me on. My ministerial training came through preaching on the hostile floor of the commodities exchanges, in what is commonly known as 'the pit.' When I preached the gospel there, the people were cussing at me, calling me names, and cursing God. If I even messed up for a second with a facial expression, they would remind me of it for weeks to come. My point is that I learned to preach in an environment in which I could not expect much *positive reinforcement* to come back. Through it all, I learned that my divine assignment was not going to be a bed of roses."

One notable act of persecution took place in November of 1984, when Dan brought his fiancée Ann down to the floor of the Commodity Exchanges. "Because of the powerful ministry of intercession that had developed in her, I thought it would be good to take her to the heart of where demonic forces were working to control the wealth of the world," explained Dan.

"I have seen things going on down there that were nothing short of manifested demonic spiritual activity. Therefore, it seemed logical to me at the time to take Ann there to do some praying against the enemy's schemes. I mean, with so much spiritual warfare happening from the devil's forces there in the midst of the Exchanges, where else should you take a 'prayer warrior' to combat it?

"When we arrived, Ann began to pray and to bind the spirits that were there. In almost no time at all, it seemed the entire attention of the demonic forces there were on my little tiny Ann. Things started happening quickly as the devil realized his 'territory' had been invaded. We actually were assaulted both physically and verbally by another trader as he shouted, 'Get her off the floor! Who brought her on the floor? Get her out of here!'

"On another occasion some years later, I took a couple of nationally known ministers, with whom I had become acquainted, to see what was going on down there. When one of them began to quietly pray—again, all hell broke loose! Traders often have 'nicknames' on the floor that they go by during trading. One such arbitrageur's badge actually read, 'Satan.' Immediately he seemed to *know* by some means that something unusual was going on in the Exchange—and he quickly traced it somehow to my minister guests. He began to shout and protest their presence on the trading floor. As the other traders became aware of his outbreak, they began to shout, 'Satan objects! Satan objects!'"

Let me assure you that, in fact, Satan does object whenever people of faith get down in the Exchange Pits and begin to use the authority of Jesus' Name against his filthy schemes.

Keep in mind also that Dan was not in violation of any rule or ordinance by having Ann and these ministers on the Exchange floor during trading hours. These individuals had been properly cleared through the necessary security channels and had permission for the access they were initially enjoying. Visitors were quite common in the "pits" to observe the workings of the Exchanges—prior to 9-11. But Holy Spirit-filled believers who were praying against the schemes of the enemy? That was NOT commonplace, neither was it welcomed by those under the sway of the enemy's foul influence.

It was in that environment of animosity, persecution, and outright hatred that Dan's ministerial grooming took place. So, do Dan's feelings get hurt when, while he is boldly preaching the Word of God (New York-style) in a church, someone sours up and gets offended?

"Actually," Dan would respond, "it does not bother me at all. If a screaming foul-mouthed trader, full of the devil, attacking me in the 'pit' could not shake me from my calling, then a prune-faced Christian certainly will not either." Amen.

CHANGING CIRCUMSTANCES

As 1985 progressed, informal spiritual discussions and Bible studies began to crop up around Dan because of his activities there on behalf of his Savior. People were drawn to his steadfast Christian witness...and they began to have questions. This gave Dan an excellent opportunity both to share Truth with them, and to grow in his own gifting as a minister of God's Word.

Dan and Ann Stratton (2004)

In the beginning of October, Dan's life took an even greater turn for the better. On October 6, 1985, Dan and Ann Stratton were covenanted together in the bond of marriage at their home church, Redeeming Love Christian Center. His lovely fiancée had finally become his beautiful bride, and he stepped into a new domestic chapter of his life. However, just a few weeks later,

Dan's new partner in life would hear news about her husband that neither one of them particularly wanted to hear.

On the 27th of that same month, Dan saw a doctor who told Ann that her husband was in extreme danger with an embolism in his leg and could die. (How would you like to hear that a few weeks after your honeymoon?) Dan was told by his doctor to "stay off the leg, take blood thinners," and that he should "quit his job and never eat red meat again"—not a good way to finish a busy month!

Fortunately, God had bigger plans for Dan and Ann's lives together than the doctor's report would have indicated. Dan never had to quit his job (which is good since he owned the company), and God saw to it that his leg was completely healed—and still is to this day. God was continuing to reward the Strattons' faith and faithfulness with His manifested grace on their behalf—something He longs to do for *all* His children...if they will only believe:

> "And Jesus said, [You say to Me], 'If You can do anything?' [Why,] all things can be (are possible) to him who believes!"
>
> (Mark 9:23, AMP)

Dan, Ann, and Danielle Stratton
(Photo by David Ebmeier, 2005)

God worked another miracle for the Strattons a few years later. Doctors told Ann that she could not have children—another report that neither she nor Dan were willing to accept. Consequently, they immersed themselves in God's Word and embraced the promises of YHWH. Agreeing in prayer, they mixed some necessary marital "works" with their faith (James 2:14-24) and expected to see the power of God manifested. In October of 1992, Ann gave birth to their beautiful daughter, Danielle Grace. Once again, *Jehovah Jireh*—the Lord our Provider—showed Himself strong on their behalf.

A CALL TO MORE

In May of 1986, Dan Stratton began to foresee the need for some type of business network geared toward uniting Christian business people with each other—and the multitude of churches and ministries who would benefit from their financial support. What is often dubbed the "prosperity message" was spreading rapidly across the nation, and Dan perceived that a "balancing piece" was needed to bring this revelation into a practical application.

YHWH (the actual proper Name of God, which He told to Moses in Exodus 3:13-15) did not want His own children to suffer lack—Dan knew that. However, he also knew that the principle of God's loving grace in material abundance being taught by these honest ministers was lacking something: the necessary business and financial elements to bring the full manifestation of this grace into the earth for His people. As an accomplished businessman and investor, Dan had seen and experienced powerful biblical truths that "normal" ministers had not.

One night, in the parking lot after a choir rehearsal, Dan had a very deep discussion with another Christian businessman, Mark Van Mater, concerning the concept that would later evolve into the ProVision Network. Standing there that night, the Lord birthed something within this Wall Street millionaire, and he began to see his own calling in an entirely new light. Things began to change in Dan's life from that day, and God has since been faithful to complete the work in this man which He alone had begun.

On April 27, 1987, God confirmed Dan's call to the Exchanges and downtown New York by blessing him with an absolutely phenomenal trading day—with over $500,000 profit. This unusual wind of the Holy Spirit on that day caused a continued "windfall" which ultimately resulted in his best trading year to that date. As Dan himself said, "God was moving in my life, and I knew I was where He wanted me."

Just a few months later in November, Dan became a full member of the New York Futures Exchange. Then again, in May of 1989, God blessed him to become a member of the Coffee, Sugar, and Cocoa Exchange. And again, in January of 1991, YHWH Himself opened up the door for Dan to join the membership of the New York Mercantile Exchange. Now that Dan had the power of God's Spirit working with him in his business labors, the increase was no longer just gradual—it was supernatural.

God had brought Dan Stratton a long way through the years. From his blue-collar family home back in Minnesota, to Yale University, to Wall Street, and now pastoring and traveling throughout the world as a minister of the Gospel. The "kingly" anointing of a businessman and investor was now being augmented by a five-fold ministry "priestly" anointing as well.

DELIVERED, NOT DEAD!

On February 26, 1993, Dan was scheduled to board a plane with his wife, Ann, on a trip out of state. Because their flight was not until just after 1 p.m., Dan had decided to go into work to his offices at the World Trade Center to get some business done the first half of the day. He was pleased to get out of the house and get down to the office for a few hours before they headed off that afternoon together.

As he traveled his way down to the Financial District, Dan was impressed on the inside, "Go home and help your wife pack." Dan had no intentions of doing that since he was delighted that he had a great excuse *not* to help with the packing. Furthermore, he kept thinking to himself, "The Lord would never tell me to not go to work. Diligence in labor is a biblical precept—so this just must be the devil trying to deceive me and keep me from doing my job!" However, the impression kept coming to him over and over as he traveled to the office—on the inside of him, not from the outside as he first assumed.

World Trade Center Towers
(Photo by David Ebmeier, 2000)

Finally, Dan said, "Lord, that has to be You because the devil would *never* try to get me to do something to bless my wife, so—whatever Your reason is—I am going home to help her out!" Turning his car around, he headed back home and surprised Ann with his arrival to assist her in the packing. He later received a surprise himself, once he found out what happened only six parking spots away from his reserved space in the parking garage under Tower One.

Dan had originally planned to leave his office about noon to meet his wife at the airport for their trip. At 12:17 p.m., about the time Dan would have been starting his car to leave, a van containing explosive materials was detonated by terrorists in an attempt to collapse Tower One into Tower Two and destroy the World Trade Center.

This first attack was not successful, however, and remarkably only six people perished in this blast. This was despite the fact that sodium cyanide was included within the explosives to murder thousands more through the ventilation system, should the Tower collapse strategy fail. Nevertheless, according to Wikipedia.org, the blast was so powerful that it blew open a thirty-meter-wide hole through four sublevels of concrete.

Given the intensity of the explosion, six parking spaces of distance would have been insufficient to protect Dan from the effects of this first terrorist attack on the World Trade Center. Dan Stratton confidently affirms today that if he had not listened to the Holy Spirit's direction to simply go and help his wife pack—he would have undoubtedly been victim number seven. Disobedience to the leading of the Holy Spirit in this instance would have proven fatal. The lesson Dan learned through this experience would later provide a foundation for equipping other believers to avoid a very similar tragedy several years later.

THE BIRTH OF PROVISION

In 1995, Dan and his team began a series of Bible studies in the Stratton home. His goal was to teach solid biblical principles to help the professionals and business people in his congregation and community to achieve their best and highest potential in their vocations. Initially named the "Breakthrough Bible Study," this business-oriented gathering would eventually evolve into what is now known as the ProVision Network (PVN) by 1997.

In January of 1999, a conviction formed in Dan's heart during a minister's conference in Texas that the time had come to retire from full-time trading and to devote his attention to the church and the development of the ProVision Network. As the year developed, many ProVision Network chapters were added, Dan's traveling schedule expanded widely, and adjustments had to be made.

Dan went from a seven-figure annual income as an active pit trader, to living off of his investment income and offerings only. Although he retained millionaire status, the sudden disappearance of that seven-figure income meant some significant changes would have to occur in how things were done in the Stratton household—and some of them were not easy to make.

Nevertheless, the Strattons began to flow with the realities of the new season they were now in. Yes, the transition to only a ministry-based income is often a sacrificial test for any family that is called to do so... even for millionaires.

HEBREW HAPPENINGS

In the late 1990's, Dan began to perceive a drawing from the Lord toward the original language of the Bible—and what many consider the original language *period*. As the calendar began its transition into the new millennium, Pastor Dan Stratton could be found delving into concordances and lexicons in his effort to mine the treasures of this rich tongue.

His efforts to explore Hebrew eventually lead him to study under the tutelage of two rabbis in the New York City area. Nevertheless, Dan is quick to inform others that he does not yet consider himself a genuine "expert" on the language, since he does not study it from the perspective of learning to *speak* the dialect. Rather, he is a *student-scholar* whose primary goal is to be able to *read* the Scripture in its original form while plunging the depths of meaning contained within individual Hebrew words and letters. He wants to understand the roots of the New Testament revelation about *Yahshua* (Jesus' actual name, in Hebrew—often spelled "Yeshua" by Messianic Jews), which is found within the Old Testament revelation that foretold His coming. Realizing that Yahshua was (and still is) a Jew has opened up volumes of revelation for this New York pastor—insights that are extremely relevant for us today.

These truths not only opened up his understanding into the richness of the Bible from cover to cover (both Old and New Covenants), but it also opened up doors of opportunities not commonly afforded to Christian pastors.

For example, some of Dan's writings made their way into the hands of some prominent Jewish leaders, and in them they discovered a man who not only had a passion for the Hebrew language of their heritage, but also for the Land of the Bible where they—and our Lord—had their affections. In the year of 2001, a relationship developed between Dan and the Israeli Consulate there in New York City. He was subsequently invited to participate in a select—and strategic—small group of Christian and Jewish leaders who met at the Consulate to discuss and pray for Israel, which he did for about a year. This all happened because of his divinely inspired affection for the Hebrew tongue.

Furthermore, Dan's church, Faith Exchange Fellowship (FEF), has benefited tremendously from their pastor's love of this ancient idiom. His increasingly powerful teaching has opened up glorious and practical insights regarding the New Covenant not often seen by many Christians unfamiliar with their Jewish roots. Additionally, a noticeable number of Jewish Messianic believers have joined their congregation—people who have embraced Yahshua as their Messiah. Some even came to that place of trust through FEF's own services and outreaches—attracted by Dan's message of a Jewish Jesus. Furthermore, even some Muslims have come to know the Savior. "We can understand a Jewish Messiah," some have said. "So we want to receive the Yahshua you preach as *our* Lord too."

Thus, those who visit the Freedom Center in New York City where FEF holds its services can see and experience a manifestation of the vivid reality found in the book of Ephesians:

> "But now in Christ Jesus, you who once were [so] far away, through (by, in) the blood of Christ have been brought near. For He is [Himself] our peace (our bond of unity and harmony). He has made us both [Jew and Gentile] one [body], and has broken down (destroyed, abolished) the hostile dividing wall between us, by abolishing in His [own crucified] flesh the enmity [caused by] the Law with its decrees and ordinances [which He annulled]; that He from the two might create in Himself one new man [one new quality of humanity out of the two], so making peace. And [He designed] to reconcile to God both [Jew and Gentile, united] in a single body by means of His cross, thereby killing the mutual enmity and bringing the feud to an end. And He came and preached the glad tidings of peace to you who were afar off and [peace] to those who were near."
>
> (Ephesians 2:13-17, AMP)

Regardless of the origin of the individuals (whether Jews or Gentiles), God has made a way for all nations to know His saving grace, and to fellowship with Him and each other through His Messiah. Though the congregation of Faith Exchange Fellowship is comprised of people of all sorts of nationalities, varying colors, and different ethnic origins, they will all tell you the same thing: Yahshua (Jesus) is Lord. (For more information about this dynamic church, visit **www.faithexchange.org**.)

THE YEAR EVERYTHING CHANGED

The year 2001 began with a strong impression from the Lord for Dan to begin teaching his congregation how to hear and obey the voice of the Lord. He obeyed. The Lord also began to deal with Pastor Dan about taking a more proactive approach to the discipleship of individual leaders in his congregation, and adding accountability standards to both the church and ProVision Network. As a result, some "sifting" took place in both organizations, and several PVN chapters were closed in the subsequent pruning. As the year progressed, Dan found that the reduction in his schedule's workload would prove to be extremely important.

On September 10th, Dan was overcome with a spirit of intercession for the church. He wept in prayer as intercession poured out of his mouth in other tongues…for hours upon hours. "Maybe it is because of so-and-so's situation," Dan told his wife—referring to a young woman whose husband had tragically died prematurely only days before. "But, I just can't stop crying!" He continued to pray.

The next day, on September 11, 2001, terrorists hijacked passenger jet aircrafts early in the morning. These madmen crashed the airplanes into a field in Pennsylvania, the Pentagon in Washington, D.C., and the World Trade Center in New York City—directly across the street from the building that housed Faith Exchange Fellowship and the offices of the ProVision Network.

That morning Dan was at an early meeting elsewhere in New York City when he received a phone call that, "a plane has hit the towers." With an overwhelming conviction that rose in his spirit, he tried to get downtown only to be told by the cabbies, "I am not going any further." He diverted his route to his second appointment at the apartment of a Christian brother with a view of the Twin Towers. They began to earnestly intercede for the people in the World Trade Center area when they were suddenly impressed to pray for "the towers to stand"—which they prayed.

Despite the eventual collapse of the Twin Towers, they stood longer than the engineers predicted they could under such circumstances—and just long enough for most of the people to escape. Subsequently, many phone calls were made to locate members of the church and friends, and people were helped in getting home from wherever they were stranded.

Miraculously, although about 80% of the congregation of Faith Exchange Fellowship either worked in that area or traveled through the World Trade Center on their way to work, no lives were lost, nor injuries occurred—even among their families! Over the days to come, testimony after testimony would come in of how people either heard the voice of the Lord directing them to safety, or how miraculous circumstances prevented them from being in harm's way.

THE PROVOCATEUR

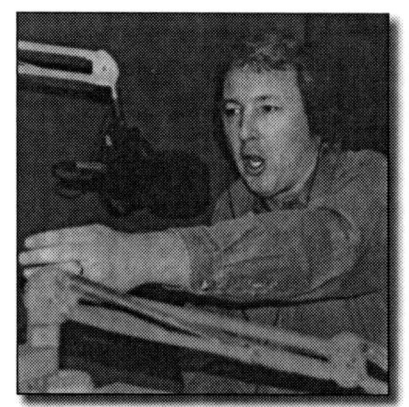

Dan on the radio
(Circa 1999)

Today, Dan Stratton travels the world ministering in churches and conferences, large and small. He and his wife, Ann, are continuing to serve the congregation the Lord used them to found, Faith Exchange Fellowship. In their new facilities located in downtown New York City, as well as at their second location in North Brunswick, New Jersey, this powerful group of believers is making a difference in the communities they serve.

The ProVision Network also continues to grow around the world as the Lord persists in blessing this unique ministry through open doors and new opportunities. Fresh relationships are formed almost daily as the ministry enhances its organizational complexity and further expands its member resources. (Additional information about the ProVision Network will be detailed in Chapter Four, as well as sporadically throughout the remainder of *Divine ProVision*. Up-to-date information can also be found on their web site at www.provisionnetwork.org.)

Regardless of which avenue Dan uses in sharing the Word of God through his unique anointing, you will find yourself provoked to self-betterment. Those of us within the ProVision Network have begun to affectionately call him "The Provocateur" because of his uncanny ability to motivate people to action. Of course, some people do not like being challenged. Some have actually been hostile toward Dan when he has dared them to abandon their excuses and come up to a higher level in their lives, businesses, and professions.

Book signing—CBA Convention in Denver, CO
(Photo by Kim Garrison, 2005)

One notable example is found in a woman who was tremendously obese at the time she first heard Dan minister. With tears in her eyes she came up after the service and literally punched him in the stomach (not to his harm, mind you) and said, "Who are YOU to tell me to reawaken my dream?!" She had come to the place where she had reasoned herself into accepting the limitations she had place on her own life. Suppressing her dreams and drowning her sorrow with food, she had developed an artificial comfort zone—until Dan came to town. After hearing his teaching, and the testimonies of other ProVision Network members, she was provoked to anger by the painful awakening of her ambitions.

However, about four months later when Dan next saw her, she was nearly one hundred pounds lighter. Furthermore, she had enrolled back into college to finish her degree, and had established a budget for her finances. Her dreams had begun the process of emerging as realities in her life—all because someone dared to provoke her to become something greater.

Dan with his co-author, Rich Vermillion (CBA Convention, 2005)

When I think of this woman and the many others who could testify similarly, I cannot help but hear the heart of God in the midst of their testimonies. His plan for us is greater than we have even dared to imagine—so should we not pursue that plan? Many would shout a resounding "yes" to that question...but do they like being provoked to excellence by someone who has been there? None of us do. Nevertheless, the wise appreciate the reproof rather than judging its source.

Provocateur. What an appropriate word to describe Dan Stratton. Synonyms include: an agitator, disrupter, firebrand, goad, instigator, revolutionary, zealot. Dan is all of these and more to those of us who enjoy and appreciate his leadership in our lives. Of course, Dan is extremely respectful of those in authority wherever he ministers—do not misunderstand me at all in that point. What I am expressing to you is the fact that we all need someone in our lives to *agitate* us out of our comfort zones, *disrupt* our meager agendas, be a *firebrand* that awakens us to action and *goads* us on to excellence in our endeavors, and who *instigates* a clarion call through a *revolutionary* application of God's Word—as a *zealot* for His will being done in our lives!

Dan is "The Provocateur" who can get the job done—that is if you decide to listen and be provoked to greatness. Provocation can be a very positive thing if you accept the "iron sharpens iron" principle of Proverbs 27:17. However, not everyone does. Those of us who have joined the ProVision Network enjoy Dan's teaching—especially when he is confrontational in his delivery. We would rather be corrected than to prove that we are "right." Since Dan has tread the dangerous marshes of commerce and economic conquest before many of us, we would prefer to receive his perspective on these hazards rather than becoming mired in the quicksands of our own opinions. Furthermore, his congregation is quick to express similar sentiments regarding his teachings ministered to them on a pastoral level—some of which golden wisdom "nuggets" find their way into our PVN meetings as well.

Thus, as you press forward into the Dan's teaching within the remainder of this volume, I can assure you that an even clearer picture of this man and his message should become evident to your perception as we journey together. As we do, expect to be provoked and encouraged to press forward into the call of God on your life—regardless of what that call may be. With the basis of the foregoing biography in mind, we will now move on to explore the uncommon revelation of this man, and allow his own thoughts to illuminate the portions of his story which I purposely left unrevealed in the preceding pages.

The four chapters that immediately follow this biography were derived through a collaborative process whereby Dan and I worked to construct a suitable foundation for the outstanding teaching contained in the remaining portions of *Divine ProVision*. Most of the subsequent chapters have been derived primarily from transcriptions of several of Pastor Dan's teachings on tape. Brimming with fascinating personal narratives, they have been edited and enhanced—organized and expanded—in order to convey the essence of his ministry and message...with his peculiar New York flavor essentially uncut and replete.

And now, without further ado, let us delve into the wisdom of my own mentor and friend. Prepare yourself now for some powerful insights into God's truth—communicated *Dan Stratton style*.

Dallas, Texas ProVision Meeting
(Photo by Jeff Pearce, 2005)

PART II

KINGS AND PRIESTS

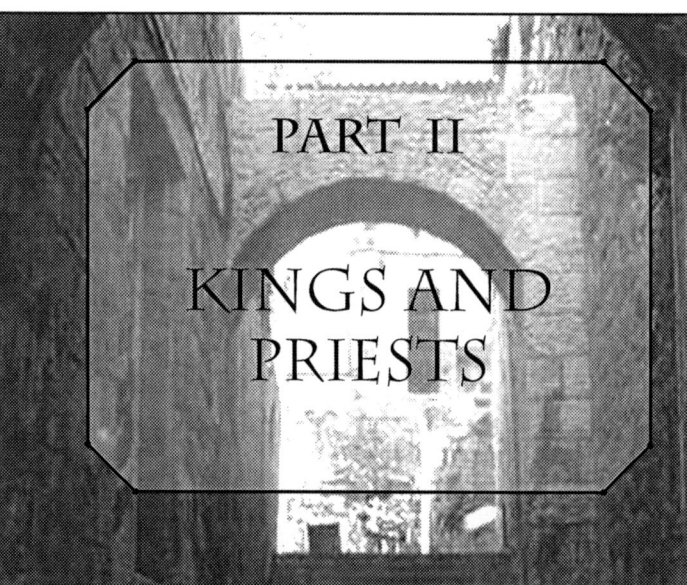

"The proper king/priest relationship must be understood by both parties in these last days, because neither one is complete without the other. Remember, ministers *perfect* and kings *conquer*. It is a symbiotic relationship that God intends to use to spread His Kingdom throughout the world."

—Yahshua—

Jesus—The Way, The Truth, and The Life.

"I came that they may have and enjoy life, and have it in abundance (to the full, till it overflows)."

(John 10:10b, Amplified)

KINGS AND PRIESTS I: FUNDAMENTALS

Without a doubt, one of the great truths that needs to be taught and understood in the Body of Christ is the fact that all believers are ordained by God to be both kings and priests:

> "And from Jesus Christ, who is the faithful witness, and the first begotten of the dead, and the prince of the kings of the earth. Unto him that loved us, and washed us from our sins in his own blood, and hath made us kings and priests unto God and his Father; to him be glory and dominion for ever and ever. Amen."
>
> (Revelation 1:5-6)

Such understanding is crucial to your success in life as a believer—for without it you cannot truly fathom God's calling and purpose on your life. Apart from understanding who you are in the Anointed Savior, Yahshua (Jesus), you will always be unable to fully grasp what great plans God has in store for your future. Furthermore, without a fundamental knowledge of this truth, you will be sorely handicapped in understanding the revelation that I will be sharing with you in the chapters to come.

As I travel around the country, I find that there

is an awesome need for believers to realize that God has anointed them to do what He has called *them* to do. God's gifts and grace abound toward *every* believer (not only those who minister in the pulpit) to do specific jobs here on the earth. The questions that need to be asked are, "What has He called and anointed me to do now?" and "What are His plans for my future?" The answers to these related questions can be more easily discovered if you first understand that there is both a priestly and kingly calling in your personal destiny, and then ascertain whether one or the other anointing predominates your life.

What does the scripture indicate when it calls us kings? It is certain that God has not ordained us to run around here on Earth with royal robes and scepters barking out orders to bewildered strangers on the street. How about priests? No, you do not need to go buy a "clergy collar" and chase your neighbors down to offer them communion either.

Let me take you on a short, guided tour of the Scriptures to expand your thinking beyond religious stereotypes, and into comprehending these dual callings that abide upon all of us that name the Name of the Lord as our Master. Then you will be better equipped to recognize which one is the stronger anointing on you, and therefore, how to identify and cooperate with His plan for your life.

A CERTAIN TRUTH

Lost among centuries of religious traditions and man-made doctrines are the realities of our "royal priesthood." This truth was lost during the time period known as the Dark Ages, and then was partially regained when the Reformation brought forth the revelation of the priesthood of the believer. However, even today, these principles have gone by the wayside in many religious circles—and the kingship of God's children has largely gone unnoticed. God has predetermined us to walk in an exalted status here on the Earth as "kings and priests" as we exercise authority in the Name of Jesus. Consider for a moment a few additional passages that identify our calling:

> "And they sang a new song: 'You are worthy to take the scroll and to open its seals, because you were slain, and with your blood you purchased men for God from every tribe and language and people and nation. You have made them to be **a kingdom and priests** to serve our God, and they will reign on the

Kings and Priests I: Fundamentals

earth.'"

(Revelation 5:9-10, NIV, emphasis added)

Did you notice that it said, "They will reign on the earth"? Obviously, this is not talking about Heaven. Neither is it exclusively referring to the Millennial Reign of Christ, when we will be ruling with Jesus for one thousand years over the nations of the earth (although it does include that) for Peter said:

> "But you are a chosen people, **a royal priesthood**, a holy nation, a people belonging to God, that you may declare the praises of him who called you out of darkness into his wonderful light."
>
> (1 Peter 2:9, NIV, emphasis added)

Notice in the passage above that you ARE a chosen people—a royal priesthood. Peter, who walked and talked with Jesus Himself before and after His crucifixion, said that we already are royalty (kings) and members of a divinely established priesthood. Most certainly, we will be reigning with our Lord over the nations of the earth during His Millennial Reign. However, our Savior is already "LORD OF LORDS, and KING OF KINGS" (See 1 Timothy 6:15; Revelation 17:14 & 19:16.) This is not a title that Jesus will have one day in the future—He is already King and Lord NOW.

Who then are the kings and lords Jesus is ruling over? Are they the unbelievers who are in leadership around the world?

No. Those who do not know Him are obviously quite reluctant to submit to His rule and authority. The "kings" and "lords" over which Jesus reigns are those who have confessed Him as their Lord and King—the believers…the Body of Christ…the royal priesthood.

Much can be said concerning the priestly and kingly functions of every believer. My purpose here in this chapter, however, is not to give you a complete theological discourse on the royal priesthood. Rather, I have two purposes:

The first is to note the basic principles of the "royal priesthood" of all believers so that there will be no unnecessary confusion about what I believe and teach among my fellow ministers—and readers.

And the second is to then take you into the deeper understanding of how I specifically use these terms to refer to those with predominant "kingly" or "priestly" anointings.

Once I get your thinking lined up with the basic tenets of these principles in this chapter, I will continue to expound upon them throughout the rest of this book. However, first, let me give you an "overview" of the royal priesthood as it applies to every believer.

BASIC FUNCTIONS

Now, when you think of the word "priest," do not allow your mind to conjure up an image from your religious background or experience. Don't let the picture of a minister with a clergy collar fog your interpretation of what God means by "priest." With all respect to my Catholic and Episcopalian brethren (whom I love very much and among whom I have many friends), I have to point out that the New Testament never uses the word "priest" with such liturgical significance regarding Christians. What then are our priestly duties as believers?

> "Be joyful always; pray continually; give thanks in all circumstances, for this is God's will for you in Christ Jesus."
>
> (1 Thessalonians 5:16-18, NIV)

All Christians are called by YHWH to spiritual services such as prayer, worship, thanksgiving, and practical acts of service on behalf of our God toward others. It should be of no surprise to any believer that God expects him (or her) to pray, read his Bible, and fellowship with others in private and public settings. Furthermore, it should not be a "shock" to anyone that God would expect His people to actively participate in praise and worship on Sunday morning (or whichever day your church meets) and serve Him within that ministry with their finances, prayers, and acts of service.

This basic universal comprehension of our duties as believers actually falls under the category of our "priestly" service before God. Additionally, this priestly function of our calling contains what the Bible calls, "the ministry of reconciliation:"

> "Therefore, if anyone is in Christ, he is a new creation; the old has gone, the new has come! All this is from God, who reconciled us to himself through Christ and gave us the ministry of reconciliation: that God was reconciling the world to himself in Christ, not counting men's sins against them. And he has committed to us the message of reconciliation. We

are therefore Christ's ambassadors, as though God were making his appeal through us. We implore you on Christ's behalf: Be reconciled to God. God made him who had no sin to be sin for us, so that in him we might become the righteousness of God."

(2 Corinthians 5:17-21 NIV)

Every person who has been reconciled to God through faith in His Son is commissioned by God to share the good news with others that they may be reconciled as well. In other words, personal evangelism is a part of every believer's priestly function in God's Kingdom. As priests under our High Priest (Yahshua—Jesus) we need to be winning souls for God. Sowing the Word of God and reaping salvations in our families, communities and work places are vital parts of our priestly duties—and great fun as well.

Beyond those already mentioned, we can say that nearly every aspect of our personal devotion before God is also a part of our priestly ministry. In fact, I think it can best be summed up by simply defining our personal roles as "priests" before God as a combination of the following:

- Our personal devotion as Christians to our Heavenly Father, especially in the home.
- Our ministry on His behalf to those who do not know Jesus.
- Our individual service towards Him regarding the Body of Christ, including service within our local churches and towards each other.

What about kings? Kingship, by necessity, involves rule and authority. God has endowed every believer with awesome authority in the Name of Jesus through his birth into the family of kings—the Body of Christ. Just consider for a moment the "power promises" of dominion that Jesus Himself promised those who would follow Him:

"Behold! I have given you authority and power to trample upon serpents and scorpions, and [physical and mental strength and ability] over all the power that the enemy [possesses]; and nothing shall in any way harm you."

(Luke 10:19, AMP)

"And Jesus answering saith unto them, 'Have faith in God.'" [Or, as many Bible column references read,

"Have the faith of God"] "'For verily I say unto you, That whosoever shall say unto this mountain, "Be thou removed, and be thou cast into the sea;" and shall not doubt in his heart, but shall believe that those things which he saith shall come to pass; he shall have whatsoever he saith.'"

(Mark 11:22-23)

"He said to them, 'Go into all the world and preach the good news to all creation. Whoever believes and is baptized will be saved, but whoever does not believe will be condemned. And these signs will accompany those who believe: In my name they will drive out demons; they will speak in new tongues; they will pick up snakes with their hands; and when they drink deadly poison, it will not hurt them at all; they will place their hands on sick people, and they will get well.'"

(Mark 16:15-18, NIV)

Kings have dominion. Dominion over the entire universe is inherent in the Name of Jesus. Since all Christians have been given the authority of His Name, we have the dominion of kings under our King—Jesus Himself. Again, seeing as He is the King of kings, we who have confessed Him as our Lord must be the kings He is King of.

Therefore, let me reiterate:

Every believer is called to be a priest before God.

Every believer is called to be a king before his King.

However, there are various degrees of anointing as "kings" and "priests."

Whenever you come to one of my meetings or listen to one of my tapes, you will hear me talking about kings and priests. Whenever you pick up one of my books, or read an article I have published, I will nearly always have some reference to one or both of these offices in the "royal priesthood." However, I am rarely referring to the priesthood or kingship of every believer when I do. Rather, I am generally talking about those who have the predominant callings and anointings in one or both of these ministries. Specifically, I am generally either referring to the five-fold minister "priests" of the Church, or the warrior "kings" God has placed in the marketplaces, governments and public arenas of the world to take territory for the Kingdom.

PREDOMINANT ANOINTING

As a believer, you need to determine if you have a dominant anointing in one or both of these areas. You must by necessity ask, "Where does my primary anointing lie?"

Those who have a dominant anointing in the "priestly" capacity may be working within the Body of Christ as a worship leader, musician, prayer counselor, or some other "ministerial" function to edify the Church. However, the primary examples of those who have the "priestly" anointing dominating their life's calling are those who operate in one or more of the following five-fold ministry offices: apostle, prophet, evangelist, pastor, and teacher. These "vocational ministers" are those to whom I am specifically referring when I mention "priests."

When I refer to "kings," however, I am talking about those whose predominant anointing lies in advancing the Kingdom of God in the workplace, government, education, business and the marketplaces of the world. These "full-time warriors" are the ones I am primarily called and equipped to identify, train, and empower. These are the ones I am referring to when I talk about the kings of the Kingdom.

Of course some, like me, have a dual call to operate within both realms. However, generally there will be only one predominant anointing manifest in a Christian's life—and if there is one, you must identify which one it is if you are to flow with God's destiny for your future. Vocational "priests" make lousy "kings," and warrior "kings" tend to slaughter sheep. Unless you are anointed in that area—do not cause problems in the Kingdom (and your own life) by venturing there.

Let me note also that neither of the two callings is more intrinsically valuable than the other, for both are necessary to advance the purposes of YHWH in the earth. Each has its own specific purpose, anointing, and calling to express the Person and ministry of Jesus to the Body of Christ and the world. Moreover, *no believer*—regardless of his position, title, financial status, calling, or fame—is considered by God to be any better than another:

> "Moreover, [no new requirements were made] by those who were reputed to be something—though what was their individual position and whether they

really were of importance or not makes no difference to me; God is not impressed with the positions that men hold and He is not partial and recognizes no external distinctions..."

(Galatians 2:6a, AMP)

Those of us with "larger" callings, who have been entrusted with greater assets, anointings and influence, simply have a greater responsibility before God. We are all in this game together—and we must all play together as a team to exercise the victory that YHWH has already given us. After all, we win, so let's play—but let us do it together, and in our own lane.

So, when I mention "kings," I am referring primarily to those with a vocational call to the workplace, business, sports, education, government, etc.—whether male or female—who have been gifted by God to excel in such arenas. I am talking about Christian leaders in the marketplaces of the world. If that describes you, then you are one of those kings.

Of course, much of what applies to kings on the larger scale concerning their dominant anointing will apply also to every believer on a smaller scale. The principles I share in this chapter, and throughout the book, universally apply to every believer in that sense. Nonetheless, I want to clarify that in this particular book, I am actually referring to "vocational" kings, since they are the ones to whom I am primarily called to minister in the topics covered.

Let me illustrate further by pointing out a few well-known kings of this "vocational" nature. These are Christians who are in places of high rank and great influence in their fields (some of them are aware of the Kingdom of God's conflict with that of Satan, and others are not):

Mel Gibson is an example of a gifted king in the film industry.

George W. Bush is an anointed king in government and politics—the most powerful one in the U.S. today, I might add.

One whose name may not be as well-known: Pat Gelsinger, who is the Senior Vice-President and Chief Technology Officer at Intel Corporation, is an example of a king in the corporate world.

Now that we have covered kingly examples, let me share with you that there are outstanding examples of "vocational priests" as well. Of course, hopefully your pastor is truly called of God to be one, and therefore would serve as an example of one with a dominant priestly anointing. Some examples of those in the Kingdom who wear the priestly mantle are: Oral Roberts, Charles Stanley, Billy Graham, Pat Robertson, Jerry Falwell,

Joyce Meyer, T.D. Jakes, Kenneth Copeland, Creflo Dollar, and others.

Now, I specifically chose to name these "priests" above because they also serve as leaders to many kings through their ministries. YHWH has always used anointed men and women to give guidance and direction to the kings throughout Scripture—sometimes even rebuke and correction. Consider the ministries of Elijah, Elisha, Deborah, and Nathan the prophet, for instance. However, the most notable thing about the leaders I named above, and many more like them, is the fact that they are learning to launch and release the kings of God to impact the communities and industries within their spheres of influence.

Kings need priests to perfect them so they can do the work of their kingly ministry with the character of Christ (Ephesians 4:11-15). By the same token, priests need kings to bring in the spoils of combat to fund the Gospel—and to provide practical knowledge and skills in the fields of their expertise that it might advance the Gospel. To put it simply: We need each other. I will share more along these lines shortly, but for now, let us build upon this foundation and take a closer look at what it means to be a king...

CHARACTERISTICS OF KINGS

We need to stop looking at ourselves and each other according to the natural eye. We must quit judging the Body of Christ in light of our religious upbringing. If we are to become the army of the Lord in these final days, then we must abandon our earthly perspective of things. This involves ascertaining from God's Word what He considers the army of the Lord to be—and then adopting that image into our thinking:

> "They run like mighty men; they climb the wall like men of war. They march each one [straight ahead] on his ways, and they do not break their ranks. Neither does one thrust upon another; they walk every one in his path. And they burst through and upon the weapons, yet they are not wounded and do not change their course. They leap upon the city; they run upon the wall; they climb up on and into the houses; they enter in at the windows like a thief. The earth quakes before them; the heavens tremble. The sun and the moon are darkened and the stars withdraw their shining. And the Lord utters His voice before His army, for His host is very great, and

[they are] strong and powerful who execute [God's] word. For the day of the Lord is great and very terrible, and who can endure it?"

(Joel 2:7-11, AMP)

The army of the Lord is strong and mighty. Who are His soldiers? Those who hear the voice of the Lord and do his bidding are His army.

His is a military force of kings—warrior kings who have a taste for battle and an ear open to their Master. Invading the territory of the enemy, these kings conquer darkness both to win souls and gather the wealth of this world for the Kingdom of Light.

What an honor it is to be in His army, to take spoils for the King of kings, and to serve him with all of our might and all of our wit! Ours is an army of royalty that marches forward in ranks and moves without hindrance. There is to be no striving between the soldiers on the left and on the right. Rather, each warrior simply has his own path, his own lane. Each soldier understands the significance of his assignment, while recognizing and respecting the God-given callings of the other soldiers in the Body. Kings edify and unite with one another to advance the Kingdom, realizing that they are all members of the Body of Christ. To try to tear each other down is an attack against the Body itself.

Kings have supernatural ability to use walls of obstructions as shortcuts to a destination. For a king, obstacles and barriers turn into roadways that get him to wherever he needs to be. Even weapons meant to hurt him cannot:

> "No weapon that is formed against thee shall prosper; and every tongue that shall rise against thee in judgment thou shalt condemn. This is the heritage of the servants of the LORD, and their righteousness is of me, saith the LORD."
>
> (Isaiah 54:17)

Kings strive to execute the word of the Lord. To do His bidding is their overwhelming joy and passion. All personal agendas are abandoned—and the desire of their King is their chief aspiration.

This is the God-nature of His kings. Our Lord is the Great King, and we are subservient kings made in His image—the sons of God. This God-nature is the product of the new birth, and the working of His Word and Spirit to equip and transform His children from glory to glory. All creation must respond to the true kings who exhibit this level of dedication and training:

> "For [even the whole] creation (all nature) waits expectantly and longs earnestly for God's sons to be made known [waits for the revealing, the disclosing of their sonship]."
>
> (Romans 8:19, AMP)

Kings pray. Kings fast. Kings give. Kings wait for instruction. Kings execute plans with emotionless accuracy. They are warriors of the Most High God and they are purpose-driven. Those kings who listen to God and obey His instructions will become almost immune to failure.

Even those situations which initially appear to be failures turn into stepping stones to promotion for the godly and obedient king. Even David hid in caves for a few years before occupying a palace. His "cave days" of perceived failure were actually training periods for his future exaltation to the throne. True kings realize that their King has a plan for their ultimate success despite the "bumps" in the road along the way.

New Testament kings are not weak—they are meek. Meekness is simply being obedient before YHWH to the uttermost. The meek love their God with all of their heart, soul, mind, and strength…and their neighbor as themselves. (Matthew 22:37-40)

When kings fall, they get up. When adversity comes, they rise up and run on top of it. The voice of the Lord goes before them and shouts, "Victory!" The Spirit of the Lord reigns in their heart; and when others faint, they do not hesitate—but they do take note and learn.

Kings wait upon the Lord to renew their strength. They run and are not weary. They walk and faint not. (Isaiah 40:31) Those who would associate with them are compelled either to keep up or to get out of the way. There is no room for doubt, indecisiveness, or vanity of talk. Kings who have embraced God's vision for them will achieve the purpose and the call that God has planted inside them.

Oh, to serve the King! Oh, what joy to honor Him with the increase of my hands and my voice! I sing praises to the Most High God! He is beautiful, righteous, and wonderful to serve. There is no evil or darkness in Him. Virtue and glory are His character and nature—and it is to my *credit* to pursue spoils for His precious Name.

—Yahshua—

Jesus—The Way, The Truth, and The Life.

"I came that they may have and enjoy life, and have it in abundance (to the full, till it overflows)."

(John 10:10b, Amplified)

KINGS AND PRIESTS II: EXAMINING THE KINGDOM

The word "kingdom" refers to the "king's dominion." It is a compound of two words. When we refer to the "Kingdom of God," therefore, we are referring to the dominion or "sphere of authority" of YHWH. This same Kingdom is also referred to as the Kingdom of Heaven in the Lord's Prayer:

> "After this manner therefore pray ye: Our Father which art in heaven, Hallowed be thy name. Thy kingdom come, Thy will be done in earth, as it is in heaven."
>
> (Matthew 6:9-10)

Without going into an exceptional amount of Scripture to illustrate this in its entirety, let me give you the essence of the struggle between God's Kingdom of Light and the kingdom of darkness ruled by Satan (then you can go and study it further on your own):

God created man in His Own image and after His Own likeness—giving him dominion and authority (Genesis 1 & 2). Essentially, God made Adam king over the entire creation, for the psalmist declared:

> "When I consider Your heavens, the work of Your fingers, the moon and the stars, which You have ordained; What is

> man that You take thought of him, and the son of man that You care for him? Yet You have made him a little lower than God, and You crown him with glory and majesty! You make him to rule over the works of Your hands; You have put all things under his feet..."
>
> (Psalm 8:3-6, NAS)

Satan deceived Eve in the third chapter of Genesis, and through an act of rebellion to the known will of his Creator, Adam gave the entire "kingdom" he had been entrusted with to the devil. Thus, the kingdom became one of darkness as a fallen angel became its master...and man his pawn. God was now on the outside looking in, and needed to reestablish His Kingdom in the earth. However, God had a plan...and another Man.

Jesus came as the "last Adam" (1 Corinthians 15) and through His death, burial and resurrection, gave us back the authority and dominion that was lost in the Garden of Eden. Our King is a warrior! He took back ownership of what was stolen from God—through triumphant conquest!

> "Blotting out the handwriting of ordinances that was against us, which was contrary to us, and took it out of the way, nailing it to his cross; And having spoiled principalities and powers, he made a shew of them openly, triumphing over them in it."
>
> (Colossians 2:14-15)

Then, once the victory was secured and the devil defeated, He commissioned His kings to exercise authority in His Name and to manifest His victory in the natural realm. In other words, like Joshua and the land of Canaan (in the book of Joshua), God has given us the Kingdom—but we must also take it.

> "And from the days of John the Baptist until now the kingdom of heaven suffereth violence, and the violent take it by force."
>
> (Matthew 11:12)

He has bestowed upon us the royal calling of God to take back from Satan's kingdom everything he has stolen from God's through the fall of man and the activities of wicked men. God's Kingdom is sown into the hearts of men through the new birth (Luke 17:21), but His Kingdom is expanded in this natural world when His people "take ground" through economic and spiritual conquest. God's creation must be reclaimed piece by piece by His kings—until the King of kings returns Himself and takes it ALL back once and for all:

> "And I saw heaven opened, and behold a white horse; and He that sat upon him was called Faithful and True, and in righteousness He doth judge and make war. His eyes were as a flame of fire, and on His head were many crowns; and He had a Name written, that no man knew, but He Himself. And He was clothed with a vesture dipped in blood: and His Name is called The Word of God. And the armies which were in heaven followed Him upon white horses, clothed in fine linen, white and clean. And out of His mouth goeth a sharp sword, that with it He should smite the nations: and He shall rule them with a rod of iron: and He treadeth the winepress of the fierceness and wrath of Almighty God. And He hath on His vesture and on His thigh a name written, KING OF KINGS, AND LORD OF LORDS."
>
> (Revelation 19:11-16, capitalization added)

Therefore, it is imperative that the kings of God's Body here on earth embrace their calling, and are activated into fruitful service on behalf of their King. For here on earth, there are two kingdoms: God's Kingdom (capital "K") and Satan's kingdom. It is the calling of kings to reclaim the property the devil has stolen and put it into the hands of God's people, and to use the spoils gathered to advance the Kingdom of God as a whole.

WHOSE KINGDOM IS IT?

The Kingdom of God obviously belongs to Him. Consequently, it is made up of people who understand and honor the Lordship of Jesus Christ (again, Luke 17:21 tells us that the Kingdom is in the hearts of men). These people are kings and priests—many of whom are called to be "vocational" royalty because of a predominant anointing in that area. Such true warrior-kings see their life's purpose exclusively in the light of their service to God through Jesus Christ.

The Kingdom of God is singular. There are not Kingdoms (plural); there is only one Kingdom of God. There is no question of ownership in this Kingdom—only one of stewardship.

Yes, one could say that there are many sub-"kingdoms" (small "k") within the Great Kingdom of our God, since we are all individually called to be "kings" before Him. After all, who ever heard of a king without a kingdom? However, such would only be kingdoms of stewardship—not ownership.

Furthermore, far too much sectarianism has been evident in the Church as individuals have lost sight of the supremacy of THE Kingdom and His glory—and have sought to build their own little "kingdoms" for their own glory. Those with such self-centered motives are not walking as true kings before their God.

Those who comprehend this struggle of division within the Body, and who reject the criticism of other "sects" within the Church, are the true kings. They may recognize that the Lord has delegated to them a sphere of influence or territory to conquer, but they do not devote their hearts only toward their own endeavors.

Those who are truly for His Kingdom spend their time meditating on how to produce for the benefit of the whole Body—and shun comparison, division, and criticism. They realize that their own assignments from Heaven are part of the larger plan of God—and they work to supply their part only as members of the larger Body:

> "For because of Him the whole body (the church, in all its various parts), closely joined and firmly knit together by the joints and ligaments with which it is supplied, when each part [with power adapted to its need] is working properly [in all its functions], grows to full maturity, building itself up in love."
>
> (Ephesians 4:16, AMP)

Additionally, these true kings (men and women) recognize other kings by their devotion to Jesus and dedication to the gifts that He has given them. Once they distinguish another king, they will celebrate that king's anointing without prejudice, and will esteem him as a brother (or sister) in the Lord. When possible, they will even seek to bless the other kings for the good of the Kingdom, while expecting nothing in return. They have a revelation of sowing and reaping (Gal. 6:7), and they comprehend the concept that whatever good they do for others, they will receive multiplied back again from the Lord.

Jesus is the King of kings and the Lord of lords. He has all preeminence!

Jesus' Name is the Name above all names. He is Lord over the church, all business, all education, all personal life, all entertainment, all media, all art, all music—all of life.

The kings understand His Lordship and the nature of His Kingdom. Furthermore, much like Joshua, they understand that even though they have already been given the promised land, they will still have to run out the inhabitants—giants and all.

DUPLICATION OF KINGS

I first came into the Kingdom of God in 1984 when I actively began to bring my supply into His house, the local church. The day I wholeheartedly entered the Kingdom was the day I began to faithfully tithe. It was on this day that I began to participate in the advancement of the gospel and to show my allegiance to God by giving of something that I had control over—my money.

At the time, I was 25 years old. It seems young now; it didn't seem so young then. I was trading commodities on the exchanges in New York City and I needed some divine intervention. "Peace" was not the active word in my life. Chaos and anxiety were my constant companions. It was not until I began paying God ten percent of my income (which belonged to Him anyway) that I started to experience the change in purpose I needed in order for peace to manifest in my life.

The giving of the tithe became my lighthouse, my rudder, and my compass. The mental struggle caused by the speed of the markets and the weight of the consequences of failure weighed heavily—except it could now be faced boldly because now it was not merely an earthly pursuit, but a quest for higher purpose. The tithe brought me into the "King's Valley." I was now one of those who fought for Jesus:

> "So he brought back all the goods, and also brought back his brother Lot and his goods, as well as the women and the people. And the king of Sodom went out to meet him at the Valley of Shaveh (that is, the King's Valley), after his return from the defeat of Chedorlaomer and the kings who were with him. Then Melchizedek king of Salem brought out bread and wine; he was the priest of God Most High. And he blessed him and said: 'Blessed be Abram of God Most High, Possessor of heaven and earth; And

blessed be God Most High, Who has delivered your enemies into your hand.' And he gave him a tithe of all."

(Genesis 14:16-20, NKJV)

But the tithe is not the only qualifying factor. A king is a king, whether he yet possesses an earthly kingdom or not. He is one who, by nature, strives for dominion. He is one who actively aims for mastery and excellence. He declares the rules and sets the boundaries. He collects the tribute and cares for his people. Historically, kings have performed this role poorly, except one King of course—Yahshua, the King of kings.

A king is formed through participation and training. He is trained in the ways of the world but is equipped with the wisdom of the Holy Spirit. Moses is a perfect example. He is trained in Pharaoh's court and then, after a period of exile, re-enters Egypt (a type of the world system) to extract spoils and deliver what really belongs to God back to Him. This is the role of the king—to redeem that which has been paid for already by Yahshua. So go out and take that which is promised! Because it is His, it is supposed to be ours.

As I mentioned before, kings are recognizable (especially by other kings)—yet, they are not easily penned. Pastors will often try to fence them in like sheep. This is not possible—NOT if they are true kings. Kings are dominion-minded; and they are called, anointed and appointed for their God-given assignment—just as many of the pulpit ministers are. (By "many," I mean that not everyone who wears the title of pastor, apostle, prophet, evangelist or teacher is called to that position by God. Some are sent by God, and others just decide to do it—for whatever reason.)

Because pastors are often ignorant of the callings of these kings, they endeavor to enclose and control them in an attempt to conform them to their concept of good "sheep" behavior. Consequently, many such kings never take their rightful place in the Kingdom—and they spend their entire lives serving the wrong "master."

It is the role of those who comprehend "kingship" to reach these men and women, and to introduce them to other kings for divine appointments, God-ordained relationships, and fellowship. It is the role of those who see this truth to listen to the heart cry of these kings and to understand that their inner voice is strong and has a great desire to build and to provide. They cry out for innovation and for discovery. They ache to give and to contend. They hear the voice of truth and they strive to set the boundaries in the right places and to make things right. As it says in the Scriptures:

> "A false balance is abomination to the LORD: but a just weight is his delight."
>
> (Proverbs 11:1)

And again, in the Message Bible:

> "GOD hates cheating in the marketplace; he loves it when business is aboveboard."
>
> (Proverbs 11:1, Message)

Covenant, conquest, and character—this is the heart of the true king.

In the book of Genesis, we see that all living things that have been created produce progeny after their own kind. Oranges beget oranges, and bears beget bears. A bear cannot produce a cat, and an orange cannot produce an azalea bush. In this manner, a pastor cannot produce a true king. He can discover a king. He can somewhat mentor a king in his understanding of the scriptures. He can mold a king and guide a king. But he cannot reproduce one.

KINGS BEGET KINGS

In times past, if you wanted to become a silversmith, your father would take you to the home of the tradesman and drop you off. In many cases, your father would pay the silversmith to take you in to learn the trade. In other cases, you would work for that man for free—in exchange for the knowledge that you would gain. This concept seems lost today. Wisdom and skill are undervalued, conformity is esteemed, and our schools have taken the individuality and art out of work. By doing so, they have also taken out of the mix the relationship between the master and the apprentice, the mentor and the protégé, the father and the son:

> "He will turn the hearts of the fathers to their children, and the hearts of the children to their fathers; or else I will come and strike the land with a curse."
>
> (Malachi 4:6, NIV)

In most cases, we have bottled creativity and boiled out the life and the ingenuity. As a result, we have taken the adventure and the fun out of the work. Without a sense of purpose and without a personal stake, there can be no fulfillment and no real sense of satisfaction. Life passes, but it is not lived or enjoyed.

The apprentice learns from the true master more than just the trade. He learns the love for work and for building something worthwhile. He learns of a life that does not exist for everyone. He sees passion and pain as they are mixed in the master's struggle to do his very best work. The apprentice is scolded and cajoled as he is allowed to observe and to work alongside this "king."

Whether we're studying a shoemaker or a city builder—the principles are the same. Shoemakers beget shoemakers, plumbers beget plumbers, and traders beget traders. However, not everyone who works leather can produce a shoe and not everyone who can bend pipe is a plumber.

To make my point even clearer, not every professor in college is a master in his field. Attending college alone does not guarantee the proper "education" for professional success.

Now, I am not "knocking" education. Nor am I suggesting that every professor is "clueless" as far as how to actually put into practice business and investment principles in real life. In fact, some business curricula, currently offered by the most credible institutions, are now based on real-world scenarios developed in conjunction with major U.S. corporations. Furthermore, it is becoming more and more common to find college educators who are actually proven experts in various business fields, but who have either a love for education or a desire to impart their experiences into a younger generation.

Nevertheless, I do want to clearly impress upon you that if you are trying to learn how to be a successful entrepreneur, you are not generally going to get that type of applied wisdom from college professors alone—especially from those who simply teach out of a textbook and have few (or no) streams of income beyond their teaching salaries.

You need to be taught and mentored by those who are already where you want to be, rather than by those who can only teach you how to get a job. You need more than mere academic knowledge—you need to learn applied wisdom from someone who has actual experience in your field. You need mentors.

Kings beget kings, and as one who sees the kingdom, I am constantly on the lookout for those who are *doers*. I am also searching for those who have the desire to *do*, and the discipline to train under those that *do* so that they can be mentored into the realm of mastery. There are those that would pay the price to stand beside the king to watch and learn—and many who would not. There are those who understand the value of the craft and the

Kings and Priests II: Examining the Kingdom

craftsman—and these initiates are valuable and need to be properly placed in positions of training.

Kings need to be taught the importance of duplication and the importance of progeny (bearing fruit). They must be reminded not to fall into the trap of myopia. They cannot be allowed to see their role as the only role or the most important role. They are not to be shackled, but they are required to reproduce. This is the role for those who have a vision for and who comprehend the kingly anointing.

The practical application for this is simple. Once a true king is discovered, much prayer is required. Prayer is essential, because kings are *focused*—and can be *offensive*. The "priest" (and I speak from first hand knowledge as a pastor and apostle) cannot afford to be offended at the kings—or anybody, for that matter.

Such offense towards the brethren causes a break in the Body—and the Body will not function properly if both sides do not provide the flexibility and the fluidity necessary for the flow of exchange. This exchange between the king and the priest is built upon trust and upon a much higher purpose than ourselves. Kings must be taught this principle of discipleship so that they will understand it over time—and they will, if both the priests and kings continue to teach the protégés how to serve and respect the mentors in exchange for training. Value for value, service for service, respect for respect—these are all involved in Kingdom building.

Kings beget kings—and there is no Kingdom without kings. There is also no effective Kingdom advancement without peace and unity. This is the role of the priesthood. The priests are to study to uphold the moral and ethical code for kingly behavior—and to proclaim it without fear, continually providing the balm of reconciliation and forgiveness.

> "When he takes the throne of his kingdom, he is to write for himself on a scroll a copy of this law, taken from that of the priests, who are Levites. It is to be with him, and he is to read it all the days of his life so that he may learn to revere the LORD his God and follow carefully all the words of this law and these decrees and not consider himself better than his brothers and turn from the law to the right or to the left. Then he and his descendants will reign a long time over his kingdom in Israel."
>
> (Deuteronomy 17:18-20, NIV)

Where do kings learn the law of the Kingdom so that their hearts will not be not lifted up in pride? From the combination of their own study of the Scriptures and the tutelage of the priests—God's chosen instruments for the perfection of all the saints (see Ephesians 4:11-16). The "priestly" instruction derived from the five-fold ministry gifts, and the king's own study of the Bible, keeps anointed kings from developing swelled heads and enlarged egos.

The priests are also to train the kings in the principles of love, faith and devotion to God—the basis for supernatural living. It is the priesthood that teaches the royal conquerors how to operate in the gifts of the Spirit, and to function as true "ministers in the marketplace"—taking spoils AND souls by the power of God. The proper king/priest relationship must be understood by both parties in these last days, because neither one is complete without the other. Remember, ministers *perfect,* and kings *conquer*. It is a symbiotic relationship that God intends to use to spread His Kingdom throughout the world.

However, let me note here for a moment also that God is raising up five-fold priests, gifted specifically as apostles (literally "sent ones"), and prophets to the church to be catalysts in the restoration of this relational understanding. "Marketplace ministries" are rising and "Davidic anointings" are emerging. Like King David who was both a king and prophet, there are those who exhibit predominant mantles as both kings and priests today.

I, of course, am one who was raised up on the battlefields of conquest—and yet now also walk with an apostolic anointing to locate, activate and empower God's other kings to do the same. Additionally, several others with a similar calling, yet their own unique anointing to do the same include: John Maxwell, Os Hillman, Michael Pink and others.

"Davidic" ministers, who walk in both realms concurrently, serve as "translators" to the Body of Christ. Since they can see both perspectives simultaneously, they are well-equipped to explain the intricacies of this king-priest relational dynamic. They can speak with additional credibility into the lives of business "kings" regarding the king's dependence on the men and women of God placed in their lives by the Lord.

Meanwhile, as five-fold "priests" themselves, they are able to explain to the ministers how to properly relate to these battle-bred warriors—who are typically not very "churchy" in their demeanors. When these Davidic "translators" are given the due regard and respect that their unique anointing deserves, they are able to bridge the gap and unite the Body of Christ into its "royal priesthood" here on the Earth (see 1 Peter 2:9).

TRUE MARKETPLACE MINISTRY

Before I close this chapter, I want to clarify that what I am teaching is NOT necessarily in agreement with some other similar-sounding teaching that you may have heard. There is a move in the United States of America that is called "Marketplace Ministry." However, their notion is that all of us that go to work in secular society are to take our faith to that place of business and wear it openly. This is good in general, but it can also be harmful when the spectrum of the instruction is too limited. Let me explain why…

Meetings are taking place in which we are told that we have a calling and it is a special apostolic calling to wherever we are. "Apostles" are laying their hands on people and are being told to "have at it" at work Monday morning after a weekend seminar or meeting. While for some people this will be fine, others will find this absolutely disastrous. Why?

First, let me point out that the broad application of the term "apostle" used by these ministers may be somewhat misleading. Ephesians 4:11 clearly states that there are "some" called to be apostles—there is a specific ministry office of an apostle and not everybody is called to it. While in the general sense, all Christians are "sent ones" (the literal meaning of the Greek word translated "apostle") into their communities, families and workplaces—there is a difference.

For some, this difference will not prove to be anything but semantics. But for others, it might prove quite painful as they discover that bona fide apostles are "earmarked" for higher levels of persecution (see 2 Corinthians 11)—and that by ignorantly intruding into that to which they are not called, they lack the grace to sustain such opposition. Again, let me elaborate further…

You will notice that many of these meetings are taking place in the South or in the middle of the Bible Belt, where it is very likely that your employer will be used to those people who proselytize. However, if your workplace is anything like mine was on the New York Commodity Exchanges—get ready for serious persecution.

I was ostracized, blackballed, openly attacked (both physically and verbally), back-stabbed and ridiculed…and there was no recourse that I could take. However, unlike many who might naively swallow such "marketplace ministry" teaching, I was self-employed and really good at what I did. Therefore, I was able to maintain my position and fight through the obstacles to eventual victory—but it was no bed of roses.

This apostolic calling is heavy and so are the costs for those who do these things. Many will lose their jobs, lose their reputations, and some will be passed over for promotion. I would say that before we send these "sent ones" into the marketplace with John 3:16-17 attached to their foreheads, we must teach them to be absolutely excellent at whatever they do in their profession. Then, they will have the credibility to minister to those who might otherwise pay them no attention—and become too valuable to lose their jobs in the process. Excellence speaks louder than talk any day.

The Body of Christ is a group of people here on this planet—people with all sorts of personalities and various problems. These are individuals with individual assignments from God, who have their own individual circumstances, challenges, and opportunities. These make up the Body of Christ.

Nonetheless, it is a fact that most of these individuals that we call "Christians" are better trained at "church talk" than "work talk"…and this is where the problem lies. We, who are leaders and seasoned in the workplace, need to teach our people how to *live their faith*—and *talk about the task at hand*. That task must be the task *that we are being employed by the company to do*. Far more opportunities come to those who truly excel in business to share their faith, than to those who talk about their faith only—while showing themselves less interested in doing the work they were hired to do.

At universities like Yale, at companies like Goldman Sachs, in the markets such as the Mercantile Exchange, in the boardrooms of Wall Street, and among landowners and bank owners, the talk is to the point and very concise: "Can you do what you say you can do…and can you do it in the time frame that you commit to?" If the answer to that question is *yes*, then you are a rare commodity—and then the conversation might turn to other matters like Jesus and faith.

Credibility is everything.

Sending people out into the marketplace without this understanding will sometimes taint the environment for those Christians who truly have pursued wisdom and excellence—and let their lives do the talking. Let us not shackle the true "called ones" with these man-made "sent ones." Not everybody that enters the ministry is called or sent by God. Like I mentioned before, some are sent…and some just *went*. This is true in the pulpit and it is equally as true in the marketplace.

There are those who are truly gifted and graced to be "ministers in the marketplace," who prove their value in the marketplace first. These are the true kings of God. I travel the country looking for men and women of this caliber. I have found a few and am proud to say that they have become my friends. Are you one of these? If so, I am looking for you. Continue reading, for now…then find me later at **www.provisionnetwork.org** so that we can connect. We have really exciting work to do for the furtherance of the Kingdom together.

—Yahshua—

Jesus—The Way, The Truth, and The Life.

"I came that they may have and enjoy life, and have it in abundance (to the full, till it overflows)."

(John 10:10b, Amplified)

KINGS AND PRIESTS III: DIVINE ORDER

Now that we have spent some time examining and expounding upon the mantles of kings and priests, let us take a few moments to examine more clearly the divine order of finances for the church, as well as the practical sides of king/priest relationships. Without a clear comprehension of how the vocational "kings" and "priests" are to function together to advance the kingdom of God, it is unlikely that the two will get along—much less create the necessary synergy to propel the visions of both into full fruition.

MEAT IN MY HOUSE

"Bring ye all the tithes into the storehouse, that there may be meat in mine house, and prove me now herewith, saith the LORD of hosts, if I will not open you the windows of heaven, and pour you out a blessing, that there shall not be room enough to receive it. And I will rebuke the devourer for your sakes, and he shall not destroy the fruits of your ground; neither shall your vine cast her fruit before the time in the field, saith the LORD of hosts. And all nations shall call you blessed: for ye shall be a

Chapter Three

delightsome land, saith the LORD of hosts."
(Malachi 3:10-12)

The most well-known passage of scripture regarding the tithe is undoubtedly the passage in Malachi above. In many churches across the nation and around the world, this text is read during offering time as an exhortation for God's people to step out in faith and "prove" God in His promise to bless the tither in all that he does. However, contained also in this passage beloved by many is the key issue of God's provision for His houses of worship—His divine order.

Considering the context of the kingly and priestly anointings in the lives of the Body of Christ, who is it that is supposed to bring the tithes into the storehouse? Furthermore, who is it that receives them? Any honest examination of scripture (here and elsewhere) will reveal that it is the priest who receives the tithes and offerings brought by the people of God.

It is not the responsibility of the vocational five-fold priests to fill the house of God with the necessary finances to get the Gospel preached. It is the responsibility of the people of God—and especially the kings—to see that the provision of God is in the house of God. The way to ensure that true "meat" is coming from the pulpit to perfect God's saints to do the works of God, is for the priests to see to it that the kings are effective in their callings as well.

One of the most hypocritical and self-destructive things the vocational priests can do is to preach against God's people pursuing the wealth of this world's system, while simultaneously asking them to support the work of God. It is when God's kings are raised up and released into their vocations as warriors for the King that they will be able to bring in the spoils of war—and make sure "meat" is flowing in God's house. Although every believer has a "kingly" responsibility to bring their tithes and offerings to the ministries that feed them spiritually, it is the vocational kings that are ordained and equipped by God to do that same service on a higher scale.

By releasing the kings of God into their calling, the priests are actually fulfilling their own mandate of perfecting the saints so that the saints can do the "work" of the ministry. In so doing, the priests are ensuring that there will be an abundant supply to meet the needs of the ministry, do outreach, and evangelize their communities. To paraphrase one minister: "Rather than hoping some millionaire would visit my church to help with our budget and programs, I discovered that I could raise up my own millionaires through teaching them the practical principles of the Word.

Now I have five, and more are on the way!"

God's divine order is for the vocational priests to be financed in their ministries through the spoils brought in by God's vocational kings. Davidic kings (who are both priests and kings) have the added flexibility to both finance the Gospel and receive offerings to further the Kingdom, beyond what their own kingly service can obtain alone. These two models present the divine order of ministry finance regarding the channel flow of Kingdom economics. History can attest that nothing else will work nearly as effectively—and often will have dire consequences.

PASTORING KINGS WISELY

It may seem that I have been somewhat hostile toward the five-fold priests at times during my teaching, but nothing could be further from the truth. I am the pastor of Faith Exchange Fellowship and an apostle to the Body of Christ at large regarding finances. I am certainly not intending to be too hard on any specific person. In fact, I am not a "respecter of persons," so I tend to come down hard on everybody when I preach and teach! My job is to minister the truth in love—somewhat bluntly, howbeit—in order to wake us up to the truth of God's word. Remember, I am one of God's provocateurs!

In that same vein, let me also add that because I am Davidically anointed as both a king and priest, and have plenty of kings within my church in New York City whom I pastor, I am in an excellent position to point out a few things that will help other shepherds in their pastoral relationships with the kings. As I said before, kings have a habit oftentimes of being *offensive*, so let's look at a few basics.

Keep in mind that kings—especially those who have very strong anointings in this area—tend to be used to being "in charge" of everything. Therefore, it is not uncommon for a spiritually immature king to come in with a "bossy" attitude that tries to run the show. Therefore, you need to use wisdom in appointing kings to church boards and leadership positions—until they have been tested and proven to be able to handle it spiritually.

Another issue is that kings are used to doing combat in the marketplaces of the world—thereby causing them to have an "edge" about them that is somewhat rugged and primitive. Pioneers of old, like Daniel Boone, were tough men who probably only bathed once a month or so. They might wrestle a grizzly for lunch, kill a hostile enemy or two for dinner, and then build a cabin to sleep in at night. They are mavericks. They are conquerors.

Similarly, the modern "kingly" pioneers have a spiritual "stink" about them that is often distasteful to priestly-minded believers, but it is actually the smell of war still wafting about them. You need to get used to that "smell," and learn to deal with their personalities with tact, grace, and wisdom if you want to keep from harming your ability to minister into their lives.

I am not in the least bit implying that you should not confront a king when one gets out of line. On the contrary, kings respect confrontation and gall. What I am saying is that you cannot expect to get them to conform to your religious ideas of what a "church person" should be—and you do not want to *write them off* and reject them because they do not fit the standard mold. That type of religious treatment is why more such "kingly" men do not attend your services regularly—they simply cannot fit into the mold that the people attempt to conform them to. Let them be who they are, celebrate their gifting, and release them into greater things through loving perfection of their character before Christ.

Finally, do not look to the kings as "checkbooks" walking about your ministry foyer. True kings can spot a "con" a thousand miles away—and they know when someone is trying to "shake them down." Boldly teach them the Word for their benefit in love—and do not look at their assets while you are doing it. Eventually, they will see your selfless love, and the spoils will begin to flow into the ministry as well.

WHO'S THE SHEPHERD?

By the same token, you kings need to get a clue about who runs the local church. Your "anointing" is no excuse to be rude, bossy and to try to run your pastor's life. It is not your place to treat your spiritual leaders as one of your employees. Many a spiritually immature king has sat down with his pastor or another minister and tried to tell him how to run things—just because that *spiritual-baby* king financially supports the ministry.

Take a warning from the life of King Uzziah:

> "And Uzziah prepared for them throughout all the host shields, and spears, and helmets, and Habergeons, and bows, and slings to cast stones. And he made in Jerusalem engines, invented by cunning men, to be on the towers and upon the bulwarks, to shoot arrows and great stones withal. And his name spread far abroad; for he was marvelously helped,

till he was strong. But when he was strong, his heart was lifted up to his destruction: for he transgressed against the Lord his God, and went into the temple of the Lord to burn incense upon the altar of incense."

(2 Chronicles 26:14-16)

Notice that Uzziah was very successful in his kingly calling when that success began to go to his head. Taking upon himself priestly duties to which he was not called, he decided that the *king* could go into the temple of God and start doing things *his* way. Too often, pastors have had kings come up to them and use their "tithe" as a weapon to try and control how things are done in the church (not that God would actually honor it as a *tithe*). However, a strong vocational priest will not stand for that, and will have no qualms about getting the king put back into his proper place:

"And Azariah the priest went in after him, and with him fourscore priests of the Lord, that were valiant men: And they withstood Uzziah the king, and said unto him, It appertaineth not unto thee, Uzziah, to burn incense unto the Lord, but to the priests the sons of Aaron, that are consecrated to burn incense: go out of the sanctuary; for thou hast trespassed; neither shall it be for thine honour from the Lord God. Then Uzziah was wroth, and had a censer in his hand to burn incense: and while he was wroth with the priests, the leprosy even rose up in his forehead before the priests in the house of the Lord, from beside the incense altar. And Azariah the chief priest, and all the priests, looked upon him, and, behold, he was leprous in his forehead, and they thrust him out from thence; yea, himself hasted also to go out, because the Lord had smitten him. And Uzziah the king was a leper unto the day of his death, and dwelt in a several house, being a leper; for he was cut off from the house of the Lord..."

(2 Chronicles 26:17-21a)

Although it is good to note the noble character of the priests in this story, the sad note here is that Uzziah was struck with leprosy and died a leper outside of God's house. Whenever a "king" intrudes into that to which he was not called, he runs the risk of finding himself "cast out" of the house of the Lord—and suffering a type of "spiritual leprosy" that prevents him from ever truly achieving the full plan of God for his life.

Furthermore, like Uzziah, he tends to lose the notoriety and benefits from his earlier success, as he becomes a "leper" in the local community—marked by God Himself for having tried to usurp the authority of God's priest. It is God who appoints. Respect that appointment.

Fortunately, there is repentance through the blood of Yahshua for you and me that King Uzziah did not have available to him during his dispensation. If you have been guilty of usurping priestly authority—or even trying to start your own church apart from a divine call—then simply repent, humble yourself before those against whom you have transgressed by confessing your sin to them, and submit to the godly authorities that He has put in your life for your perfection. God can and will get you back on the right track if you will first humble yourself so that He can lift you back up (1 Peter 5:5-6).

PART III

LAYING THE PROPER FOUNDATION

"God has based His whole kingdom on mysteries. But they are mysteries that we are supposed to discover. These things are hidden *in* God *for* us— that we would have the *inside* information, while the devil is left out in the cold trying to figure out what God is up to in our lives."

—Yahshua—

Jesus—The Way, The Truth, and The Life.

"I came that they may have and enjoy life, and have it in abundance (to the full, till it overflows)."

(John 10:10b, Amplified)

RUNNING WITH THE PROS

Chapter Four

There are two words you are going to see throughout the rest of this book that must be fully understood before you continue into the meatier teaching of financial conquest for the Kingdom. It is necessary that I draw your attention to them for just a brief moment because these are pivotal words that I will elaborate on throughout the book in one way or another.

The two words are: "ProVision," and "proactive." The first is the network of kings that I have formed by the direction of the Lord to advance His Kingdom; the second is the thing you will need to become if you want to achieve anything of value. We will begin with the first...

"PROVISION"

As was mentioned in Rich's biography about me earlier, I founded a Christian business organization called the "ProVision Network" (PVN) as a vehicle to gather kings together—for reasons I will share shortly. To introduce to you here what the ProVision Network is, let me first clearly state what it is *not*. Contrary to what some might assume due to its name, PVN is *not* a multi-level network marketing opportunity. Rather, PVN is a 501(c)3 non-profit, Christian business networking organization—and a financial resource center for believers.

Although we certainly have network marketers who join PVN and we encourage them to glean from our resources and teaching, the ProVision Network is not itself such an organization. Furthermore, we have established policy regarding network-marketing activities within PVN as to what activities are appropriate, and which are not. (However, we will detail those guidelines in a later chapter geared toward network marketing within this book.)

Originally, this entity began as a Bible study in our home called the "Breakthrough Bible Study" in 1995. It was later renamed after quickly outgrowing our house and spreading to other locations—growing into the multi-chapter ProVision Network that continues to expand in scope and sophistication today.

In grasping the concept of the ProVision Network, consider for a moment the English word "provision," which has a variety of meanings and applications. The first thought that generally comes to most Christians' minds is that of a "material sustenance and financial supply." The reason we capitalized "ProVision" in such an unusual manner is to reflect my desire to emphasize the two elements "pro" and "vision" for the purpose of distinguishing how the two are interrelated.

"Pro," as a prefix in a word, is properly defined as "to move forward, to lead forth, project, produce, etc..." It is a prefix that indicates that something is "for" something else. That it will promote, propagate, and move to the forefront whatever it is "pro."

On the other hand, "vision" refers both to the ability to see, as well as that which is seen. Specifically, we as Christians understand that "vision" refers to the divinely inspired picture that God gives us, which reveals a plan He has for our lives. One can say that a person is a "visionary" if he seems to have the ability to see what is yet unseen—with an eye of faith that fully plans to see that vision come to pass. From pulpit to pew, every believer has a God-given destiny that Heaven wants to manifest in his life. Faith, coupled with prayerful intimacy with God, enables the Spirit of God to paint that vision on the inside of the person so he can see it with the "eye of faith"—and then see it come to pass.

The network is named "ProVision" because we are simply "for" you and "for" the vision God has given you. We want to promote the cultivation of your gifts and talents as a king, and see you successful in every area of your life—spiritually, mentally, physically, emotionally, socially—and financially. The "ProVision Network" is simply the vision that God has given me to facilitate the callings of the kings in the Body of Christ. In so doing, we are also serving the five-fold ministry "priests" by expanding the economic resources of their ministries through the activation of these fiscal warriors.

ProVision Network (PVN) is a Christian organization designed to unite the Body of Christ through business people, entrepreneurs, professionals, and companies who are dedicated to financing the harvest through churches, ministries, and outreaches—whether local, national, or international. Our desire is to see all believers taking their rightful place of dominion in the marketplace.

PVN provides a database and an environment that connects believers with the people and information they need to convert their God-given dreams into reality. This is accomplished through networking an array of professional and financial resources, and conducting monthly chapter meetings on the Internet and in physical locations around the world. The purpose is to inventory, develop, and endorse those individuals who make their supply and talents available to God and to one another.

We believe most emphatically that everything that the Body of Christ needs is already in the body! Doctors, lawyers, plumbers, landscapers, bankers—whatever gift and/or occupational talent is needed, God has already provided within His Church. All we need to do is identify and inventory those people-assets, while networking them to compound their effectiveness for the Kingdom.

One of the primary tools we have developed to accomplish the inventorying and networking of God's kings is our web site. With its user interface, new members of the ProVision Network complete member profiles that inventory their professional strengths, abilities, goals and achievements—as well as upload specific information about their companies, products and services into our web mall.

Then this data is available to the other PVN members through a variety of search methods to allow them to connect with the people whose skills, products, or services they may need. Other features, such as our member bulletin board, and employment opportunities areas, also form a catalyst to connect believer with believer, king with king—in order to advance the Kingdom together.

The goal of ProVision Network is to empower Christians to succeed in their "kingly" callings, and therefore enlarge their monetary giving to their local churches and other ministries—financing the end-time harvest. The web site, PVN study materials, and chapter meetings are just some of the tools we utilize to accomplish this.

ProVision Network is a business organization designed to help meet the needs of Christian businesspeople, entrepreneurs, professionals and others to ensure that their God-given dreams may be established. As PVN grows, it will have a profound effect on the economy of the Christian church around the world. This network of believers, working together, will take massive amounts of capital from the world's system and build businesses for the Body of Christ, which provides for God's vision in the earth.

For those who do not feel that their primary anointing is as a "king" in the marketplace, PVN offers tremendous services regarding personal finances, debt reduction, mortgages and refinancing services, insurance, and even budgeting assistance—all through our ever-expanding membership base. The products and services we need are already in the Body. Furthermore, whatever vocation God has called you into is needed in the Kingdom. All the ProVision Network does is help connect Christians with Christians who provide the services and products that each of them needs—within the framework of an accountability structure that helps to ensure that those who purport to do a thing, can actually carry out their promises.

What do we believe doctrinally? We believe in the uncompromised Word of God from cover to cover. We believe that there is only one vision, and that is God's vision. Our job is simply to line up with and take our place in the assignment that He has given us.

Let me also call attention to the fact that we teach on the importance of tithing and giving to the local church—and that as business people, our ministry is in the marketplace. We are submitted to our pastors and are committed to helping finance the campaign to see that every person on the planet is given an opportunity to know Jesus as Savior and Lord. In short, the two primary foundational scriptures upon which the vision of PVN is built are found in the books of Proverbs and Habakkuk:

> "Where no counsel is, the people fall: but in the multitude of counselors there is safety."
>
> (Proverbs 11:14)

> "And the Lord answered me, and said, 'Write the vision, and make it plain upon tables, that he may run that readeth it. For the vision is yet for an appointed time, but at the end it shall speak, and not lie: though it tarry, wait for it; because it will surely come, it will not tarry.'"
>
> (Habakkuk 2:2-3)

By providing the kings an appropriate atmosphere and vehicles (such as the Internet) for networking, we enable them to find credible counselors for the ventures they embark upon—thereby seeing the vision they have written down (such as a business plan) fulfilled to God's glory. That, in a nutshell, is an introduction to the ProVision Network—and many more things will be said to elaborate in the chapters to come.

PROACTIVE

"Proactive" is, unfortunately, not a word in most people's vocabulary—but it is extremely important to the investment and business communities. Most of my elaboration on this word will take place within the remainder of this book, as you find it is one of my favorite words—apart from those found in the Bible. However, I wanted to draw your attention to this term, and define it briefly, so that throughout the rest of this book you will find the Holy Spirit driving its meaning into your consciousness—and its characteristics into your behavior.

We already looked at the prefix "pro," so let me draw your attention to the second part of the word..."active." To be successful in any endeavor, you need to get *active* about something. You need to be moving. You need to be exerting energy—spiritually, mentally, and physically. "Active" is defined as "lively, physically mobile; engaged in practical activities; energetic, busy" (Webster's Universal English Dictionary). However, just being busy does not mean you are being *effective*, or accomplishing anything at all!

To be "proactive," you are being busy *for* something. You are moving toward something. You are moving forward and leading forth with a specific goal in mind. You are producing...you are accomplishing...you have taken the challenge, and you are doing what is necessary to see victory in the end.

The opposite would be the "let's wait and see what happens" mentality; the "hope my ship comes in" mentality; the lack of any initiative and enterprise. Proactive people do not *wait* for something to happen, they take the steps necessary to *make* things happen. As Christians, this means first being proactive in the spirit, then proactive in the mental realm, and then finally proactive in the physical realm as you move forward to accomplish that which He has laid out before you. Essentially, as a believer, you need to learn how to be powerful in three realms...

THE THREE REALMS OF POWER

Too often, my brothers and sisters, Christian people fail to realize that they are in fact living in three realms of existence at one time…the spirit realm, the soul realm, and the material/physical realm:

> "May God himself, the God of peace, sanctify you through and through. May your whole spirit, soul and body be kept blameless at the coming of our Lord Jesus Christ. The one who calls you is faithful and he will do it."
>
> (1 Thessalonians 5:23-24, NIV)

God, Who is three Persons in One, has made us after His Own image and likeness—three persons in one. You are comprised of your spirit, your soul (made up of your mind, will, and emotions) and your physical body. Each portion is endowed with certain characteristics that enable it to function within its realm of authority and existence. To be truly powerful as either a priest or king, you will need to be proactive in all three realms of existence—however, most people are not.

For many believers, they are so out of tune with their spirits and so ignorant of God's Word that they are completely unable to tap into the supernatural power of God to overcome the obstacles that stand in their way. For others, they are so focused on prayer that they never obey the Holy Spirit's promptings to make progress in either of the mental or physical realms—and so their prayers continue unanswered.

All the "heroes" of faith in the Bible began in prayer with a foundation of a strong emphasis in the realm of the spirit—but they were also always expected to obey God with either seeking out information, or taking certain "steps" of faith in the physical realm to see the power of God manifest.

Although I will elaborate on this considerably more in subsequent chapters, let me summarize here that successful Christians are proactive Christians—and supernatural believers are proactive in all three realms of existence. They are proactive in the *spirit* through prayer, reading the Word, and the confession of their faith; they are proactive in the *soul* realm by studying their fields—learning the natural knowledge and terminology of their vocations; they are proactive in the *physical* realm by acting on that which the Spirit, through their prayer and the acquiring of knowledge, has directed them to do—obeying Him with their deeds by doing what they know to do.

Since all biblical truths and processes are *circular* in nature (note Isaiah 55:10-11, and John 16:28, for example), this one is no different. You begin in the spirit, follow His leading to gather information into your soul, then once His Wisdom has prompted you to act on that knowledge, you carry through in the physical realm with your actions. Then you return to the Word, prayer and the confession of your faith for more wisdom and instruction and begin the process again. Actually, you never leave the spirit realm for you must always be in communion with your Father. Nor do you cease to develop the soul or become inactive in the physical realm—except for periods of rest, of course.

As you continue throughout this book, this principle of proactively pursuing success in the *three realms of power* will become clearer. However, now that we have established in these introductory chapters the foundational concepts and terminologies that will help you to flow with my message and ministry, we will continue from here into the meatier pieces of God's revelation of financial conquest for the Kingdom—within the proper perspective of His Word and ways.

—Yahshua—

Jesus—The Way, The Truth, and The Life.

"I came that they may have and enjoy life, and have it in abundance (to the full, till it overflows)."

(John 10:10b, Amplified)

WHERE IT ALL BEGINS

What are you called by God to do with your life? Do you know? Have you ever even thought about it? I hope you have, because your Creator has a plan for your life.

You may be called to business, ministry... perhaps a profession like a doctor, engineer or teacher—or maybe even a "blue collar" worker who wins souls while doing his trade (a very honorable calling, indeed). Money is not the issue here—because God will reward whoever follows His plan for his life, if he will walk in God's wisdom and counsel. The question is one of divine fulfillment, destiny, and purpose.

What are you?

Who are you?

Life has very little purpose until one has received from Heaven the divine seed of his destiny—and has put his entire being into the pursuit of its fulfillment.

One minister said, "Faith begins where the will of God is known." If you think about it practically, that statement has tremendous merit. When you know what God has called you to do, you have the potential to fearlessly walk it out. Doubts and fears will try to enter in, but if you hold on to what God has said to you and do not let go, you can with a joyful heart complete the mission God has assigned for you to carry out. You might be saying, "Well then, how do I find out what God's will is for me?" I am glad you asked! For that is where it

Chapter Five

all begins.

REVEALED MYSTERIES

God has based His whole kingdom on mysteries. But they are mysteries that we are supposed to *discover*. These things are hidden in God for us—that we would have the "inside information," while the devil is left out in the cold trying to figure out what God is up to in our lives. God has always had the intention of revealing His plan—His mysteries—to His people so that we may flow with Him and fulfill all His purposes in our lives:

> "For I do not want you, brethren, to be uninformed of this mystery…"
>> (Romans 11:25a, NAS)

> "Now to Him who is able to establish you according to my Gospel and the preaching of Jesus Christ, according to the revelation of the mystery which has been kept secret for long ages past, **but now is manifested**…"
>> (Romans 16:25-26a, NAS, emphasis added)

> "We do, however, speak a message of wisdom among the mature, but not the wisdom of this age or of the rulers of this age, who are coming to nothing. No, **we speak of God's secret wisdom**," [KJV-"the wisdom of God in a mystery"] "a wisdom that has been hidden and that God destined for our glory before time began."
>> (1 Corinthians 2:6-7, NIV, emphasis and note added)

> "Behold, **I show you** a mystery…"
>> (1 Corinthians 15: 5, emphasis added)

> "And **He made known to us the mystery** of His will, according to His good pleasure, which He purposed in Christ…"
>> (Ephesians 1:9, NIV, emphasis added)

> "It is the glory of God to conceal a thing: but the

honor of kings is to search out a matter."
(Proverbs 25:2)

God is not hiding anything from us. Rather, He has hidden everything *for* us within Himself, that only through fellowship and communion with our Creator can we truly know His Will for our lives. Anything other than His Will shall ultimately prove futile if we attempt it and will result in a withholding of rewards for us in Eternity. The effort will have been simply wasted time, energy, and money.

The Scripture that should jump into your mind now is, "Unless the Lord build the house, they labor in vain that build it" (Psalm 127:1). If we do not get His plan first, then we are in danger of expending much time and resources—only to either fail miserably, or to discover that it was completely in vain, since it was not His plan for our lives in the first place.

"Well, how then do I discover God's plan for my life? How do I tap into that mystery hidden in God for me?" you might ask.

Simple: We look into the Word of God—His divine instruction book for how the universe operates—and simply follow His directions.

One beautifully woven passage of Scripture that provides us a portrait of how we press into God for comprehension of our divine purpose is found in the prophetic book of Habakkuk. There we find a prophetic metaphor for how we press into God for this revelation.

From the beginning of this prophet's intercourse with God in the very beginning of Chapter One, he asks YHWH a series of questions. Actually, we could say he was really *whining* and *complaining* to God—as so many of us have done in times past. However, the prophet then makes an interesting statement as to how he will endeavor to press into God for the answer to his questions:

> "[Oh, I know, I have been rash to talk out plainly this way to God!] I will [in my thinking] stand upon my post of observation and station myself on the tower or fortress, and will watch to see what He will say within me and what answer I will make [as His mouthpiece] to the perplexities of my complaint against Him. And the Lord answered me and said, Write the vision and engrave it so plainly upon tablets that everyone who passes may [be able to] read [it easily and quickly] as he hastens by. For the

> vision is yet for an appointed time and it hastens to the end [fulfillment]; it will not deceive or disappoint. Though it tarry, wait [earnestly] for it, because it will surely come; it will not be behindhand on its appointed day. Look at the proud; his soul is not straight or right within him, but the [rigidly] just and the [uncompromisingly] righteous man shall live by his faith and in his faithfulness."
>
> (Habakkuk 2:1-4, AMP)

How do we hear from God? How do we press in to discover the mysteries of His will for the Church—and even our own individual lives? We begin by getting in the metaphorical "prayer closet," climbing the tower (so to speak), standing our watch in earnest heart-felt prayer before our mighty and loving God, and then waiting for the Lord to speak to us His reply.

"Does God speak to people today?" one may ask.

> "The man who enters by the gate is the shepherd of his sheep...and the sheep listen to his voice. He calls his own sheep by name and leads them out. When he has brought out all his own, he goes on ahead of them, and his sheep follow him because they know his voice."
>
> (John 10:2-4, NIV)

Remember, "the Lord is our Shepherd" (Psalm 23:1).

Yes, most emphatically, Jesus Christ still ministers to, and communicates with, His Church corporately—and to the individual people He loved and saved as well.

"How does He communicate with us?"

Notice what the prophet said in verse one above, "...and will watch to see what He will say within me..." God lives in His people by His Spirit, and that same Holy Spirit will talk to our hearts—if we listen, as the prophet did, to His voice speaking on the inside of us. The question is not whether or not He *will* speak. The question is rather, "*What* will He speak to our hearts?"

I have found by experience, and can confirm by the testimony of Scripture as well, that most of the time He will begin by correcting us. The King James Version translates Habakkuk 2:1 as, "I will stand upon my watch, and set me upon the tower, and will watch to see what He will say unto me, and what I shall answer when I am reproved." It should come as no shock to any of us that God is smarter than we are, knows more than we do, and is always right—even when we cannot comprehend it. Our thinking is almost always the reason we find ourselves in a mess or outside of God's will for our lives. Therefore, it is necessary to first of all allow Him to straighten out our proud carnal minds before any further instructions can be given to us. The most important thing for us to remember is that when He reproves us, we watch to see that we respond to Him appropriately…

> "Whoever loves discipline loves knowledge, but he who hates correction [KJV-'reproof'] is stupid."
> (Proverbs 12:1, NIV)

Wow! You would almost think God was from New York City as "bold and brash" as He decided to make that Scripture. But, for those of you who prefer a "nicer" word of instruction, try this one on for size:

> "For the commandment is a lamp, and the whole teaching [of the law] is light, **and reproofs of discipline are the way of life**…"
> (Proverbs 6:23, AMP, emphasis added)

The NIV says, "The corrections of discipline are the way *to* life." So if you cannot receive correction and reproof, whether directly from God or through people, then you have barred yourself from the "way of life," and are quite "stupid"—according to God. (Again, that may seem a little too direct for you, but you have to admit that God—the *Original* Provocateur—certainly has a way with words!)

Remember the fourth verse of our passage in Habakkuk?

> "Look at the proud; his soul is not straight or right within him, but the [rigidly] just and the [uncompromisingly] righteous man shall live by his faith and in his faithfulness."
> (Habakkuk 2:4, AMP)

The word "soul" used in the passage above refers to our mind, will and emotions—not to be confused with our spirit, which has been born again through faith in Jesus. Therefore, God will speak correction and reproof to our hearts through His Word, Spirit, and even other people. We need to be open to that correction and repentant when it comes—otherwise we are in pride. (See 1 Peter 5:5.)

We never want to be hostile or indifferent to His correction. We need to be continuously open to His reproof…and instantly repentant when it comes. That openness to His divine realignment of our lives (and heads!) puts us under the waterfall of His grace—which includes His wisdom, direction, and provision—and is infinitely bigger than Niagara Falls! (I don't know about you, but I need more than a "dripping faucet" of God's grace to get everything done that He has called me to!)

INSTRUCTIONS PLEASE

Once our hearts are right (through true repentance) and our heads are straightened out (through reproof), God will follow up with the much-desired instruction. In fact, let me give it to you another way.

Do you remember sitting at the dinner table with your parents as a kid? It seems to me that most people can relate to the fact that no matter what delectable things were set on the table, there was always some sort of "food" that was "good" for you—but you did not particularly care for it at all. However, if your household was like most, eating "good-for-you food" always seemed to be a requirement before the real good stuff was to follow—and you certainly were not going to get second helpings or dessert until it disappeared off your plate!

Using this metaphor, once we have eaten the asparagus (or whatever "food" you personally detested as a child), He will let us have more steak, barbecue beef ribs, mashed potatoes—and even throw in some dessert too—but only *after* we have eaten our vegetables! Otherwise, we can sit at the proverbial "table" until we turn blue and fall off our chairs—and not get another word from God on the subject—until we have finished digesting that word of correction He wants us to eat first. Again:

> "…God resisteth the proud, but giveth grace to the humble."
>
> (1 Peter 5:5b)

Then, once we received the instruction, this verse we read before in Habakkuk tells us that we must "write the vision and make it plain." We need to write things down so that we have a clear record for ourselves—and for others—to follow.

That is how we do things in the proper order. We seek God alone as our source of vision and destiny. We dedicate ourselves to prayer, wait upon

Him for the answers to be revealed in our hearts, and receive any reproofs He gives us (repent!). Then we receive the instructions that follow and write them down. Once they are written, we can begin to run with the vision God has given us.

Now, for whatever areas of your life in which you are seeking God's wisdom, the whole process described above may take several hours, days, even weeks, months, or years. However, if we develop a constant "walk" with God, it will often be a matter of continual fellowship and communion, rather than seeming like a laborious task or tedious endeavor.

Back to this chapter's initial question: "What are you called of God to do with your life?" You now have the understanding necessary to discover your personal "paths of righteousness" as ordained by God for your days here on the Earth.

Are you called to be a king before God—taking territory for the Kingdom in an anointing for spiritual and economic combat?

Is your calling to be one of God's priests—serving Him as a five-fold minister and perfecting the saints?

Perhaps your driving destiny is to serve as one of those in a "king's court" to help him or her advance the Kingdom for the glory of His Name. That is not a bad calling when you consider how well paid Solomon's court servants were (1 Kings 10).

Maybe you are a "Levite" who ministers with the five-fold "priests" to see that the service of God's house is done according to divine excellence. Whatever your specific God-ordained assignment is in life—you have one. The key is to discover what God has called you to do with your life in every area—including as a spouse, parent, and member of your community.

Unfortunately, many do not follow the simple path of persistent prayer that I laid out above—and fall woefully short of their divine potential as a result. To some, this process seems too ethereal (in their thinking) for the practicality of it to register on their minds.

For others, it seems excessively difficult to press into God in prayer until the answer comes. And for many others, it just seems like too much time is "wasted" searching God for the answers rather than finding them some "easier" or "quicker" way. If that is your thinking, then you have not yet comprehended the true source of complete peace…

—Yahshua—

Jesus—The Way, The Truth, and The Life.

"I came that they may have and enjoy life, and have it in abundance (to the full, till it overflows)."

(John 10:10b, Amplified)

THE SOURCE OF TRUE PEACE

Are you looking anywhere other than God for insight into your destiny? Unfortunately, many Christians are.

Rather than seeking YHWH to clarify the issues of our lives and His calling on us, too many of us are so busy watching each other that we cannot ascertain from God what we are supposed to be doing. We will never determine God's will by comparing ourselves with others, or duplicating what they are doing. We must discover His plan within us, and there we will find His grace given to us to accomplish that plan.

Others look to the world system for answers to their destiny—such as science, psychology, or even the world's religions. My friend, the world system is destined to be thrown as a beast into the Lake of Fire for all eternity. Does that sound like a good source of information for direction in your life? (See Revelation 19:19-20)

Still others think that the answers they seek about themselves are found in their parents, their friends, their coworkers—but again, these are simply ways we compare ourselves with each other to find purpose:

> "...but they measuring themselves by themselves, and comparing themselves among themselves, are not wise."
>
> (2 Corinthians 10:12)

When we do look elsewhere, we fail to

Chapter Six

recognize that the things originating in Divinity can only be discovered and revealed through that same Source. Since there is only One God, and His plans for your life were Created by Him "before you were formed in the womb," (Jeremiah 1:5) who else can supply the keys that will unlock the mystery of your created purpose?

Now that should immediately trigger to your remembrance the Scripture where Paul exhorts Timothy to, "Stir up the gift that is within you." (2 Timothy 1:6) We stir the "gift" up within us by stirring ourselves up in prayer and devotion to God. In order to discover God's will for our lives, we must put Him first.

Let's get into the Hebrew language a little bit here.

"Shabbâth shâlôm" is how the more devout Jewish people greet each other. They don't just say, "Shalom," which is Hebrew for "peace." They say, "Shabbath shalom" which has a much fuller meaning.

Shalom by itself is a powerful word, meaning "complete peace." It is a peace that comes from being absolutely whole—with nothing lacking, missing or broken in any area of your life—spiritual, soulical, material, familial, or any other way.

However, *Shabbath* is the Sabbath—the day God designated for rest and reflection on Him. It refers to the idea of going to God in worship, and setting a whole day aside to study the Word, to be with your family… and to set your priorities straight. Within the Hebrew word *Shabbath*, as combined with the word *shalom*, is the powerful concept of going to God first—before you can expect wholeness. In other words, when a Jew says "Shabbath shalom," he is conferring upon another the blessing of a complete peace that permeates every area of life. However, that can only be derived from entering into a God-centered rest—where only He is your source of entirety. The "formula of peace," therefore, can be loosely expressed as:

faith = confidence = rest

"Faith" is "confidence" (in God), which is the source and essence of bona fide "rest." God is the only One Who can truly make you complete. He is the only One Who can unite the broken pieces of your life and make you an entire person again—or more accurately, for the first time in your life.

Such a state of true "totality" can only come by entering into His rest and discovering that perfect peace "which surpasses all understanding" (Philippians 4:7). That is why in the New Testament Book of Hebrews (which was written to the Jews of that day—who knew these truths intimately), Paul exhorted his readers:

> "Therefore, since the promise of entering His rest still stands, let us be careful that none of you be found to have fallen short of it. For we also have had the Gospel preached to us, just as they did; but the message they heard was of no value to them, because those who heard did not combine it with faith. Now we who have believed enter that rest [*Shabbath*]...It still remains that some will enter that rest, and those who formerly had the Gospel preached to them did not go in, because of their disobedience...For if Joshua had given them rest, God would not have spoke later about another day. There remains, then, a Sabbath-rest for the people of God; for anyone who enters God's rest also rests from His own work, just as God did from His. Let us, therefore, make every effort to enter that rest, so that no one will fall by following their example of disobedience."
>
> (Hebrews 4:1-3a, 6, 8-11, NIV, notes added)

Men, can you imagine buying your wife an engagement ring that you spent a ton of money on...only for her to never wear it? You pay thousands of dollars for it, but when you give it to her she says, "Oh, that's so very nice," and then puts it in a safe somewhere and never puts it on her finger.

In a sense, God has bought you an engagement ring.

He paid for it with His Own Blood, and gave it to you as a gift to be prized above all! Those abilities, aptitudes—and even the anointing in your life—are all a part of that "gift" from the Bridegroom to His Bride, the Church, of which you are a member. They are there for you—but they are also there for the rest of us as well.

They are to be valued...they are to be esteemed...those gifts are to be USED.

That is what the whole parable of the talents found in Matthew Chapter 25 is all about. He has placed inside you an individual, magnificent gift; it is ridiculously powerful, awesomely limitless, and amazingly unique. But if you do not *Shabbath*—if you do not go and climb your tower like Habakkuk and desperately pursue God for the understanding of what that gift is…you are dishonoring Him.

Now, let that sink down into your spirit.

Furthermore, let me add that we need to make God our priority on a daily basis, not just on Sunday. The Bible says that if we acknowledge Him in *all* our ways, then He will direct our paths (Proverbs 3:6). Discovering what those paths are comes through spending time meditating on Scripture, getting quiet before God and letting Him speak to your heart, worshipping Him, and fellowshipping with other believers.

As you practice learning to hear God's voice (which usually comes in the form of something being dropped in your heart and accompanied by the peace of God), you will eventually become skillful at it. You will recognize the voice of your Good Shepherd when He speaks to you. This concept will become more real to you as you meditate on Scriptures referring to hearing God's voice and following it. And when you know that the plan you have is from above, you can in total confidence and faith take the steps He leads you to take. Before you know it, you are living out your destiny.

Along the way, however, you will still be required to paint the picture of that destiny with the words of your own mouth if you are ever to see it become a reality. It is when you discover that words become things, that you find the "gas pedal" to propel your life to your divine destination…

—Yahshua—

Jesus—The Way, The Truth, and The Life.

"I came that they may have and enjoy life, and have it in abundance (to the full, till it overflows)."

(John 10:10b, Amplified)

WORDS BECOME THINGS

Chapter Seven

The Hebrew word *dâbâr* is a very significant declaration from God as to how things really work in this universe. It is the Hebrew word for "word," and is the primary term used throughout the Hebrew portions of Scripture to refer to God's Word, as well as the "Word of the Lord" spoken by the prophets. But, beyond that, this term also means a "thing"—or the substance of what was spoken. Remember God's recount of how He created all "things"?

"In the beginning God created the heaven and the earth...And God **said**, Let there be light: and there was light...And God **said**, Let there be a firmament in the midst of the waters, and let it divide the waters from the waters...And God **said**, Let the waters under the Heaven be gathered together unto one place, and let the dry land appear: and it was so...And God **said**, Let the earth bring forth grass, the herb yielding seed, and the fruit tree yielding fruit after his kind, whose seed is in itself, upon the earth: and it was so...And God **said**, Let there be lights in the firmament of the heaven to divide the day from the night;…And God **said**, Let the waters bring forth abundantly the moving creature that hath life, and fowl that may fly above the earth in the open firmament of heaven…And God **said**, Let the earth bring forth the living creature after his kind, cattle, and creeping thing, and beast of the earth after his kind: and it was so…And God **said**, Let us make man in our image, after our likeness: and let them have dominion over the fish of the sea, and over the fowl of the air, and over the cattle, and over all the earth, and over every creeping thing that creepeth upon the earth. So God created man in his own image, in the image of God created he him; male and female created he them."

(Genesis 1:1, 3, 9, 11, 14, 20, 24, 26-27, emphasis added)

Eight times in twenty-seven verses, God tells us that He "said" and it was "so," or came into existence. God's creative *method of operation*—His "M.O."—is clearly shown to us to be that He speaks a thing, and the thing becomes a reality.

Have you ever noticed that this entire planet still operates by words?

If you own your house, what proof do you have of that ownership? Only words that are written down on paper (called a "deed"). What signifies your ownership of the car you drive? Another document filled with words. On what basis can you—or anyone else—declare that you are married to another person? The words spoken in the presence of witnesses (the marriage covenant), and additional words written down on a piece of paper (the marriage certificate—if issued by your state).

Evident to all who will honestly contemplate it is the fact that this universe was created by words (as Genesis testifies) and that it completely functions yet today by words—as experience will confirm. This truth is also evident in the very nature of the Hebrew word *dabar*; words…that become things. In fact, by God's definition, the words you say are things as well:

"And God said, **Let us make man in our image, after our likeness: and let them have dominion**…"

(Genesis 1:26a, emphasis added)

"And Jesus answering saith unto them, Have faith

Words Become Things

in God. [In the original Greek language and many cross references, literally '...have the faith of God"] For verily I say unto you, That whosoever shall **say** unto this mountain, 'Be thou removed, and be thou cast into the sea;' and shall not doubt in his heart, but shall believe that those things which he **saith** shall come to pass; he shall have whatsoever he **saith**."

(Mark 11:22-23, emphasis and notes added)

You and I were created in the image of God, and as such, we have that same creative force of faith on the inside of us that He does—howbeit not nearly as well developed! What you speak from a heart filled with faith will ultimately become the things you speak.

Did God believe those things He said in Genesis would come to pass as He spoke them? Of course He did! Therefore, since you and I are created in His image and after His likeness, we are by design created also to speak our future into existence.

You already speak to your circumstances and surroundings all the time—unconsciously. In fact, when Genesis 2:7 says that "man became living soul" from the breath of life given him from God's breath, the literal Hebrew meaning of that phrase is, "and man became a speaking spirit."

What happens when someone's car will not start some cold morning? He speaks to it! And generally, the words are not ones fit to be written here, let me assure you.

Put money in a vending machine, and if the desired product does not come out...you'll probably find yourself having a one-way conversation with the dumb thing. Why? You are created by God to be a *speaking spirit*. It is in your very nature to talk to things. That is why God has told us to speak things that are in agreement with Him—and that we will be judged one day for those times when we have not:

> "Your words have been strong and hard against Me, says the Lord. Yet you say, What have we spoken against You? You have said, It is useless to serve God, and what profit is it if we keep His ordinances..."
>
> (Malachi 3:13-14a, AMP)

> "For by your words you will be justified and acquitted, and by your words you will be condemned

and sentenced."

(Matthew 12:37, AMP)

Speaking God's Word about ourselves and about those around us will always be found profitable to us in the long run—and enable us to receive approval from Jehovah God when we stand before Him.

Furthermore, when you say, "I am the righteousness of Jesus Christ," (2 Corinthians 5:21) or "I am the head and not the tail; above and not beneath," (Deuteronomy 28:13), etc., you are bringing your life into divine alignment with His creative order. You are not simply declaring those things so that someday they will happen. Rather, what you are doing is "calling things that be not as though they were," like Abraham did according to Romans 4:17. You are speaking in the present tense because, from God's eternal perspective, it is already done—and you are simply lining yourself up with that which is already granted to you. Your words are becoming the things that connect your future with His plan.

The Scripture says, "Beloved, I wish above all things that thou mayest prosper and be in health even as thy soul [the mind, will, and emotions] prospereth," (3 John 2). When you understand the divine pattern of creation—and your part in it—things will begin to "click" in your head and your soul will begin to prosper from that revelation. Once you realize that your entire life is made up of words, you can begin to grasp the basic truths you need to get yourself on the right path to fulfilling your God-given purpose in life.

When you begin to "speak to the mountain to be removed," you may not sense anything happening at first. However, because faith is developed by hearing the words of your own mouth (Romans 10:17; Joshua 1:8), just the act of saying it will, over time, cause it to become real to you—on the inside of your being. Then it is only a matter of time before things begin to change in your life for the better, as your words continue to line up with His Word—and His revealed plan for your life.

Although what I shared in this chapter about *dabar* being "words that become things" might sound somewhat "deep" to many who might read this, I want to take you even deeper into the Hebrew construction of this particular term. Therein lie even greater secrets of the Kingdom concerning your prosperity…

—Yahshua—

Jesus—The Way, The Truth, And The Life.

"I came that they may have and enjoy life, and have it in abundance (to the full, till it overflows)."

(John 10:10b, Amplified)

WHAT MOVES YOU?

What moves you to better yourself, or, in other words, to prosper? Stop for just a moment and do an honest evaluation of your heart. What moves you? Money? Opportunity? Security? Adventure?

Those things are all well and good—in their *proper* perspective. However, by themselves, they are evidence of a self-centeredness that will limit your true potential in God.

"Oh, no, Brother Dan! I don't care for any of those things! In fact, I don't really even want to prosper beyond my current state!"

Then you are even *more* selfish than those whose motivations are solely focused on their own personal goals and achievements. Consider what Paul wrote about the Body of Christ:

Chapter Eight

> "For just as the body is a unity and yet has many parts, and all the parts, though many, form [only] one body, so it is with Christ (the Messiah, the Anointed One)...For the body does not consist of one limb or organ but of many...**And if one member suffers, all the parts [share] the suffering; if one member is honored, all the members [share in] the enjoyment of it."**

(1 Corinthians 12:12, 14, 26, AMP, emphasis added)

If those in meager circumstances continue to walk in that condition, they are causing the entire Body of Christ to suffer with them through their abasement. However, if they rise above that place of insufficiency and lack to a place where they have more resources than they could possibly use personally, then they can use their overflow to bless the entire Body. Their abundance then becomes a supply to those who are in lack, and the Body of Christ is enhanced and enlarged as a result.

But those in lack are, in effect, not carrying their own load—and are forcing the rest of the Body to take up the slack for them. They are essentially a liability to the Church of Jesus Christ in the sense that they siphon off resources that could have been used toward spreading the Gospel.

Additionally, they are not adding their own share to the overall condition of the Body either—they are not fulfilling their own potential and therefore are not ministering to others materially and spiritually to the degree they ought. In effect, they are somewhat crippled limbs on the Body of Christ—neither able to help others or themselves—and yet receiving nourishment from the rest of the Body that should be going toward productive uses.

Now that is a hard word to hear—especially from a Wall Street millionaire, Ivy League preacher from New York—but it is what you *need* to hear if I am to shake you out of your self-deceit and get you on God's path of increase for your life.

"I am not deceived!" you may protest.

Well, let me ask you something: Do you really believe you do not want to prosper? Let's get real for a moment and really consider that question.

Do you get envious or "testy" when someone else gets a promotion, a new car, a pay raise, or a new house? Do you judge them? Do you criticize them?

How about when good things come *your* way? Do you get excited when your boss offers you that new job…or when you get a pay increase…or when you find an item on sale?

When it gets right down to it, God created you in HIS image and likeness—and He is a Person Who likes to increase!

He created the laws of seedtime and harvest that makes the entire world flourish…He is the One Who made the streets of the celestial city with gold so pure you can see through it…He is the One Who sent His Son to die on the cross—so that He might be the "Firstborn among many brethren"! (Romans 8:29)

Let's stop playing games here...of course you want to prosper. You are made in the image of the most prosperous being of the universe—YHWH Himself! It is in your DNA! It is the very makeup of the core of your entire being! Wake up! Reject that hypocritical religious mind-set the devil sold the Church hundreds of years after the Resurrection of the Messiah. Its very origins are from Eastern religions—not the Scripture. A few Bible passages here and there taken out of their context does not justify a "poverty is holy" doctrine—not when there are hundreds of Scriptures from Genesis to Revelation that contradict such a "doctrine" on every point!

My friend, there are billions of people in this world who are on their way to Hell, and we need every resource and every gift God has given His Church to get this final harvest into the Kingdom before the door closes on time once and for all—and we do not have much time. We certainly do not have time to be carrying the weight of broke, sick, "busted and disgusted" Christians who on one hand tell us how "holy" they are for letting us do all the work—and bad-mouthing us on the other hand for having more than $20 in our pocket.

We love you, and we'll minister to you in whatever way we can to get you up and on your feet. But we also need you to receive correction, instruction, and exhortations—and get with the program!

Let's discover our full potential in Christ! Let's get properly educated both spiritually and financially so that we no longer put our money in "bags with holes in them" (see Haggai 1:6).

Let's get our bills paid through the application of biblical principles—with plenty more left over for us to help someone else get up and join the fight with us too!

—Yahshua—

Jesus—The Way, The Truth, and The Life.

"I came that they may have and enjoy life, and have it in abundance (to the full, till it overflows)."

(John 10:10b, Amplified)

GETTING DEEPER

Now, I have not forgotten about those of you who have self-centered and superficial motivations driving you toward your goals. Money, opportunity, security, and adventure are all good things in their proper place. (Hey, I've had a boatload of them all in my life through the years!) However, as *motivations* these can be quite deceptive and lead you astray. You need to have the proper godly motives and purposes to support you as a firm foundation—then God will add to you all the money, opportunity, security, and adventure you can handle!

> "Beloved, I wish above all things that thou mayest prosper and be in health, even as thy soul prospereth."
> (3 John 2)

> "But seek (aim at and strive after) first of all His kingdom and His righteousness (His way of doing and being right), and then all these things taken together will be given you besides."
> (Matthew 6:33, AMP)

Chapter Nine

Just prior to this verse in Matthew, Jesus talked about how the world seeks after material things—and even noted that we need such things in our lives (see verse 32). However, He stated that the principle of their acquisition is based entirely on having our hearts and labors toward the things of God first. Then, we will have "prosperous souls" as John mentioned above, and these cause both material prosperity and health to be manifest over time in our lives.

Are you ready to receive some of this for yourself?

Good! That is what I am here for. That is my calling—to minister revelation concerning financial conquest for the Kingdom of God.

Now, let's go into some more depth on this same Hebrew word, *dabar*, and see what Kingdom principles God has for us that will cause our motivational foundation to be solid and sure—and entirely based in righteousness.

The first letter of *dabar* is the Hebrew letter *dâlet*, which looks to most English-speaking people like an up side down "L" with a little bit of a lip on one side:

ד

(dâlet)

It is the fourth letter of the Hebrew alphabet and it resembles the picture of a man who is leaned over—which symbolizes a man who is willing to carry other people's burdens. Consider these words of Jesus as recorded in John:

> "Then said Jesus unto them again, 'Verily, verily, I say unto you, I am the door of the sheep. All that ever came before me are thieves and robbers: but the sheep did not hear them. I am the door: by me if any man enter in, he shall be saved, and shall go in and out, and find pasture.'"
> (John 10:7-9)

Remember for a moment that when Jesus walked the Earth two thousand years ago, He did so as a Hebrew man—a Jew. Here in this passage, He was addressing Jewish religious scholars, as well as a crowd of Jewish people. When Jesus said, "I am the Door," He was making a metaphorical reference for their benefit regarding things that these people knew intimately as a part of their culture, language and spiritual heritage as decedents of Abraham. Jesus was really saying, "I am the *dalet*." He was saying, "I have come to carry your burdens, so come to Me. I will carry your burdens if you come through this door." For my Christian readers, this should immediately bring to mind two additional passages of Scripture:

> "Come unto me, all ye that labour and are heavy laden, and I will give you rest. Take my yoke upon you, and learn of me; for I am meek and lowly in heart: and ye shall find rest unto your souls. For my yoke is easy, and my burden is light."
> (Matthew 11:28-30)

> **"Let this mind be in you, which was also in Christ Jesus**: Who, being in the form of God, thought it not robbery to be equal with God: **But made Himself of no reputation, and took upon Him the form of a servant**, and was made in the likeness of men: And being found in fashion as a man, **He humbled himself**, and became **obedient** unto death, even the death of the cross. Wherefore God also hath highly exalted Him..."
> (Philippians 2:5-9a, emphasis added)

If we are to be "highly exalted" by our Heavenly Father, then we must first follow Jesus' example and take upon ourselves this servant-like spirit of humility. The way up, is actually by going down:

> "Humble yourselves therefore under the mighty hand of God, that he may exalt you in due time..."
> (1 Peter 5:6, KVJ)

"Now, what in the world does all of this have to do with financial prosperity?" you might ask.

Becoming wealthy is not just a simple matter of confessing that money will come to us—although our words are important, as I have already shown you. No, if I want money to come to me, this is how it will happen:

I must meet somebody else's need.

Did you get that?

Most credible people will tell you that proper marketing is the backbone of any commercial endeavor—and real marketing is all about your saying, "I've got to figure out what you need, and then you give me money so that I can give it to you." That is business and commerce in its essence. Since the foundation of the world, nearly every financial transaction has resulted in one form or another from the simple concept of finding needs and fulfilling them.

Money is not going to come to you abundantly just by people running up to you and putting it in your hand (although I have had that happen a time or two). That is not how the natural economies of this world work—nor is it how God's economy functions. Money and wealth are consistently generated through *exchange*. Money changes hands…products and services are conferred—this is how successful economies function. Even Jesus taught that the way of financial increase was through trade:

> "Again, it will be like a man going on a journey, who called his servants and entrusted his property to them. To one he gave five talents of money, to another two talents, and to another one talent, **each according to his ability**. Then he went on his journey. The man who had received the five talents went **at once** and **put his money to work** and gained five more. So also, the one with the two talents gained two more. But the man who had received the one talent went off, dug a hole in the ground and hid his master's money.
>
> "After a long time the master of those servants returned and settled accounts with them. The man who had received the five talents brought the other five. 'Master,' he said, 'you entrusted me with five talents. See, I have gained five more.'
>
> "His master replied, 'Well done, good and faithful servant! You have been faithful with a few things; I will put you in charge of many things. Come and share your master's happiness!'
>
> "The man with the two talents also came. 'Master,' he said, 'you entrusted me with two talents; see, I have gained two more.'
>
> "His master replied, 'Well done, good and faithful servant! You have been faithful with a few things;

Getting Deeper

I will put you in charge of many things. Come and share your master's happiness!'

"Then the man who had received the one talent came. 'Master,' he said, 'I knew that you are a hard man, harvesting where you have not sown and gathering where you have not scattered seed. So I was afraid and went out and hid your talent in the ground. See, here is what belongs to you.'

"His master replied, 'You wicked, lazy servant! So you knew that I harvest where I have not sown and gather where I have not scattered seed? Well then, you should have put my money on deposit with the bankers, so that when I returned I would have received it back with **interest**.

"'Take the talent from him and give it to the one who has the ten talents. For everyone who has will be given more, and he will have an abundance. Whoever does not have, even what he has will be taken from him. And throw that worthless servant outside, into the darkness, where there will be weeping and gnashing of teeth.'"

(Matthew 25:14-30, NIV, emphasis added)

Now, before I elaborate on the principle of exchange from the above passage, let us take a look at the starting capital these servants were entrusted with by their master:

Some Bible references will leave you the impression that these men were not given a very large quantity of cash to work with—but that could not be farther from the truth! Keep in mind that most of the references used (such as Strong's Concordance, Vine's Expository Dictionary, Smith's Bible Dictionary, etc…) are one hundred or more years old. Since many Bible footnotes are based on these or similar sources, they likewise can leave the impression that these sums were not significant. Things have gotten a bit more expensive in the last century, so let me reveal what Greek words are used in this passage, and then we can assess a reasonable value to the sum entrusted to these stewards.

Originally, a *talent* was the Hebrew word *kikkâr* (Strong's #3603), which in the economies of Abraham's day indicated a certain *weight* of something (about ninety-one pounds, or forty-one kilograms today)—primarily precious metals such as gold and silver, exchanged in commerce. However, as coinage became the standard of economic trade over time, this term transformed to become a reference to a *quantity* of coinage, rather than the *weight* thereof.

The specific Greek word used here in this New Testament parable for "talent" is the word *talantŏn* (Strong's # 5007), which, in Roman coinage, was equivalent to 6,000 *denarii* (plural for *denarius*—a silver coin used at the time of our Savior). In fact, the Greek word translated "money" in verse twenty-seven above is the word *argurion* (Strong's # 694), which literally means "silver." So to be candid, we are talking about a rather large *pile* of silver coins when the Bible says that their master gave them each a talent or more to invest.

Now it would be difficult to assess an exact value in contemporary buying power—especially in a book—since commodities like silver fluctuate over time. However, given that a single silver denarius weighed a little less than a quarter of an ounce (or 5.4 grams in metric), then we can determine that 6,000 denarii weighed about seventy-one and a half pounds (or 32.4 kilograms). Considering that the price of silver in today's market is at about $7 per ounce when this text was written, that means that the master gave his first servant about $40,000 to invest, the second $16,000, and about $8,000 to the third! (In Euro, that is about €32,000; €12,800 and €6,400 respectively.)

Anyway you look at it, any of those amounts are significant starting capital for three new traders in the market! There were a few times I could have used an endowment like that myself in my own early days as a commodities trader.

Now, let me get back to explaining the principle of exchange:

The Greek word translated "put his money to work" in the New International Version translation above, and "traded with the same" in the King James Version, is the word *ĕrgazŏmai* (Strong's #2038), which means to "toil," "labor," or to "work with something." Notice how this verb is used in other Bible translations of this same passage:

> "The man…began immediately to **buy and sell** with it."
>
> (TLB, emphasis added)

"Without delay the one who had received the five

talents went and **employed them in business,** and gained five more."
(Weymouth's New Testament, emphasis added)

"The servant who received the five bags of gold began immediately **to invest the money** and soon doubled it."
(NLT, emphasis added)

"...the servant with the five thousand coins **used them to earn** five thousand more..."
(CEV, emphasis added)

"...The servant...went at once and **put his money to work**..."
(NIrV®, emphasis added)

It is a scriptural fact that Jesus taught more about finances (i.e. money) than any other subject—except redemption itself. Over half of His parables dealt in some form with proper handling, stewardship, and attitudes regarding money. Here in the famous "parable of the talents," Jesus laid out for us in stark detail how money is earned and multiplied—through *exchange*.

Now, I know that there are some brethren out there who teach the principles of God's economy as though the only thing you have to do is tithe, give some offerings, and get out of the way before the Brinks truck runs you over as your harvest comes in. That is not how the Bible teaches it, however. Neither is it how some of the more respected prosperity teachers explain it. No, you need to "put your hand to" something so that God can bless it (see Deuteronomy 28:8, 12).

The people for whom the true "prosperity message" works are those who apply the principles taught to their businesses, professions and financial affairs—and allow the biblical principles of exchange to work for them even as the laws of seedtime and harvest do. In fact, if you do not "sow some seed" into your business and investments, then the seed you sow into the Kingdom of God through tithes and offerings will have a limited ability to return to you since you are neglecting significant portions of Scripture in your daily conduct.

Let me say this in another way: If you do not invest capital into your business and investment portfolios, then you are cutting off much of the "returns" you would have received from your investments into the Kingdom through your tithes, offerings, and acts of charitable giving. The channels of your harvest from the seeds you have sown into the Kingdom of God are primarily (but not exclusively) your business, professional and investment endeavors—much like Israel's primary channels of increase came through their agricultural efforts, professional trades, and commerce once they entered Canaan.

When God told them "I'll open up the windows of Heaven and pour you out a blessing" (Malachi 3:10), they heard, "Your fields will be watered, your crops will come in, and your every business enterprise will prosper." If you are expecting money to drop on you from Heaven, you will be waiting a long, long time—and ultimately wind up very disappointed in the end.

Now, I am not saying that God will not use miraculous means to supply your need from time to time. However, such spectacular supernatural interventions generally occur when either people are in locations without resources (such as when Elijah was fed by ravens) or when He needs to pull one of His kids out of a jam before his or her world caves in! God never intended for His people to live from miracle to miracle—but to eat the good of the land! (Isaiah 1:19)

Even Israel found that the manna no longer rained down from Heaven once they entered into their promised land—it was simply no longer necessary. He intended for them to use the resources He provided through the land of the Canaanites, given to them via military conquest. His desire was that they would use those assets to establish their own livelihoods and form the economy for the entire nation—using the principles of exchange to increase more and more.

Essentially, the biblical laws of exchange open up conduits for the blessings of the laws of seedtime and harvest to flow through. Both sets of laws compound the effects of the other—exponentially—and the benefits of both dwindle rapidly in direct proportion to the extent that the other is lacking in your life.

Furthermore, both laws "hang" on the spiritual law of love in order to function:

> "'Master, which is the great commandment in the law?' Jesus said unto him, "'Thou shalt love the Lord thy God with all thy heart, and with all thy

soul, and with all thy mind." This is the first and great commandment, and the second is like unto it, "Thou shalt love thy neighbor as thyself." On these two commandments hang all the law and the prophets.'"

(Matthew 22:36-40)

All spiritual laws are mutually dependent on each other to function to their maximum capacity. However, only two spiritual laws reign supreme as the foundation for all the others—"Love the Lord your God with all your heart, soul and mind," and "Love your neighbor as yourself." Consequently, although the laws of exchange and the laws of seedtime and harvest depend on each other to bring maximum blessing, neither will work at all without love:

> "If I give all I possess to the poor and surrender my body to the flames, but have not love, I gain nothing."

(1 Corinthians 13:3, NIV)

LOVE IS HUMBLE

Now, let's bring this back to the biblical principle of humility in the context of business; because without true humility, you will simply not have the grace to see God's system of increase work in your life—especially your finances. You need to ask yourself, "How can I humble myself to look through the eyes of my brother to see a need that he has, and then continue to humble myself so that I can meet that need? How can I get my eyes off of me and onto someone else's situation so that God can show me the opportunities that await us both?"

Humility is not being a wallflower. Humility is *carrying someone else's burden*. Sometimes it takes great boldness to take on a burden. Sometimes it takes a big personality to do it. Really, humility (that is, humility for others) has to do with exposing and using your gift at full blast. Biblical humility is a willingness to subjugate your life to use the gifts inside of you to benefit others.

The funny thing is that humility oftentimes leads to greater things because in order to help other people, you have to become bigger and bolder. How else can you serve others greater unless your capacity for service increases? As you humble yourself in service to others, you will be expanded and enlarged. Through the process, you often become "larger than life" in other people's eyes, and they begin to believe in your abilities. That is why the Bible exhorts us in two very distinct passages of Scripture to:

> "Humble yourselves in the sight of the Lord, and he shall lift you up."
> (James 4:10)

and

> "Humble yourselves therefore under the mighty hand of God, that he may exalt you in due time."
> (1 Peter 5:6)

So the way *up* is indeed *down*.

Oftentimes, however, when our brothers and sisters in Christ come into situations in which they seem to be going backwards, some criticize them and say that they are "not in faith" and not doing the right things to gain the victory in those situations. When we do that, we are killing the very oak trees (which are explained in the chapter entitled, "Acorn, Baby!") that would be supplying the fruit for years to come. Such a fault-finding mind-set comes from a lack of understanding the principle of having to go down before you can go up. Remember:

- You have to re-tool to get better.
- You have to bend your knees before you can jump.
- You have to pull your arm back before you can strike a blow.
- A seed has to "die" before it can grow. (John 12:24)
- And you have to tear down, before you can build back up:

> "There is a time for everything, and a season for every activity under heaven: a time to be born and a time to die, a time to plant and a time to uproot, a time to kill and a time to heal, a time to tear down and a time to build, a time to weep and a time to laugh, a time to mourn and a time to dance, a time to scatter stones and a time to gather them, a time to embrace and a time to refrain, a time to search and a time to give up, a time to keep and a time to throw away, a time to tear and a time to mend, a time to be silent and a time to speak, a time to love and a time

to hate, a time for war and a time for peace."
(Ecclesiastes 3:1-8, NIV)

Understanding the truth of God's seasons, and how He uses humility to raise people up higher, will cause us to be far more compassionate toward others who are in a time of trial—and to be comforted ourselves when it is our season. Of course, there are times when people are "missing it" in their faith or application of God's Word to their lives—but far more often than is realized, people have to take a significant step down before they find the elevator that will take them to the top.

I know I am getting hard on you as I readjust your thinking here, but you must understand that the Word of God is not just for doctrine and for righteousness, but it is also for reproof and correction as well (2 Timothy 3:16-17). Loving others is not passive. True "loving" is giving and serving—it is proactive. So many times, we are looking for our "harvest of blessing" without really understanding what we have to go through to get there.

We may have to "walk through the valley of the shadow of death" in order to come to that table where we are seated in the "presence of our enemies with our cups running over" (See Psalm 23). There might be a few distractions along our path—a few "bumps" in the road.

I have actually been criticized about what happened to our church building during the "9-11" World Trade Center attack, and for other setbacks I have experienced. People have said, "Well, Dan, if you were anointed, your building would have never been blown up. If you were anointed, your church would be so much bigger. Those Muslims could not have bought that other building you were pursuing out from under you. If you were anointed, you would have known these things."

Wake up and get in touch with reality!

I have never been in business or in sports where I have not been confronted on some level—where I did not have to win some fight. Unlike these critics, I have read my Bible:

David had to beat Goliath. (1 Samuel 17)

Moses had to face Pharaoh. (Exodus 3 through 15)

Abraham had to leave everything and walk out into the wilderness. (Genesis 12)

Even Jesus had a wilderness experience!

"Jesus, full of the Holy Spirit, returned from the

Jordan and was led by the Spirit in the desert, where for forty days he was tempted by the devil... When the devil had finished all this tempting, he left him until an opportune time. Jesus returned to Galilee in the power of the Spirit, and news about him spread through the whole countryside."

(Luke 4:1-2, 13-14, NIV. See also Matthew 4:1-11 and Mark 1:12-13)

If Jesus was purposely led by the Holy Spirit into the wilderness for a time of testing before the launching of His earthly ministry, is it too hard to comprehend that the same thing might happen to you as well? You must understand that such wilderness experiences—and your abilities to handle them—are training grounds, preparing you for the huge things that God has planned to accomplish through you. That way, when the divine opportunities come, you have the wisdom to do what you are supposed to do on a larger scale.

Humility is the foundation of true prosperity and promotion—and is found quite stunningly in just the first letter of the Hebrew word, *dabar*—*words that become things*. Moreover, the other two letters of this three letter Hebrew word also contain "hidden" truths for us to explore.

—Yahshua—

Jesus—The Way, The Truth, and The Life.

"I came that they may have and enjoy life, and have it in abundance (to the full, till it overflows)."

(John 10:10b, Amplified)

EXCHANGE

Chapter Ten

The second Hebrew letter of the word *dabar* that we need to examine is *bêth*, which is the second letter of the Hebrew alphabet:

(bêth)

Since the Hebrew letters are also its numerical system, this particular letter also means "two," implying exchange. Whenever two or more people come together and interact with one another, there is always some form of exchange taking place.

Furthermore, *beth* is the first letter of the Hebrew word for "house"—implying that this is "where you live." So when we examine the concept of "humility" expressed by *dalet* (the first letter of *dabar*), we find that the second letter tells us that it is not some kind of outward false humility, but it refers to living a humble life all the time. We need to live in humility "24/7."

Sure, we can go to church and worship God and sing, "Holy, holy, holy. Praise Him!" and act really spiritual in the house of worship. However, do we then go home and criticize everything that happened at church and the way people treated us?

We need to have humility and integrity at home—when nobody is looking. We need to act as true sons and daughters of God by displaying His nature of love all the time.

That letter *beth* also refers to the fact that you cannot have things go from the supernatural to the natural *by yourself.* This is where the power of agreement comes in. It takes two (or more):

> "Again, I tell you that if two of you on earth agree about anything you ask for, it will be done for you by my Father in heaven. For where two or three come together in my name, there am I with them."
> (Matthew 18:19-20, NIV)

Remember, contained within *beth* is the idea of exchange. Sure we need to come to the place where we acknowledge our need for God's "super" on our "natural" to live the life He has destined for us. But we also need to humble ourselves and admit we need others in the Body of Christ to be successful as well.

It takes humility to acknowledge our total dependence on God.

It takes humility to admit our interdependence on each other.

It takes humility to serve other people.

Then *beth* tells us to "bring it home" and act that way all the time—with our own families, not just at the church house. That is another level of humility, still.

Furthermore, this letter tells us that we are not supposed to live by ourselves because we need relationships. *Relationships form the basis of exchange.* That is why widows and orphans are supposed to be cared for. Many people live by themselves and say, "Leave me alone. I don't want to be in agreement with anybody. I've got my own life. I can do it all by myself." That is not the way it is supposed to be, and you cannot get to where you need to go being a one-man or one-woman show.

TOGETHER WE PROSPER

If you are married, you understand that love is not a constant state of bliss all the time. I do not have to tell married couples that there are times when your emotions are on "cloud nine" and others when reality has set in. For the rest of you, let me illustrate this from my own youth...

When I was 19, my love for a particular girl dominated my mind. I thought she was just beautiful. My heart would "pitter-patter" when she walked by. I could not wait to call her. But whenever we went out to dinner, a change would occur. She might say, "Why are you wearing that shirt? Don't eat those potatoes, eat the asparagus. Put your napkin on your lap," etc. Suddenly the "ooey gooey" thoughts returned to earth and became really practical.

That is the way we are in the Body when we are endeavoring to work together. It will be all exciting when we first come into contact and exchange business cards, but after a while, we get to know each other and have to put up with some personality traits that might grate on each other's nerves. When you get into a relationship with someone, your weaknesses will begin to show up if the other person is strong in those areas. Instead of feeling threatened, inferior, or getting offended when that happens, you must admit to having shortcomings so that others can help you in those areas.

As I mentioned in an earlier chapter called, "Running with the Pros," I believe that everything you need as a Christian is already in the Body of Christ. The problem is that those within the Body are not talking to each other. It is like a dysfunctional family. We need to be doing business with each other as best as we can. For example, if you know a Christian who does nails, then support that person instead of going to the world. If you know a Christian florist, then buy your flowers from that person. Look for Christian businesses and buy products and services from them.

Somebody might say, "Well, I want to save myself $400." That person is not seeing the big picture, which is to build up the Body of Christ. Although there are times when a Christian over-inflates his prices, seeking to rip people off, those who are honest, fair, and excellent in their vocations should be supported by others in the Body. The more that we help each other expand and prosper our businesses—and the more we see each other as family, the more the Gospel will get preached.

"Why?" you might ask.

When the individual members of a local church increase financially, then the Church corporately experiences increased prosperity as well:

> "And if one member suffers, all the parts [share] the suffering; if one member is honored, all the members [share in] the enjoyment of it."
>
> (1 Corinthians 12:26, AMP)

RELATIONAL PROSPERITY

We must understand that all of the prosperity that God is going to bring to the Body of Christ will come through the cultivation of relationships. It will come through people. What happens sometimes in larger churches is that the people do not talk to each other! They sort of have a relationship with the person in the pulpit, and they give their money, but because people are quirky, needy, or impolite, or because they don't seem to share common interests, nobody gets to know each other. Do you know what word doctors use to describe a condition when members of a body do not communicate with each other?

Paralysis!

There are far too many "paralyzed" congregations in the world attempting to carry out the Great Commission! (See Mark 16:15-18) We need to get the "members" communicating with each other so that the local church body can function with some sense of biblical "normalcy." We need to understand that our prosperity is dependent on our removing their burdens and destroying their yokes:

> "And it shall come to pass in that day, that his burden shall be taken away from off thy shoulder, and his yoke from off thy neck, and the yoke shall be destroyed because of the anointing."
>
> (Isaiah 10:27)

> "For because of Him the whole body (the church, in all its various parts), closely joined and firmly knit together by the joints and ligaments with which it is supplied, when each part [with power adapted to its need] is working properly [in all its functions], grows to full maturity, building itself up in love."
>
> (Ephesians 4:16, AMP)

The "yokes" and "burdens" that afflict and oppress people are destroyed when individual believers use the specific "power adapted to [their] needs" and minister that anointing to the other parts of the Body. Your prosperity hinges on freeing up others in the Body, so they can maybe go and find a divine appointment for you. God wants to free us all! Jesus freed us by coming down to our level—and then doing the work that His Father had called him to do. When we humble ourselves and serve others with our God-given gifts, talents and anointings, then we will likewise be doing the work of Jesus—and find our own deliverance within the deliverance of others. Unfortunately, what often happens is we want to *talk*, but we do not want to *do*.

WEALTH BUILDING 101

Now in sharing these things with you, I want to make sure you start thinking towards wealth, and not just towards "ministry," (at least what you *think* is ministry). I am not saying that ministry is not a necessary thing for us to focus on, but ministry does not make any money in and of itself. In fact, true bona fide Gospel ministry can only go so far without money.

Nor am I talking about forms of "ministry" where you are feeding the poor, or clothing the naked—that is another thing entirely from what I am talking about here. What I am describing to you is the individual members of a local church body (and the Body of Christ as a whole) using their own particular gifts and abilities to strengthen each other and meet needs among themselves. I am describing believers humbling themselves to discover the needs of others—and then offering their goods, services, and abilities to meet those needs. In other words, what I am trying to impress upon your mind is the fact that:

Meeting other people's needs leads to great wealth.

When you, out of a heart of servanthood, reach out and help fill a void in someone's life, it is right and just for that person to compensate you. For example, if you are a carpenter, and someone needs some remodeling, then it is right, just and fair for that person to pay you for your services. He or she needs remodeling; you have the tools and skills necessary to meet that need. And through a common medium of exchange (i.e. money, or the barter of other goods and services in return) the person compensates you for your labors. These exchange-types of relationships are win-win connections that benefit both parties—and that can last a lifetime when they are cultivated within Christian covenant.

Just think what would happen if we all started doing business with each other, completely ethically on a high level of integrity, and were committed to doing business together on a regular basis! The financial flow through the Body of Christ would be astounding! However, notice that I mentioned that it would have to be built upon both *biblical ethics* and *integrity*.

Anybody can come to our ProVision Network meetings. However, they have to set a firm standard for themselves of treating people right and having a high level of integrity in their business practices if they want to have unbridled liberty to do business within our network. We have an understanding in PVN that we all need to look out for each other by listening and finding out what is going on in people's lives—and to help each other to be overcomers in every area.

However, that interpersonal relationship development also tends to expose those who have substandard business ethics as well. We will try and work with them—if we can, to get their practices in line with the Word. Nevertheless, we will not allow dishonest people to create havoc among the believers either. Such a cultivating, yet protective, atmosphere is an environment where relationships can flourish.

Strong associations are built within the context of covenant.

DON'T LET GO!

I have a profound revelation of relationship and partnership. I know that you are an important part of what God is going to do in the earth today. And I also know that I have a vital piece to impart into you, so that you can be properly cross-pollinated to do what you are called and gifted to do. It is a powerful opportunity that we have. Let us fight this fight and run our race, and let us expose ourselves to the greatness of God and the bigness of the gifts that are within each and every one of us. And let us trust others to help us instead of dwelling on disappointments, discouragements, betrayals, and all the other painful experiences we have gone through.

The most challenging thing in our lives is holding on to God-ordained relationships, no matter how rocky things get. When you have messed up, or when you have not "hit the mark" or the standard, or when your expectations of someone did not get met exactly the way you wanted them to, how do you peacefully continue in a relationship?

Jesus told those who believed on Him, "If ye continue in my word, then are ye my disciples indeed; And ye shall know the truth, and the truth shall make you free." (John 8:31-32) A "disciple" is a "disciplined one"—spiritually, physically, mentally, socially, emotionally, and financially. We are to be "disciplined ones" in relationship with each other as well.

If we mess up, then we can look each other in the eye afterwards, repent to the one we have wronged, and go on—because we know we are the righteousness of God in Christ Jesus (2 Corinthians 5:21) and love will cover a multitude of sins (1 Peter 4:8). We also know that we are not

Exchange

allowed to quit or disqualify ourselves for making a mistake, or for not living up to certain expectations.

No church will ever be one in which everybody likes everyone else there. But when we come to understand covenant, our capacity to love each other will grow:

> "But now are they many members, yet but one body. And the eye cannot say unto the hand, I have no need of thee: nor again the head to the feet, I have no need of you."
> (1 Corinthians 12:20-21)

Even the things that you do that irritate me are put there by God to make me stronger, like the sand in the oyster making the pearl. If we can see our differences in this way, we will experience a lifestyle of "iron sharpens iron," rather than allowing the spirit of division to come in and sabotage God's great plan for us. (See Proverbs 27:17)

My function in the Body of Christ is to help each person to enter into his calling by teaching on the following Bible-based topics:

- Fearlessly pursuing the will of God,
- Discovering one's God-given gifts,
- And the necessity of covenant relationships to make it all happen.

Getting your financial life in order is not simply about having "three steps" to getting out of debt and "five steps" to getting your budget together. It is about our coming together and helping each other. In sports, no championship team I ever played on was one in which every player liked all of his other teammates. It never happened.

My job is to instill in you a relationship. Unless you have my same personality, you are going to have to get big enough to love a crass, bold, poor boy who went to Yale and Goldman Sachs; who screamed and yelled on the floor of the exchanges.

In the same way, I have to learn (and have learned) to love people who are always "fixin' to get ready" to do things. It is an issue of increasing our capacity to love one another, walking in covenant, and showing appreciation for others in the Body who may be very different than you in many respects.

Guess what? If we were all alike, we would not need anybody:

> "If the whole body were an eye, where would the sense of hearing be? If the whole body were an ear, where would the sense of smell be? But in fact, God has arranged the parts in the body, every one of them, just as He wanted them to be. If they were all one part, where would the body be? As it is, there are many parts, but one body. The eye **cannot** say to the hand, 'I don't need you!' And the head **cannot** say to the feet, 'I don't need you!' On the contrary, those parts of the body that seem to be weaker are indispensable..."
>
> (1 Corinthians 12:17-22, NIV, emphasis added)

Nineteen years ago, I was at a national Christian men's event at the University of Maryland. The minister taught on the Blood Covenant and about the importance of relationships and partnerships, and the fact that we cannot prosper without them. But what has happened to us, with the emergence of mega-churches in the United States, is that the churches have become so huge that although the *pastors* have relationships within the church, the *people* in the congregation do not know each other! And the ones in the pews are the church, the Body of Christ.

We need to fight through our inadequacies. We need to stretch ourselves and meet our brothers and sisters in the Lord! Some people are hoping for someone to lay hands on them and to then have $400,000 just come into their mailbox the next day. Although God is able and willing to send manna down from Heaven in extreme circumstances, this is certainly not the norm. Rather, it is through relationships that He has told us to cultivate that we will see His provision manifest in our lives on an ongoing basis.

PART IV

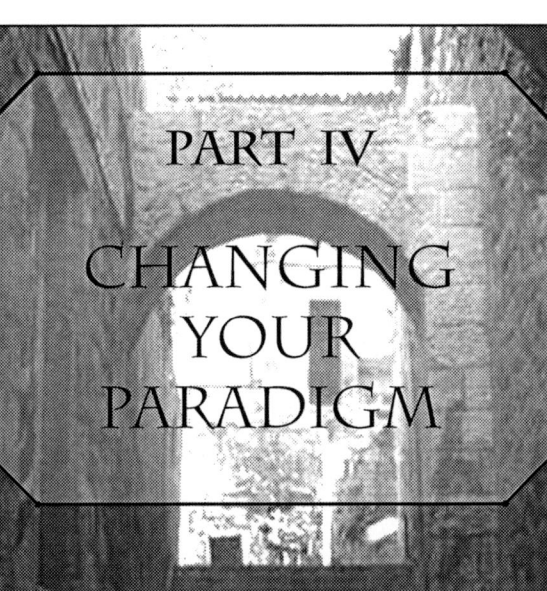

CHANGING YOUR PARADIGM

"Many people think that the economic realm should be like the recreational league. It is true that everybody gets to play, but most people do not qualify for promotion and success simply because they neglect to do what is necessary to get there."

—Yahshua—

Jesus—The Way, The Truth, And The Life.

"I came that they may have and enjoy life, and have it in abundance (to the full, till it overflows)."

(John 10:10b, Amplified)

SOUTHERN HOSPITALITY?

Have you ever thought what it would be like to be completely fulfilling the will of God for your life? Sometimes Christians think everything is going to be just wonderful when they are doing what God has called them to do. This is especially true for those who come from an area where everybody is so polite and nice to each other—like the Deep South, for instance.

Down in places like Louisiana and Texas (where I often minister) someone would rather smile and tell you he "loves you with the love of the Lord" rather than let you know you are on the wrong track heading toward disaster, or that you need to repent and get your life together—or even that your pants are unzipped and you are publicly humiliating yourself! Things that are profitable for others often go unsaid because of the social practices of so many regions of the world.

The danger with such a culture of "social politeness" is that some people would rather be polite than to tell others the truth they need to hear that could help them succeed in life. Some would rather err on the side of saying nothing, and being (what they call) "polite" to avoid hurting others' feelings, than to say what they know to be right. Rather than saying what could possibly save somebody's life and cause the listener to prosper, they become "politely mute" and the necessary truths continue unspoken. Because such behavior is ingrained into the culture of the Bible Belt here

Chapter Eleven

in the United States, Christians tend to forget the biblical exhortation from Ephesians Chapter Four:

> "Then we will no longer be infants, tossed back and forth by the waves, and blown here and there by every wind of teaching and by the cunning and craftiness of men in their deceitful scheming. Instead, **speaking the truth in love**, we will in all things grow up into Him who is the Head, that is, Christ."
>
> (NIV, verses 14-15, emphasis added)

Nowhere in the Bible does it give us a license to be phony with one another. Rather, the Scripture overflows with exhortation and instruction to be honest, forthright, and up-front with those to whom we have been connected in the Body of Christ.

I cannot personally identify with anything but being direct and up-front with people. If there is one common characteristic among typical New Yorkers, it is that they are generally "up front" with everybody—although it is fair to say that it is not commonly "in love" when they speak their mind. However, as Christians, we need to universally adopt the habit of being crystal clear and forthright with each other—in the love of God that He so generously shed abroad in our hearts by the Holy Spirit who was given to us! (Romans 5:5)

Why would so many Christians rather walk in such a façade of "politeness" instead of the truthfulness and honesty the Bible commends?

Simple: usually it is because they fear that the person would respond with something like this, "Who are you to say something like that to me? Only 'So and so' has the right to say that to me!" In other words, they allow self-interest and fear of man to prevent them from helping the other person.

My friend, sometimes God tells us to proclaim things that are not very easy for others to swallow—oftentimes they might "spit" it back up with animosity toward us as they choke on the message. Nevertheless, whether they like it or not, we must speak the truth to each other in love. Quite frankly, most of the time the other person will ultimately end up respecting us far more for our sincere love and honesty than they ever would for the phony one-dimensional relationship so often offered by most people. Consider what God said in 1 John 4:18:

> "There is no fear in love; but perfect love casteth out

fear..."
(1 John 4:18a)

"The one who fears is not made perfect in love."
(1 John 4:18b, NIV)

If you truly love the other person, you will speak the truth to him without any regard for what he might think or say in return. To put in quite bluntly: If you are afraid to speak beneficial truth to another person, then you do not truly love him with the love of God—despite any claim you might make otherwise.

Now, personally, I am not about to withhold truth from you that I feel is in your best interest. To do so would be to go "cross-grain" of the very fiber of my being. It is against my very nature to sugar coat, or "beat around the bush," and I could never do that to someone I love in Christ.

With that said, the real reason I exposed this issue of false politeness among Christians is because I want to minister another necessary truth to you for a while—in love, of course. Bear with me in my continued provocateur-type of bluntness as I press further into some additional issues that need to be addressed in regard to financial conquest...

WHAT YOU FIXIN'?

One of the things that I have discovered in my travels to Texas to minister is that New Yorkers are not all that popular there. (Could you have guessed?)

We are too brazen.

In fact, we are also too fast and pushy...too bold...too strong...and way too "straight to the point."

Now, all that might be true (from a Texan's perspective), but let me share with you one thing that we New Yorkers definitely are not:

We are not "fixin'" to do anything.

For those of you not familiar with the southern colloquialism, "fixin'," a Texan friend of mine once defined it as, "getting ready to begin to commence to about to start something." That might be a very colorful and accurate definition of that southern word—Texas-style, of course—but may I simply call it what it truly is?

Procrastination!

We New Yorkers are *not* known for procrastination—and we are certainly not "fixin' to get ready" to do anything!

We are used to doing things in a "New York minute," (a simple snap of the fingers), and we say things like, "Let's get it done!" It is a whole different mentality than what one finds in the southern parts of the United States. Yet God has sent me to various places in Texas and other southern states to cross-pollinate and impart into those areas some sense of urgency—especially in regard to ministry, business, and commerce.

My friend, it is way past "fixin'" time! If that word is in your vocabulary, lose it—quick!

Prospering in God is not simply about placing your tithe in the offering bucket on Sunday morning, and then going home to wait for a stack of one-hundred-dollar bills to "supernaturally" show up at your house on Wednesday night! It is about putting into practice all the principles of God's Word—tithing included—but, also the principles of diligence, hard work, the use of wise counsel, proper stewardship in investments and business...and even the practice of being truthful and open with each other.

As it has been prophesied recently through a credible man of God, five-fold ministry gifts (apostles, prophets, evangelists, pastors, and teachers) are going to begin to be manifested more fully and completely in the Body of Christ. This should come as no shock to anybody who is familiar with God's Word:

> "And he gave some, apostles; and some, prophets; and some, evangelists; and some, pastors and teachers; For the perfecting of the saints, for the work of the ministry, for the edifying of the body of Christ: Till we all come in the unity of the faith, and of the knowledge of the Son of God, unto a perfect man, unto the measure of the stature of the fullness of Christ..."
>
> (Ephesians 4:11-13)

"How many ministry gifts are there?" one might ask.

Five.

"For how long were they given?"

Until the entire Body of Christ comes into the unity of the faith, and of the knowledge of the Son of God, and to the point of being a complete and "perfect" man.

"What is a 'perfect' man?"

Complete Christ-likeness.

I can say with all surety that I have not personally arrived at that point in my walk with the Lord. Moreover, I can most emphatically say that neither have you—and especially not the entire Body of Christ simultaneously. That will not happen universally in the Church until Jesus appears to catch us all away:

> "Dear friends, now we are children of God, and what we will be has not yet been made known. But we know that when he appears, we shall be like him, for we shall see him as he is."
>
> (1 John 3:2, NIV)

Until that soon-approaching day occurs, God has ordained imperfect men, operating by the anointing of a perfect God, to minister into our lives those things we need to be perfected "from glory to glory" into the image of God's dear Son (2 Corinthians 3:18).

My friend, I am one of those ministry gifts God has sent into your life. I am one of those imperfect ministers sent by God to the Body of Christ to fulfill a specific purpose—His purpose, to bring about a certain portion of that "perfecting" process. I have both fresh revelation and abundant grace imparted into me by the Holy Spirit, to effect certain changes in your life that will help you to grow up into that "full stature."

However, I have to admit that this "gift" does not come "wrapped" in the standard paper (at least by some people's standards). In fact, I am not like most of those in my own circle of ministers: I am Yale educated, which could define me as an "Ivy League" preacher—and from Wall Street, no less!

Trust me; I can assure you that I am considered quite weird in many circles.

"Yale educated?" It is not easily accepted. Some seem to think that if you do not go to some well-renowned Bible school that you are not even filled with the Holy Ghost!

I come from Wall Street, Goldman Sachs, working eighteen years on the exchanges—fighting against some of the toughest business people you have ever seen in your life! There on the floor of the commodity trading "pits" of New York City was some of the worst kind of backstabbing that could be found anywhere. When millions, billions, even trillions of dollars are changing hands, people can get brutally cutthroat—let me tell you!

Some days when I returned home, it felt like I had been given a forced tracheotomy while at work that day!

I had to make a thousand decisions every twenty minutes just to stay alive—much less to prosper there! Because of all of this, my mind does not work like this "fixin' to get ready" stuff. It is just not in my genes! I simply cannot think any other way than, "Let's get this thing done now! Let's make it happen now! Let's make a decision...NOW!"

This is one of my strengths. This type of mentality helped make me a very successful commodities trader. And this strength of mine is what God wants to cross-pollinate into some of my more fixin'-minded brethren who need to learn how to take the initiative, make some decisions, and get some things done...NOW!

There is an entire world out there going to Hell and we need to do something about it...NOW! We need to stop "fixin'" to do things, and start fixing some things in our lives, businesses, churches, and nations...NOW! These changes are necessary to bring in the harvests on the seeds we have sown, the wealth of the sinner which is laid up for the just (Proverbs 13:22), and the goal of every promise of God—the final harvest of souls before the End of this Age and return of our King. All this needs to happen—NOW! And to do it, it will take initiative, decisiveness, and determination to get these things done.

Now, lest you think, "Boy, that braggart from New York is really full of himself," let me also acknowledge here that I am fully aware that I do have weaknesses of my own. As I said before, I am one of God's imperfect vessels, chosen by His will and grace, to minister into your life from those things He has given me. I understand that I have weaknesses and shortcomings. However, I also understand that where I am weak, someone else is strong—and I am willing to admit my weaknesses that I might benefit from the strengths of others through covenant relationships.

In this same way, where another person is weak, I want to be there to help him with my strengths. This is what I am doing— empowering you in areas where you may be anemic. This is what relationship is all about. It is not about personalities, it is about covenant.

Let's face it; you may not like me and my bold tirades about speaking the truth in love and getting things done. I may not like your, "Maybe next week we'll have a cup of tea...if I feel like it" mentality. But together, we can help each other fulfill the plan of God for our lives—if we'll let the other speak loving truth to us that we may change for the better.

This brings us back to my initial question at the beginning of this chapter; "Have you ever thought what it would be like to be completely fulfilling the will of God for your life?"

If you think about it for even a moment, you will realize that it will take something more energetic than "fixin'," something more honest than "polite," and something more others-oriented than the typical one-dimensional relationships so common in the Body of Christ today.

We need each other.

That bears repeating…we N-E-E-D each other!

I need your gifts, talents and calling manifest to the fullest extent possible so that I can draw from what God has given you that I might be made the fuller thereby.

> "For because of Him, the whole Body (the Church, in all its various parts), closely joined and firmly knit together by the joints and ligaments with which it is supplied, when each part [with power adapted to its need] is working properly [in all its functions], grows to full maturity, building itself up in love."
> (Ephesians 4:16, Amplified)

However, that also means that you need some things from me—like my bold, brash, "let's get it done" New York mentality, so that you might draw from my strengths and be enlarged thereby as well. Only together can we, and the entire Body of Christ, become all that God has destined us to become.

יהוה

—Yahshua—

Jesus—The Way, The Truth, and The Life.

"I came that they may have and enjoy life, and have it in abundance (to the full, till it overflows)."

(John 10:10b, Amplified)

ACORN, BABY!

Chapter Twelve

Where are you in your walk with the Lord? Selah. (Stop and ponder that for a moment.)

It is not enough to just stand there and sing from the old hymn, "Just as I am...." Sure, He loves you just as you are. But if you love Him, you are not going to *stay* just as you are. God is seed-minded, but He does not just see a seed—He sees a harvest. When He created you, He saw every spiritual and physical child that you would have down through all generations. When He looks at an acorn, God does not see the acorn itself—He sees the *forest* that will come from it. The DNA of a forest is in that little acorn.

Why do I hold ProVision Network meetings all the way across the country when sometimes only a handful of people show up? *Acorn, baby!* All I can do is tell you what you are supposed to do. It is up to you to do it.

I don't know about you, but I am going for it! We are going to buy buildings on Wall Street next to the New York Stock Exchange. We are going to build a "Freedom Center," so that whenever any ministry comes they do not have to pay the millions of dollars they would normally have to pay to be able to come to New York.

The Gospel is not going to be in some back room; it is going to be in every boardroom and talked about every day. This is not just some "idle talk." It is going to happen. Recently, we dedicated space right on Fifth Avenue for an investment bank that is being built. The declaration of its founding partners has been, "We will create a new paradigm of business where trillions of dollars will flow into the Kingdom. Never again will a young church need to fight and to hunt to raise funds!" These things are happening *now*—not just somewhere off in the future. All of these great things started as simple seeds.

This takes us back to the word *dabar*. Its last letter is the Hebrew letter *rêsh*:

ר

(rêsh)

This Hebrew letter has a powerful meaning springing from its use in the word *zerah'*, the Hebrew word for "seed." We Christians often think of "seed" in terms of *money* or *time*. However, the word *zerah* actually refers to *risk*—it is sowing a seed away from you, or pushing a seed away from you so that it dies:

> "Verily, verily, I say unto you, Except a corn of wheat fall into the ground and die, it abideth alone: but if it die, it bringeth forth much fruit."
>
> (John 12:24)

Or, as The Message paraphrase states it:

> "Listen carefully: Unless a grain of wheat is buried in the ground, dead to the world, it is never any more than a grain of wheat. But if it is buried, it sprouts and reproduces itself many times over."
>
> (John 12:24, Message)

Zerah involves "casting your seed upon the water" and taking chances. (See Ecclesiastes 11:1). Every seed that you sow should extend you beyond where you are, to where you can go.

For example, I am trained to sing opera. In order to do some very difficult things in opera, you have to go beyond what you think you can breathe. You are literally finding breath in your legs! They say you have

Acorn, Baby!

more breath in your body than you think you can hold in your lungs. So you learn to stand over the core of who you are as you are singing, and when you think there is nothing left in you, then you sing two more measures before you breathe. And then when you stop singing (whoosh!), the breath is back. How is that? You gave out all that you had...and then you were filled back up. Then you can go back and do it all over again. It is a miracle!

That is an example that illustrates this point in natural terms. The problem is that most of us in the Body do not extend ourselves when it comes to our personal gifts, like I did when I sang opera.

Mothers understand this idea of having to always go the extra mile—any mother who has nursed a newborn baby knows that it is possible. That brand new baby needs to eat every two or three hours, no matter what time of day or night, and no matter how exhausted the mother is. Even when Mommy is sure she cannot take another sleepless night, she somehow always is able to push herself one more time to provide nourishment for that baby.

I want you to consider this concept of stretching yourself as it pertains to the financial arena. I am talking about getting out there in the realm of risk and moving out of your comfort zone. I am talking about not being afraid to step out into your personal gifting—and humbling yourself to get involved with projects beyond your own capabilities. That is when things are going to get exciting, and that is when you are going to move into the million-dollar-flow.

If you do not have a plan and a project—some goal you are working towards—do not expect the money to show up. And you are not going have a big enough plan for millions of dollars if it is all about *you*—and you alone. God is not going to bless your little "get a Cadillac and vacation in the Caribbean Islands" plan. Those things will only be by-products of a much greater plan.

> "Let each of you esteem and look upon and be concerned for not [merely] his own interests, but also each for the interests of others."
>
> (Philippians 2:4, AMP)

As you seek to stretch yourself beyond your limits, be advised that not everybody is going to encourage you. For example, not everyone has the same taste—especially in music. You can be an outstanding soprano opera singer, and people in Texas listening to you will be saying, "Whoa!

Would you please stop?! Please give me some country music!" You can become extremely successful and even earn awards for your talents. You can become the best that you can be, but there are still going to be folks who just can't appreciate you and your giftings.

As I began to increase by taking different steps, I learned to deal with something that we are taught about extensively in the Word: *how to overcome fear*. Fear is an enemy...and it is one that we can defeat.

I jumped on a plane with $500 in my pocket to go attend Yale University. I got in a car with no money in my pocket and drove to New York City to interview for jobs. I started my own business on the Commodity Exchange, where everybody else was dealing with millions of dollars, even though I only had about $3,000 in my pocket. (Every trade was critical! If I lost $500, it meant beans, hot dogs, and rice for me for a week!)

So fear comes. It is really going to come when you begin to understand this concept of sowing seed. If you are properly sowing the seeds that you are supposed to be planting, it should grab you a little bit in your chest. It should make you gasp. It should be a stretch for you. When you are at the point where your tithe is tens of thousands of dollars, it might make you have to take a deep breath from your gut when you think about the Mercedes Benz that you could have bought with that money. That is where trusting in God comes in.

If you do not have that jab inside you—if you are sitting there with your normal $25 tithe check (or whatever is "normal" for you), and you are just plunking it into the offering bucket, you are not into *dabar dabar*. You are not into "words becoming things"; you are not "calling those things that be not as though they were" (Romans 4:17).

So, to summarize some of what we have learned over the previous few chapters: We are to humble ourselves, have integrity in our house, operate in the activity of exchange (which involves the understanding that you cannot do it all by yourself), and sow seed (which includes taking risks and stepping out in faith). Our God is huge! He lives in you—and your staying "small" is a sin!

> "...**greater** is he that is in you, than he that is in the world."
>
> (1 John 4:4, emphasis added)

You cannot have a "begin-to-be-fixin'-to-get-ready" attitude. I don't care if you are a housewife, you need to be "calling those things that be not as though they were," and "studying to show yourself approved, being a workman able" (2 Timothy 2:15). You need to get your dream back out; get yourself transparent again; start taking risks again. All of that glorifies God and produces the forest that is destined to grow from the acorn that resides on the inside of you!

—Yahshua—

Jesus—The Way, The Truth, and The Life.

"I came that they may have and enjoy life, and have it in abundance (to the full, till it overflows)."

(John 10:10b, Amplified)

ME, A PASTOR?

Chapter Thirteen

During a recent church service I attended, the worship leader began to deal with the concept of "inadequacy" and not seeing ourselves as being good enough—not ever feeling like we were the ones who would be picked first. Believe me, in the environment that we have created in the Body of Christ, it is easy to feel that way.

We can sometimes think that the only ones who are anointed are the ones who are on the platform, and that we are supposed to devote our lives to supporting *them*—that we were born to help them preach the Gospel around the world. But the truth is that no calling is more important than any other. Whatever God has called *you* to do should be treasured and cultivated, no matter how small it seems.

Sometimes your God-created gifts and callings are not always very obvious. You may be called to do something that you think you are not qualified for in the least bit. I am the pastor of Faith Exchange Fellowship in New York City. I would not even be pastoring a church if another pastor whom I highly respect had not laid hands on me and called me "pastor" in 1993.

Not that the minister "put" the call of God on me, but God used him to steer me into a direction that I was not considering going in. Actually, I tried *not* to be a pastor. I did not think that it was a part of my temperament or a part of my make-up. I am very different than the Bible-Belt ministers—even though I am totally filled with the Holy Spirit, I love the Word of God, Jesus is my Lord and Savior, and I believe in healing and miracles. When I submitted to the call, I started to bear good fruit.

Recently, we had a twenty-year-old girl raised from her deathbed by the power of God. There have been amazing financial miracles and many marital breakthroughs at our church. We have had kids who grew up in the worst neighborhoods who, because of the Word of God being ministered to them through our church, are going to some of the finest junior high and high schools in the area.

Concerning financial ministry, it is necessary to teach the practical side to go along with the spiritual. We have about six people in our congregation who had come to us because they knew there was an anointing on our ministry for finances. They were headed into foreclosure on their homes and we were able to help them by teaching them to understand that foreclosure and bankruptcy were not the only options. Now they are sitting on hundreds of thousands of dollars in cash because they were able to sell their homes, get better jobs, and do some other things as a result of thinking a little bit differently.

There is one young lady in particular that I would like to use as an example: She is a mom who home-schools her kids, and who also used to have a nursery/daycare-type of business she ran from her home. A number of years ago she had bought a home and had eventually come to the place where she was not able to make "ends meet" financially. She eventually came to us at Faith Exchange Fellowship, though she did not initially tell us much detail about what was going on in her life. She made a very wise decision to come for counsel and asked, "Pastor Dan, what do I do?"

So we sat down and talked a little bit, and I asked her, "When did you buy your house?"

She replied, "I bought it in 1992 before my husband died."

"Okay," I said, "you bought your house in 1992…how much in arrears are you on your house payments?"

She answered, "Oh, I am about $7,000 behind…but, you know, the mortgage company is coming to take my house soon, and I'm just going to let it go into foreclosure."

"And when did you buy that house?"

"1992," she repeated.

I protested, "You've got a little bit of equity in that house."

She cocked her head to one side and asked, "What do you mean?"

Somewhat shocked, I asked, "What do you mean, 'What do I mean?'?!!"

"No really," she said, "what do you mean?"

She just did not know. She is a sweet lady who just did not have any comprehension of the fundamentals of real estate and those aspects of personal finance.

So I said to her, "We'll raise the money in the church, and we'll get you the seven grand, and help you." Now, I do not normally do that, but in this specific instance, the church knew this woman very, very well—so we just actually took up an offering and let her have some money to use in this particular situation. So, we were able to keep her out of foreclosure on this property on one condition—which I made her agree to before we raised the money.

"Okay, we'll raise the money to help you out, but you have to agree to one condition first."

She said, "Well, what's the condition?"

"You have got to sell your house."

She exclaimed, "I am not going to sell my house!"

Now, just a few moments before she was willing to let her home go into foreclosure and have it taken away from her altogether. Yet, somehow the thought of selling it outright seemed to her a shocking idea.

So, I said to her, "You do not have a good enough job to keep carrying that house note. You can't afford the house—that is why you have almost lost it. So the condition for us to bail you out of your dilemma is that you have to sell your house."

She protested again, "I am not going to sell my house!"

"You have to sell the house…because I am NOT giving you seven thousand dollars in six months—again!"

So, in tears she finally agreed, and I said to her, "Let's go get your house appraised."

She had paid about $185,000 for this house in Queens back in 1992—which was quite a bit of money back then for the house. However, it turned out that the house was now worth about $421,000! She almost lost that appreciated equity in foreclosure; and was even planning to do so willingly—that is, before she found out how much money she was going to get out of it. Suddenly, she was very willing to sell it!

When that woman first came to us she could hardly write a check for $15. Now, she was just recently able to write a $20,000 tithe check from the profit of the sale of that home—simply because she put into action biblical, yet practical, financial counsel.

But that is not all: This dear woman was able to pay off some other bills and is now completely out of debt. Her new living arrangement is more affordable and appropriate for her situation. And because she honored the man of God and actually practiced the counsel we gave her, God has blessed her with a new job that earns her four times what she was making before—higher than anything she had ever made in her life.

She got herself out from disobedience…out from under fear…and now she has $180,000 sitting in the bank, with only a small amount of rent to pay. She is now even getting ready to buy and sell homes for investment income because of what she learned in saving her own house through godly counsel and the humility of obedience.

These people who have come to our church abandoned that fearful mind-set and came out of that previous arena of bad financial advice. Someone is always willing to give you advice—with a catch. Some people want you to pay them so they can restructure you for their bankruptcy fees or refinance fees and put you in all sorts of different traps. You need to make sure that you are getting godly counsel from people of integrity to prevent such things from happening in your life. Part of my calling is to help keep God's people out of the financial traps the enemy has for them.

I am a sent one. In 2001, another minister of the Gospel laid hands on me and said, "You are an apostle to New York City" (although I was already a "sent one" before he laid hands on me). All of us are different as far as how the anointing manifests through us. What I am called to do is to proclaim the Gospel that Jesus is Lord—the Lord over everything, including finances—directly to Wall Street, and to allow that anointing to flow through me to attack the heart of the love of money, which is the root of all evil. That type of assignment is not for novices.

Someone who is just starting to learn to play baseball starts out getting together with his friends in the park. He learns the basic rules—three strikes and you are out; first, second, and third bases, where the players need to be positioned, etc. He knows what the rules are; he can kind of hit; he can kind of throw. That is one level of playing baseball. But then when it is time to go play the Yankees, he had better know how to get out of the way of a curve ball and to do his job if he does not want to get laughed off the field.

Me, a Pastor?

God wants to take us to the top level of financial spiritual warfare. More than just being an issue of spiritual warfare, that money belongs to God; it is also ours because what is His is ours. God is trying to get you to do amazing things. He is saying, "Now is the time, and, yes, I am going to do it, but I am not doing it without you. I am doing it *through* you."

Many times, we are still waiting around for God to do stuff. In actuality, we already know what to do, but we are feeling under-qualified or inadequate. The fact is we need to allow our steps to be ordered of God—not step but step<u>s</u>. It is not a matter of saying, "Well, I'll take one step and then see what God's going to do." The steps of a good man are ordered of the Lord (Psalm 37:23). We need to keep walking!

—Yahshua—

Jesus—The Way, The Truth, and The Life.

"I came that they may have and enjoy life, and have it in abundance (to the full, till it overflows)."

(John 10:10b, Amplified)

COPY CAT FEVER

Chapter Fourteen

My job as a minister of the Gospel is to encourage you to understand one major thing—you are not going to get financial prosperity by imitating others; you are going to get it by simply being *you*. You are going to get it as you—Jesus-sized (which is way bigger than "super-sized"). Your monetary breakthrough is going to come through your opening up and releasing your gifts. Paul said to Timothy, "Stir up the gift that is within you" (2 Timothy 1:6).

That brings me to a point about the "pursuit of happiness," which you will read more about in chapter twenty. It involves the necessity of being *proactive*, because no one else is going to stir that gift up for you. Forget sitting out there and waiting for some prophet of God to discover you. Do not sit there thinking, "Well, you know I am really talented, and that minister should know it. If he really hears from God, he will just say, 'Hey you over there! Get up here…'" That might sound silly, and I would not have to say this if it were not going on in the Body of Christ, but it is.

There is an increase that is about to take place in the Body for which we are supposed to set the pace. People are going to do it at different levels and at various speeds. It is going to start to happen financially, and some of us will grumble and say, "Why am I not out there leading the pack? How come they're over there making it in real estate and I'm not?"

If you are not proactive, you are going to slip into a habit of following people. You might look at someone and say, "Oh, I'm going to try to do what that person did. That guy did well with that coffee shop;" or "I'm going to try this because they were successful at it;" or "Maybe I'll go out and preach because Brother So-And-So does pretty well."

No, you have got to be proactive and get down to what God is releasing in you. Do you remember the lesson of Habakkuk 2:1? You need to get alone with God, climb your "tower," watch on your watch, and then listen to what He tells you because He is going to correct you and get you on track. As much as He loves you, He will tell you when you are missing it. He sees more and is *smarter* than you are.

Will you admit that? Will you admit that you are not the smartest person you know? This is a huge problem with "good old boys." They think, "I've been there. I've done that. I've bought the T-shirt. I've heard Dan Stratton preach before. There ain't nothin' he can teach me. I know everything he knows. I can write a book about the things he doesn't know!"

If you are one who thinks that way, you are going to miss the point. God is trying to minister to you and bring you the missing piece of information and the divine connection that you need. You cannot receive those things from God if you are just sitting back criticizing everybody else. And you cannot criticize people and love your brother at the same time—that is impossible for a true Christian. If you have that type of wrong, critical mentality, you will not be able to walk in God-ordained dominion and enter into the prosperity God has for you.

Each of us needs to ascertain through prayerful time with God what His will is for our lives. I want you to pursue, chase down, and refuse to do without your happiness, without your fulfillment, without your desires of your heart being fulfilled—all of which come from walking in God's will. I want to see you finish your race, run your course, fight the good fight of faith, and stand in the presence of Jesus and have Him say to you, "Man! You did well!" (See 2 Timothy 4:7 and Matthew 25:21.) As I have said before (and it bears repeating), sometimes we can get too caught up in judging ourselves by looking at the fruits of others.

> "We do not dare to classify or compare ourselves with some who commend themselves. When they measure themselves by themselves and compare themselves with themselves, they are not wise."
>
> (2 Corinthians 10:12, NIV)

Each of us has been given divine appointments and assignments that are unique. I cannot really do what I am called to do, without your doing what you are called to do, and vice versa.

God has shown me in places all over the Bible the concept of having to do our part. We have to get some things done. The prosperity message has been declared, but now we have to do it. We have to "believe the love" and walk it out:

> "And we have known and believed the love that God hath to us. God is love; and he that dwelleth in love dwelleth in God, and God in him."
> (1 John 4:16)

God has called me to "take ground" on Wall Street. The real estate there is very expensive to acquire, and that is a place where God's people taking over will be contested. But God is bigger than any obstacle, and the only thing I have to overcome is my desire to judge the assignment. There is a temptation to start thinking, "It's not happening fast enough. The congregation that God has given me there to pray this thing through just doesn't seem rich enough." But if I stay focused on the Scriptures and realize that my job is to give and to serve, then the fruit will manifest.

This same rule applies to you concerning whatever God has called *you* to do. In the Body of Christ, there is no room for *copy cats*. Every calling is vitally important if we are to function together to get the job done for the Kingdom. So do not try to be like someone else and attempt to duplicate what *they* are doing. Remember, the greatest thing you can do with your life is to be the *original* that God has destined you to be.

—Yahshua—

Jesus—The Way, The Truth, and The Life.

"I came that they may have and enjoy life, and have it in abundance (to the full, till it overflows)."

(John 10:10b, Amplified)

STUDY THE EXPERTS

Chapter Fifteen

If God has put a vision in your heart that you really want to pursue, then find someone else who is already doing it and learn from him. One of the best ways to become something is to find people who are already that and study them:

> "He that walketh with wise men shall be wise: but a companion of fools shall be destroyed."
> (Proverbs 13:20)

Or as The Message paraphrase so "quaintly" expresses it:

> "Become wise by walking with the wise; hang out with fools and watch your life fall to pieces."
> (Proverbs 13:20, Message)

Now, if you are a sixty-one-year-old lady, you cannot play shortstop for the New York Yankees—I don't care how much you study Derek Jeter! You have to be realistic about what you are able to achieve, and then get around those who are where you want to be.

When possible, find those you can get close to. However, that is not always an obtainable goal. Therefore, a more common way of getting to know successful people who have done what you want to do is by reading any books they have written. Study everything that they have either written or said on tape. You need to learn what they know because just simply wanting to be like them is not going to help you.

Also, let me note that many times not everything that successful people excel at is revealed in their books because people who know how to "do" things well, are not always good at teaching how they did them. They do not know why or how they do what they do; they just do it. Those are ones you simply need to make an effort to get around and take note of what they do, whether they are verbally teaching you or not. Sometimes those people do things that just come naturally to them—things they do not do consciously—that move them towards success, which are things you can often observe by watching them.

We are called to take dominion in the marketplace. Sometimes, however, we can be too *churchy* for our own good. I am not saying that you can be too *holy* for your own good—because *we need to be holy*. We need to be right with God and stay in His presence. However, what I am saying is that we need to be able to speak the marketplace language.

That does not mean that you use curse words, but rather that you know how to speak the language of the business that you are involved in. If you are in real estate, then you need to know real estate terms and how that business works. If you are in the cleaning business, then you need to know about that field. If you are in international marketing, then you need to be up to speed on how to talk that language. If you are aspiring to be an author, you need to learn everything you can about publishing—before you even write the book, much less try to talk to a publisher. (My publisher wanted me to add that last one in there.) In short:

Whatever business you are in, you have to know about it.

Just knowing about spiritual things is not enough to put you over. You must have practical knowledge of the type of business you want to pursue in order to be successful.

Furthermore, if you are entrepreneurial or have some "witty inventions" (Proverbs 8:12), you must be able to communicate your concepts in writing. You must improve your writing skills. The Scriptures are very clear about the fact that your vision has to be written down:

> "And the LORD answered me, and said, Write the vision, and make it plain upon tables, that he may run that readeth it."
>
> (Habakkuk 2:2)

In order to improve your writing skills, you must do two things. You must read books written by good writers—especially ones written by those who are in the field that you are in. The second thing you must do is practice your writing skills—by actually *writing*.

Jesus wants you to be excellent in all that you put your hands to. I am not saying you should disregard reading your Bible and spend all your time on business books. On the contrary, you must read your Bible and put God first place in your life. Also, as Christians we have the advantage over the world of being able to hear the voice of the Holy Spirit and receive His wisdom as we make decisions in the marketplace. However, you must realize that when God speaks to you, he will speak to you in the language of the occupation or the endeavor in which you are trying to succeed. The more of the vocabulary you know, the more God can teach you about that field.

One way of being in a position to learn first hand what a successful person does is by volunteering to work for him. After all, a person who goes to college does not get paid for it. So although it is better if you can get a paid position working for your mentor, if there are not any such jobs available there, do not take "no" for an answer. Go ahead and volunteer there. In most cases, you do eventually end up getting paid, as long as your heart is right and you work hard and are producing.

However, receiving a paycheck is not the goal. The objective is to become a person who is "worthy of his hire" (Luke 10:7). You really do not want the *money*; what you actually want is the *ability* to do what *attracts* the money. People are always trying to grab the money first, which leads to an entitlement mentality—where those who get a position expect to get paid *just for showing up*, whether they actually do their job or not.

That type of selfishly lazy attitude keeps them broke (while they might be confessing the whole time that because they tithe, money comes to them). It also disqualifies them from being worthy candidates for being able to ever get close to the successful people that God wants them to have a relationship with—which is a key ingredient in their prosperity. Anyone who wants to achieve great things must realize that there will oftentimes be self-sacrifice involved, which actually is simply an investment into his future. It is an opportunity to receive priceless training from the experts.

AN EAR FOR OPPORTUNITY

One of the best places to find opportunities as a Christian is by joining a ProVision Network chapter in your area. However, even if you are not a part of the ProVision Network, start paying attention to what is going on around you when you are at church. Rather than coming in with your agenda, simply go to church with your ears open.

The gold is in what you hear.

You will start hearing about opportunities and about needs that you may be able to meet. Do not get yourself trapped by the same person every week...and do not *be* the same one every week cornering someone else.

If you want to stumble across opportunity, you must be an excellent listener. There are some who never get the gold nuggets because they want to talk about how smart and successful they are. I have people in the ProVision Network who think that Jupiter would fall out of the sky if it were not for them, and that somehow God used them to hang the moon. They think that the whole world revolves around them. Well, it does not revolve around any one of us. You already know everything you know! So stop doing all the talking. If you want to learn and be exposed to new, fresh opportunities, then you must have an ear for them.

For example, someone could be saying that he is in the market for a new car. To some, that would just be an ordinary comment. However, to someone who gets referral fees from selling cars, that particular statement would set off bells and whistles in his mind. That person constantly has an ear to listen out for those who want to purchase an automobile because he gets compensated (and should) for such a transaction.

A lot of times, someone comes into a conversation so fired up to do all the talking that he cannot hear what God is trying to say to him through someone else. Braggarts are not the only ones who blab excessively. People who are too stressed out and need-minded also tend to talk too much. In an effort to talk their way into somehow getting an answer to their problem, they fail to realize that God wants them to listen to somebody else who has the solution that they need.

The great Italian scientist, Galileo, once said, "I have never met a man so ignorant that I could not learn something from him." This type of mind-set should encourage you that you can get nuggets of wisdom wherever you go. By the same token, it is also helpful for someone who is the "smartest person he knows" to realize that he needs to open up a little bit, become transparent for a change, and admit that he does not actually know everything. The answer to your challenges in life might come through somebody else—and they probably will, but the only way you will receive the help you need is if you have ears to hear and are slow to speak. You might be surprised at the opportunities that are all around you if you will simply *listen* for them.

—Yahshua—

Jesus—The Way, The Truth, and The Life.

"I came that they may have and enjoy life, and have it in abundance (to the full, till it overflows)."

(John 10:10b, Amplified)

SENDING OUT YOUR SHIP

Chapter Sixteen

I mentioned before that John 4:16 says, "And we have known and believed the love that God has toward us. God is love, and he that dwells in love dwells in God and God in him." Even though the New Testament was originally written in the Greek language, it was written by Jews who thought in the context of Hebrew revelation and culture. So you can go look up a New Testament word in the original Greek, and that will give you shades of meaning that the original translators had.

On the other hand, it is good to then locate a synonym in the Hebrew language and take it all the way back to the Hebrew meaning. So when we say, "believe the love," if you were a Hebrew-speaking believer from that time period, the word '*âhab* (Strong's #157) would immediately come into your mind. That word means, "I will give; I will serve." That is the definition of "love" in the original Hebrew meaning.

Love is not an intangible thing. It is an action word that means, "I will proactively make your life better." So to believe "I have a responsibility," and "I am going to move my feet," is to believe the love. God has already done something magnificent on our behalf—He sent Jesus to the cross. Now He is waiting on us to truly love Him (in the active sense of serving and giving), and to love each other the same way.

> "A new command I give you:
> Love one another. As I have

loved you, so you must love one another."
(John 13:24, NIV)

"Greater love hath no man than this, that a man lay down his life for his friends."
(John 15:13)

"There is no fear in love; but perfect love casteth out fear: because fear hath torment. He that feareth is not made perfect in love."
(1 John 4:18)

There is no fear in true biblical serving and giving. Fear comes when you think about not getting anything back. Fear comes when you give and think that you will not get a return. Fear can come when the person you are giving to does not appreciate the love that you are giving to him and does not reciprocate.

Again, a believer is proactive. A believer is honorable towards people who do not deserve it. Jesus came and died for sinners. His spotless Blood was shed for people who did not deserve His precious sacrifice. If we are going to imitate and live like Jesus, then we must become proactive in spite of the people around us and of how they react to us.

I am going to be the best husband I can possibly be, no matter what my wife says to me. I am going to be the best father I can possibly be, in spite of how my children behave. And for some of you, "I am going to be the best employee I can be—I don't care what a jerk my boss is." That is what "believing the love" is. At the end of the day, you cannot control anyone else but *you*.

This is related to your financial breakthrough. There is no fear in that, but perfect, mature love casts out the fear (1 John 4:18a). If you stay on it, love is going to cast the fear out. Remember, this verse of Scripture also says that fear has torment, and he who fears is not made perfect in love (1 John 4:18b).

How do you get rid of the fear? Love!

However, if you do not have the right definition of love, which says, "I will give. I will serve," you will become hesitant. You will be on the heels of your feet, waiting. Conversely, if you are in true biblical love, you will be on the balls of your feet, going forward. Love moves forward. God is moving towards you and you need to be moving towards Him.

Sending Out Your Ship

Moreover, the Word tells us a key to how we can defeat fear on every level:

"We love Him, because He first loved us."
(1 John 4:19)

We love Him because He was proactive towards us. We are proactive towards Him because He was proactive first. We are made in the image and likeness of Jesus. If you want someone to be a certain way towards you, then you should first be that way towards him. That is sowing (action) and reaping (result). That is the Gospel of the Lord Jesus Christ.

We are often just standing around waiting for someone to bring our ship to us. But friend, for that to happen, we need to start sending ships out to other people! Furthermore, we need to start looking around for other people's ships and help them connect with their destinies. When you do that, people will start looking around to help you find yours.

This brings me to another point. People need to be monetarily compensated for helping solve the problems of others. We need to be a body of integrity and be appreciative when someone helps us. If you are ungrateful and are not willing to pay anybody to do anything, then do not expect people to come "running" to your aid. Somebody might be crying out saying, "Nobody helps me! Boo, hoo, hoo."

Maybe that is because you have never said, "Thank you," in the right way. Maybe if you slap a fifty dollar bill into the hand of the guy who helped you save five hundred dollars by giving you a good referral—some other blessings might come your way as well.

"If anyone says, 'I love God,' yet hates his brother, he is a liar. For anyone who does not love his brother, whom he has seen, cannot love God, whom he has not seen."
(1 John 4:20, NIV)

Or, if a man says, "I give and serve God," but he withholds from and hates his brother, he is a liar. You cannot serve God, love Him, and be in the flow of this unconditional covenant unless you are truly reaching out to as many people as God instructs you to reach out to. When you have a lifestyle of sending out "love ships" to others, your fleet will be on its way to your shore.

—Yahshua—

Jesus—The Way, The Truth, and The Life.

"I came that they may have and enjoy life, and have it in abundance (to the full, till it overflows)."

(John 10:10b, Amplified)

NO PAIN...NO MONEY!

Chapter Seventeen

Are you called to be a financial warrior for the Kingdom? If so, it will take a bigger mind-set than the cowardly demeanor that religion has often forced into some people's thinking.

"What do you mean?" you might ask. Let me illustrate...

I generally provide opportunities for people to share about themselves at my ProVision meetings around the country—to give people an occasion to let others know what businesses or projects they are involved in. But, it seems that whenever I give people the "floor," they usually talk like this (in sort of a sheepish tone of voice):

> "I've got this really good business idea. (You know, by the way, I am a tither.) The business idea that I have...I mean...it's going to help a lot of people. It's holy. The idea, well...I just want you to know, it's not for me."

They are literally apologizing every time they talk about the things they have set out to do. You cannot come out into a place of being a financial warrior having an apologetic mind-set—not if you expect to win.

An example of that would be like my playing football and hitting somebody (in the way that is normal in football) and saying, "Oh, I'm really sorry about that! Your nose is bleeding. Can I get you a handkerchief?" No way! I am happy about it! I knocked him on his bottom, his nose is bleeding, and his helmet it broken. I plan to do it again on the next player!

Some ladies reading this may be wondering what I am talking about. They might think I am being too rough. Well, ladies, you are coming into a "man's world" in marketing, and you do not get to change it. As a provocateur, I am trying to get you to understand that you are going to have to put a sharp "edge" on yourself and expect to get your proverbial "nose" bloodied in business.

We are not going to sit there and say, "Oh, sweetheart, we'll give you the deal; you're nose is bloody. You're a nice little lady. You get the deal. We're going to start a program in the government where you get preferential treatment." When you get your way into deals like that, you might get an inside track, but you do not get any better. Maybe one or two percent of the ladies will be able to play the game and are okay with getting their noses bloody. A woman is not going to be successful in the business world unless she understands some of the dynamics of what a man's world is like.

When I got hit in the face with a loss of $25,000 on the opening trade of the day, not one person in that pit came over to encourage me. Nobody came to me and said in a pitiful voice, "Oh, Dan, I saw that trade when the market dropped twelve and a half cents on you. Are you okay, Dan? I bet you got your feelings hurt. Oh, my gosh! We should go eat a piece of cake or something to make you feel better. Maybe if you call your brother...he's always so good for these times." Guess what, there is a whole different mentality out there.

You must get over into the place where you are going to start thinking about *dominion*, and you know the stuff that happens is not always going to be good—so deal with it. Otherwise, we are going to have a lot of unnecessary conversation that will do nothing but set us back further.

We in the "Word" circles have been trained extremely well in confessing the right things and in thinking big, and all of those messages are essential. But you cannot win any kind of fight with one fist, which is the preaching side. The other fist comes into play when those of us who walk in the "kingly" anointing start defending and attacking in another direction.

Our mentality is a little bit rougher than what the church really allows. Why aren't the wealthiest people and the biggest "champions" of the marketplace in the church? Because they do not fit. They have a killer instinct that is not cool. They might be a little bit crass; they might actually fire people from their businesses once in a while. They have the stink of war on them that most people cannot tolerate.

You may think I am being a little too rough. I *am* being rough, but it is because I know what it is like out there. I have had my butt kicked (and even synonyms to "butt"). When you get out there, you will see that they use bad language. Sometimes they even write it in the contracts! I go to buy buildings, and many times the sellers lie in the contracts.

You can't just say, "Oh, I'm not doing business with them anymore because their behavior is ungodly." Guess what, a lot of times the deals you do out there will involve people doing ungodly things. Wake up! We are in the world—just not of it. We are trying to motivate a church to go to war! We sing and talk about "love" a lot in our services, and there needs to be a lot of love because out there, we are in a battle.

Let me illustrate what I am saying in another way: Every little child in your town gets to play in the "recreational league." This is the sports association where nobody cares who wins and everybody gets to participate in every inning. Most of the ladies like that. They think that is the way it is supposed to be. "Little Johnny" always gets to play, nobody's feelings get hurt, and all the mommies are happy (except those who understand kingship and our royal calling—see my chapter on *Women Warriors*).

But then there is the traveling team…

This is the team that plays in a league where they actually play the games to *win*. In this league, standings (wins versus losses) are tracked, scores are kept, and there is usually a "championship" game that separates the best team from the others. This is the level at which skill and ability become prerequisites for acceptance to the team.

However, the mommies whose children did not make the traveling team might get upset that their kids cannot go. They might suddenly switch over into thinking that "self-esteem issues" are more important than qualifications. But the truth of the matter is that the parent of one who did not make the traveling team needs to ask himself *why* his child was disqualified. Did he practice as much as the others? Is the child eating right? Is he getting enough sleep? Is the child actually gifted for the sport? You see, *everybody* can play on the recreational league, but a child needs to meet *certain criteria* in order to be able to play on the traveling team.

The higher you go in any particular sport, the more you must qualify and the fewer participants you see. Once the players reach the high-school level, the team that started out with ninety members is now down to nine. Only the select few who trained hard, prepared themselves, and are gifted for the sport, will play at the top levels.

Many people think that the economic realm should be like the recreational league. It is true that everybody gets to play, but most people do not qualify for promotion and success simply because they neglect to do what is necessary to get there. I cannot promise you success if you will not hear what I am saying—and train yourself. As much as I want everybody to play, I know that many people who read this are "quitters" at the very base root of who they are. But if you are one of those people who has the habit of quitting, be comforted in the fact that it is a trait that you can *change*—through determination and faith in Jesus Christ:

> "…for everyone born of God overcomes the world. This is the victory that has overcome the world, even our faith."
> (1 John 5:4, NIV)

—Yahshua—

Jesus—The Way, The Truth, and The Life.

"I came that they may have and enjoy life, and have it in abundance (to the full, till it overflows)."

(John 10:10b, Amplified)

BROADWAY BLUNDER

There is a story of an actor in New York who could not get a job anywhere. He was mad at his agent, and his agent told him, "Maybe you should just go to LA. Maybe you could get some work out there." So he went to Los Angeles and got work, but it was at a Hallmark store instead of somewhere in the acting field. However, over time, his agent was finally able to secure him a part in New York.

The agent called the actor and said, "Will you come out to New York? I got you a part."

The actor, who was a little skeptical, asked, "Well, what's the show?"

The agent said, "It's in Les Misérables."

"Whew! It's in Les Misérables! What's the part?"

The agent replied, "Well, it's only got one line and you're only on for one scene in the third act."

The actor said, "All right, but it's in Les Misérables! It might lead to something bigger! I'm on Broadway! This is really cool. I'll fly back, no problem. What's the line?"

"It's 'Hark! Is that cannon I hear?'"

So he knew his line by heart. All he had to do was just show up and stand in one spot until they called him out. He was to come out, and after the cannon blast, he was to simply exclaim, "Hark! Is that cannon I hear?" So he knew what to do. He

Chapter Eighteen

was a *trained actor* in his mind. So he got on the plane, sat down and started practicing, "Hark! Is that cannon I hear?" He was saying his line different ways, with the emphasis on different words to decide on which way he liked best.

"Which one did you like best?" he asked the lady sitting next to him on the plane.

"The third one," she replied.

"Yeah, I like that one best too!" he confidently agreed.

He arrived in New York and all the way over to the theater in the cab, he kept rehearsing his line, "Hark! Is that cannon I hear?"

"The third one," the cabby confirmed to the young actors delight.

Arriving at the theater, he got himself in make-up and costume and was so excited about being on Broadway. He watched the first act, then the second act. Finally, in the third act the stage manager pushed him out on stage. There he stood on stage. They were all singing in the spectacular fight scene at the end. The guns were popping. He was waiting for his cue. All of a sudden, he heard this phenomenal BOOM! He jumped in the air and said, "What was that?!!!"

My point is that you can sit in church and prepare and know exactly what to say, but when the time comes to shoot the shot, or to make the presentation, you need a little bit more in you than simply knowing your lines—and probably much more than you think you do right now. You need to know how to *use* that knowledge skillfully. That comes from having a respect for people who have done what you want to do and from listening to them.

Often, someone might look at me or some other person of wealth and influence and say, "Man, I want to someday have what that guy has!" However, they do not understand the axiom:

You do not want what other people have *earned* ...

...without first receiving what they have *learned*.

If you suddenly had a fortune dropped in your lap without first learning the principles of economics and financial management, you would blow it almost as fast as you received it—just look at most lottery winners, for example. Furthermore, if your character is not developed to the point of being able to handle the wealth, you will probably lose *yourself* in the process:

"For the turning away of the simple shall slay them,

and the prosperity of fools shall destroy them."
(Proverbs 1:32)

The Bible says, "Study to show yourself approved unto God," that we would be "workmen worthy of our calling" (2 Timothy 2:15). The Word of God is fit for doctrine, for reproof, for correction, for instruction, so that it should make the man of God perfect and thoroughly furnished for every good work (2 Timothy 3:16-17). "Study" is not just taking a glance in a book and closing it. Study is long and continual. Too many people stop reading books when they leave school. Learning should be a life-long process.

God is a Spirit, but He is also the Master. He is the God of all spiritual law; but He is also the God of all natural law. He requires you to be a master in the realm of the spirit, in covenant with Him, but also to be a master in the natural. You are made in the image and likeness of God. I hear the confessions that go forth from the church, especially during worship, such as, "We bless Your Name. You are King of kings and Lord of lords. You are a mighty God!" But our confession of those things is not what makes them real. They are *already* real.

The things from the Word that we are being taught to confess are already true—namely that we are prosperous. The Bible says, "Beloved, above all things, I wish that you prosper and be in good health" (3 John 2). Does the Scripture stop there? No, it continues, "...even as your soul prospers."

Your soul is comprised of your mind, will, and emotions. Did I say anything about your spirit? I did not mention a thing about your spirit, did I? What has been left out is the "...even as our soul prospers" part. If the end of that Scripture is omitted, then even though the first part of the Scripture—about your prospering—is still true overall, it is not true for *you*.

Mark 11 is still true:

> "For verily I say unto you, That whosoever shall say unto this mountain, 'Be thou removed, and be thou cast into the sea;' and shall not doubt in his heart, but shall believe that those things which he saith shall come to pass; he shall have whatsoever he saith. Therefore I say unto you, What things soever ye desire, when ye pray, believe that ye receive them, and ye shall have them. And when ye stand praying,

forgive, if ye have ought against any: that your Father also which is in heaven may forgive you your trespasses. But if ye do not forgive, neither will your Father which is in heaven forgive your trespasses."

(Mark 11:23-26)

When you say to the mountain, "Be thou removed and cast into the sea," and you believe in your heart and do not doubt, that mountain is going to move! But when it does move, you must be prepared ahead of time. Remember the actor who got the part in Les Misérables that I mentioned? He only had one line. It seemed so easy. But when the cannon went off, he was not prepared and blew his chance of a lifetime.

You see if the mountain moves, and you cannot make your way through the new valley, what good is that mountain relocating? It does you no good. So when you begin to pray and believe God for the secret desires of your heart, you had better begin to study. You need to find out about what's on the other side of that mountain you've been speaking to. You had better begin to equip yourself with the capacity and think everything through.

You had better find mentors. Hunt them down! Perhaps even pay them to teach you! Work for them for free! Do whatever you have to do to learn what they know, because you don't know everything you need to know to be able to do the job that you have never done before. You need the information ahead of time because you really do not know what to expect until you get there.

Keep in mind the actor who was presented with a great opportunity and thought he was prepared just because he had practiced his lines over and over again. When the time came for him to step out and do what he was supposed to do, he was caught off guard because he did not expect things to occur quite the way they did. He knew the cannon was going to go off, but he did not expect the cannon to be like *that!*

The story could have had a different ending if he had been able to talk to some folks who had previously acted in that play. They could have warned him about the "BOOM" so that he would not have been caught off guard. Without realizing it until it was too late, the actor needed a mentor. Don't wait until you're on stage in front of hundreds or thousands of people before you get the point! Track down mentors for yourself (and appreciate the ones God has already put in your life), whether you *think* you need them or not. Trust me, you *do!*

—Yahshua—

Jesus—The Way, The Truth, and The Life.

"I came that they may have and enjoy life, and have it in abundance (to the full, till it overflows)."

(John 10:10b, Amplified)

PREPARING FOR DIVINE APPOINTMENTS

Chapter Nineteen

God has divine appointments scheduled for us that we know nothing about. He has plans for our gifts to make room for us and to bring us before great men (Proverbs 18:16). Because of this, we need to stay in a constant state of *readiness* so that when those times come, we can ride that wave of blessing—instead of it 'ssmacking us in the face and laying us up on the beach unconscious!

Some years ago, I was presented with a "once-in-a-lifetime" opportunity. I had been invited to give the invocation at the 76th Annual Meeting of the Drug, Chemical, and Allied Trade Association. As I stood at the podium inside the Grand Ballroom of the Waldorf Astoria, I could feel a sense of history. The room was filled with 2,500 leaders from the pharmaceutical industry. The recently-knighted former mayor of New York City, Rudolph Giuliani, was to later address this elite group. But at that moment, there was a tongues-talking, healing-believing preacher standing at the microphone.

I knew from past experience that most clergy chose the path of least resistance and stayed "religiously neutral" when they knew that the crowd was mixed with all sorts of people from various religious backgrounds. I decided not to emulate that. I swam against the current in the world's river of "social correctness" instead. I began to address the people, "Good evening. I have been asked to give the invocation tonight. I want to do exactly what I have been asked to do, so I looked up the word 'invocation.' The word means, 'to address in prayer calling on the Supreme Being for assistance and protection.'"

I then looked at Mayor Giuliani and told him that I had been praying for him for a long time and that we had been disappointed when he decided not to run for the Senate, but now in hindsight we could see that God had a more important role for him—handling the aftermath of the "9-11" attacks. I then leaned into the microphone and said, "I am a Christian. And, in keeping with the true definition of the word 'invocation,' let us pray. Heavenly Father, God of Abraham, Isaac, and Jacob, I come to you in the Name of Jesus…" I then continued the prayer the way you and I normally would. At the end of the prayer, the room was hushed and in agreement.

Prior to speaking that night, I could see the hand of God moving. Believers from the top ranks of the Trade Union were coming to me and letting me know that they had seen my wife and me on TBN or on various television programs. They were thrilled about the fact that for the first time ever, a born-again preacher was to give the invocation. After I had prayed, the president of the association and many of the members of the board of directors came to me to talk about their faith and to ask me about our work at Ground Zero, where the World Trade Center Towers had fallen.

This experience has given me the confirmation of what I have believed for a long time—God has His people *positioned*. God has strategically placed people in relevant industry positions for kingdom purposes. The adversity that Faith Exchange Fellowship experienced at Ground Zero was a part of God's positioning us to be able to reach more people with the Gospel.

Not only did we have the opportunity to pray for the leaders of the pharmaceutical industry, but God also brought us before some of the leading Christians in the entertainment industry and in charity work. We also were blessed to participate in a monthly inroad to the Israeli Consulate there in New York. A prerequisite for such divine opportunities is sensitivity to the precious voice of God and to His plans and purposes. We need to remain tenderhearted to God's every command to us so that, through us, He can reach all people for His glory.

God has His people positioned for those great things that He has predestined for them to reach. We need to open the lines of communication and have a vision which includes those believers who have been placed in every political and economic arena. Contacts are being made on a very high level, which is going to lead to the networking of believers in some very influential places in the religious, economic, and political realms.

When you say to the mountain, "Be thou removed and cast into the sea," or when you are praying for God to deliver into your hands a better job or a business opportunity, you need to also pray that you have eyes open to see, that you are teachable, and that you are ready when such blessings come. You train like a warrior, like a "king"—spiritually, physically, mentally, emotionally, socially, and financially. You prepare all the way across the board. You have to train the whole person, not just be an intercessory prayer warrior.

You have got to develop relationships—even if some are *painful!* God has a divine appointment for you that is every bit as exciting as meeting any well-known person. He has a wonderful, awesome plan for you, but if you do not prepare for it, and you just sit around watching other people prosper, you are going to be terribly sad at the end of the day.

> "The sluggard craves and gets nothing, but the desires of the diligent are fully satisfied."
> (Proverbs 13:4, NIV)

On the other hand, if you diligently prepare for the great things that the Lord has revealed are in your future, you are going to experience more joy and satisfaction than anything else can bring. Instead of your "one-line" assignment ruining your career (like the actor), you will be ready and successful when your shining moment comes. And as you are faithful with little, God can trust you with bigger things:

> "His master said to him, 'Well done, you upright (honorable, admirable) and faithful servant! You have been faithful and trustworthy over a little; I will put you in charge of much. Enter into and share the joy (the delight, the blessedness) which your master enjoys.'"
> (Matthew 25:23, AMP)

—Yahshua—

Jesus—The Way, The Truth, and The Life.

"I came that they may have and enjoy life, and have it in abundance (to the full, till it overflows)."

(John 10:10b, Amplified)

THE FLIP SIDE OF FREEDOM

Chapter Twenty

I love the founding documents of our nation—for the United States is a nation originally founded by risk-takers. Those founding fathers had an indomitable desire to be free, and Americans still have this type of attitude today.

We have just got to be free. People cannot tell us what to do. We are pioneers; we are mavericks. We are human beings who have this desire to be free and to make our own way successful. The American historical documents were written by people who felt that way. They were pulling at constraints put on them by people who were unfairly telling them what to do. They even wrote in this nation's Declaration of Independence a phrase that resonates in my spirit today; and that is, "the pursuit of happiness":

> "When in the Course of human events, it becomes necessary for one people to dissolve the political bands which have connected them with another, and to assume among the powers of the earth, the separate and equal station to which the Laws of Nature and of Nature's God entitle them, a decent respect to the opinions of mankind requires that they should declare the causes which impel them to the separation.
> We hold these truths to be self-

evident, that all men are created equal, that they are endowed by their Creator with certain unalienable Rights, that among these are Life, Liberty and the **pursuit of Happiness**...."

(The Declaration of Independence of the Thirteen Colonies – July 4th, 1776)

The founding fathers had a revelation of the fact that the pursuit of happiness is a *right*. "Happiness" is something that you proactively hunt out...seek after...track down. Neither your spouse, nor your children, nor anyone else is going to be able to give you your happiness. You have got to go out and get it.

Your financial freedom comes the same way. I want you to be one hundred percent financially free. In fact, I want you to be free in every area—spiritually, physically, mentally, emotionally, socially, and financially. That is really what "prosperity" is, and that is the way that you need to judge your life.

Too often people judge their own level of prosperity by only how successful they are *financially*, and then they are disappointed when they do not measure up to the level of their desires. On the other hand, if their personal "mission statement" is to have success in all of the areas I have mentioned above—and they keep stock in those areas—then every day they will have something to rejoice about.

Something good will happen to you daily if you look at your life as a whole—spiritually, physically, mentally, emotionally, socially, and financially—and if you are being proactive. You stay proactive by deciding, "I will give; I will serve. I will give; I will serve," and by creating goals in all six realms of prosperity—not just financially. "Financially" is coming. Finances are coming. But before you can get there, you need to understand what true freedom is.

The Hebrew word for "freedom" is *nâqâh* (Strong's #5352) and it has a remarkable dual meaning. On the one side, it means, "jubilee; free from all obligations." That is powerful. That is what we have been taught to think about—"I'm free from all obligations. Jesus has made me free." In fact, as we have mentioned before, Jesus' Name in Hebrew is *Yahshua*—and the meaning of that Name is "deliverance, victory, and salvation (whole-life prosperity, here and forever)."

Furthermore, the "jubilee" had to do with debt-cancellation:

> "And you shall hallow the fiftieth year and proclaim liberty throughout all the land to all its inhabitants.

> It shall be a jubilee for you; and each of you shall return to his ancestral possession [which through poverty he was compelled to sell], and each of you shall return to his family [from whom he was separated in bond service]. That fiftieth year shall be a jubilee for you..."
>
> (Leviticus 25:10-11a, AMP)

But there is a second part to the meaning of the Hebrew word for "freedom"—and without the "flip side," you cannot truly have freedom from all obligations. This second meaning of *naqah* is found in the Bible when the word is translated as being "purged from iniquities." This refers to being purged from thought patterns and from habits that lead you off the mark and back into the obligations you were released from.

The first step to having a prosperous soul is always to realize that God is smarter than you. He is trying to speak to you on your level about concepts that are *not* on your level. He knows that the answers to the problems that you have are not on the plane of your understanding; if they were, then you would be able to solve them yourself.

In order for you to attain the answers you need, you have to come up. You have to get bigger in your thinking. How do you do that? By fellowshipping with someone who has a little bit of a different perspective than you do. "Jesus Christ, the same yesterday, today, and forever," is also, "new every morning." (See Hebrews 13:8 and Lamentations 3:22-24.) Sometimes reality is found in a paradox; you can have two seemingly contradicting thoughts in your mind, even though they are both true.

In the same way, if you want to be totally "free," you must accept both sides of the coin—*free from obligation*, but also *purged from bad habits*. Someone might be thinking, "Oh, I like 'free,' but I don't like, 'purged.'"

The Scripture did not say you were going to particularly *enjoy* the methods God uses in perfecting you. The Bible *does* say that we are to "humble ourselves in the sight of the Lord" that we may be exalted (James 4:10; 1 Peter 5:6).

People have often said, "Do you mean I've got to go down in order to go up? I don't want to do that!" But as we covered in detail earlier in the book, *humility is the foundation of promotion*. Have you ever tried to jump up without being down first? It is not going to happen. If you want to throw a ball, you must first bring it back and then drive it forward. A seed has to go down and die; then once it dies, the root goes down deep into the soil—first. And when it comes to experiencing total and complete freedom, you are going to have to be purged of some old bad habits before a permanent change can take place.

Let me illustrate: Suppose you want to improve your body's overall shape and appearance. Someone can give you liposuction. You can get the fat suctioned right out of your body. But if you do not change the way you eat, it will be an *annual* operation.

It works the same way in your finances. I can come into your house and look at your credit card bills, and with the "stroke of a pen" write a check that will wipe your slate clean. But if you refuse to change the way you spend, the way you invest, the way you think, and the way you buy, we are going to have to do it every single year—and guess what, I am not doing it! (And don't write me and ask me to either.)

We can preach from Luke 4:18-19 about how the Spirit of the Lord is upon us (in Christ), and how we have been anointed to preach the Gospel (the "good news") to the poor, to bring sight to the blind, to see that the lame will walk, to raise the dead, and to proclaim the acceptable year of the Lord—the Year of Jubilee (which includes debt cancellation and freedom from all bondage in any way). However, what most people would do with that message is take that to mean "free from obligation." What we really want is a miracle debt cancellation!

We want somebody else to wipe out our credit card debts. We want someone to wipe out our mortgage. We want everyone that we have borrowed money from, including friends and family, to forgive us of all the debts. All of that is freedom from obligation—but that is a lop-sided view of freedom. True, well-rounded freedom includes not just deliverance from our circumstances. Remember, the other part of the Hebrew definition for "freedom" is to be "purged from iniquities"—purged from bad habits and from unprofitable decision-making processes.

If you are set free from your debts one day, but you do not get delivered from bad spending habits and from other detrimental financial habits, it will not be long before you are right back into debt again. Going back to our liposuction example, if you do not stop going to greasy fast food places and eating other things that put weight on you, you are going to have to get liposuction again. Contrary to popular belief and all the commercials on cable, liposuction hurts! (Not that I know from personal experience, but those who have had it done say it is painful.)

My point is that you cannot simply go after the end result without first purging yourself from the bad habits that got you into the mess to begin

The Flip Side of Freedom

with. Many people come to me wanting me to just fix their problems. But when I start teaching them about the purging process—which attacks the root instead of just the symptoms—they reject it and think, "This just does not sound like the answer to my problem. I think the answer to my problem is in his back pocket, frankly! Either that, or he knows someone who could cut me a check! In fact, I heard from the Lord that he owes me a million bucks!" Don't laugh; this stuff really happens to me—frequently!

However, let me share with you that you really do not want what I have earned. You want the things that I am sharing with you right now. You want the wisdom and knowledge of those of us who have successfully made it to where you want to be, so that you can get there yourself. If you get what I have *earned* without the knowledge that originally obtained it, then you'll wind up like the multitudes of lottery "winners" who found themselves more bankrupt *after* they won the money. They did not have the wisdom to get the money honestly in the first place, so they certainly did not have the ability to hang on to it once their "winning ticket" dumped it in their laps.

Look, the same things that I am teaching you through my books and the teachings available through the ProVision Network are the same tools that we wealthy people use when we are up against the trillion-dollar giants from whom we are trying to buy buildings. They are the same tools we use when we are in negotiations on deals in the political realm as well—to keep us relevant in that society. How do we even get to go to those meetings? How do I get to go eyeball to eyeball with Rudy Giuliani, or with the top bishop of the Episcopalian church, or with Mayor Bloomberg? How does somebody get that far? He gets there because he has *prepared* for it, *positioned* himself for it, and *networked* for it. He thinks about it, gets ready for it, and proactively pursues it.

This is also where our praise towards God should come in.

Biblical praise is proactive—you know God is listening so you want to minister to Him. It is speaking aloud of all His goodness, faithfulness, and mighty acts—with or without music. For the most part, we do that out of an unction that is one-way. Even though He is ministering back to us and gives us our very breath, praise is simply when we choose from the bottom of our hearts to give to Him what we have. When we do that, we invoke the inhabitation of Jesus.

Praise is one of the chief ways from Scripture that we can use to proactively initiate God's intervention on our behalf:

> "But thou art holy, O thou that inhabitest the praises of Israel."
>
> (Psalm 22:3)

> "As they began to sing and praise, the LORD set ambushes against the men of Ammon and Moab and Mount Seir who were invading Judah, and they were defeated."
>
> (2 Chronicles 20:22, NIV)

There are people who have received bad reports from physicians concerning terminal illnesses. One person in such a condition might get opinions from five different doctors. If that patient believes the five doctors and simply accepts the diagnosis, he would probably *die*. Furthermore, if he does not continue to praise God and invoke the inhabitation of Yahshua (which, again, means "deliverer") he cannot expect to have any significant divine intervention occur in the midst of his situation.

There is always a way out if you stay in praise. That is the power of praise. It is not just a matter of saying, "Hallelujah! Praise You, Jesus! Blessed be the Name of the Lord!" If you want the Deliverer to come in and change things for you, you must praise with an expectation of deliverance. You are praising with your eyes open, expecting something to change, bringing you into the *naqah*—freedom—that God has for your life.

—Yahshua—

Jesus—The Way, The Truth, and The Life.

"I came that they may have and enjoy life, and have it in abundance (to the full, till it overflows)."

(John 10:10b, Amplified)

WOMEN WARRIORS

Chapter Twenty-One

With all my exhortations and teaching about being "kings," it would be easy to lose sight of the fact that I am including the women in this. Thus, within the context of the rest of this book, Rich and I thought it would be ideal to include a chapter devoted exclusively to women. Our purpose is two-fold: to first establish the fact that women are most certainly intended by God to be warrior-kings just like their male counterparts; and secondly, to address a few specific issues that I have encountered in my years as a pastor and the founder of the ProVision Network.

Now, it is likely that some women might jump straight to this chapter before reading any other parts of the book. To those of you who have, let me reiterate that this chapter is given within the context of this entire book. Consequently, I encourage you to be sure you allow the rest of *Divine ProVision* to set the contextual basis for this chapter. Thus, I encourage you to not interpret any point or issue made herein hastily without also reading the other sections of this text as well. If you want to read this chapter first, that's fine. Just be sure to go back and read the others too.

Let me also note here that Rich and I realize that the women who read this particular discourse come from a variety of different backgrounds and perspectives. Some are already established in their warrior-king roles within their respective fields, while others are aspiring to enter the battlefields of professional and economic conquest. Some are married, others single, or perhaps divorced. Some were raised in one generation, others in another. So, take what applies to you, and disregard what does not.

Finally, you will quickly notice as you continue beyond this point that we have included large quantities of Scripture within these pages. Thus, it would behoove *both male and female readers* to remember that as ministers, Rich and I are only called to teach you from the Bible—not to write it. Consequently, we have endeavored to convey to our readers not a "male" perspective of these issues—but a *biblical* one.

Of course, as men, there are some issues that we can (and did) address in order to bring certain issues to light for consideration by all readers. Nonetheless, we exhort everyone to maintain an open mind and spirit to the biblical exhortations at least—regardless of how you view our personal observations.

WOMEN ARE KINGS TOO!

Let me begin by being very clear here: I want to see the women of God rise up with warrior spirits and take ground for the Kingdom! The kingly anointing that we have been discussing throughout *Divine ProVision* belongs to them as well. Theirs is the calling to rise up in power and do warfare for the KING OF KINGS—and do so as well as (or better than) any man. Moreover, the Bible is quite clear that women are most certainly a part of Kingdom warfare:

> "For as many of you as have been baptized into Christ have put on Christ. There is neither Jew nor Greek, there is neither bond nor free, there is neither male nor female: for ye are all one in Christ Jesus. And if ye be Christ's, then are ye Abraham's seed, and heirs according to the promise."
> (Galatians 3:27-29)

In Christ, there are no "male and female" distinctions regarding the kingly or priestly anointings that belong to every believer in the Body of Christ. There is only one Body, and women are just as much a part of it as men—and actually outnumber us, if we are to be straight about it. Consequently, the same types of anointings and callings are available to the women, as well as the men, as God's servants.

In the English language, it is a shame that the term "man" has become synonymous with the term "male." However, in biblical thinking, *man* refers more to our species in God's creative order than to any gender reference. In fact, when God created Adam, He said, "Let Us make man in Our image, and after Our likeness...so God created man...male and female created He them." (Genesis 1:26-27) "Man" within the creative order, would be better translated "mankind" or "human being" in modern thinking. In fact, the Hebrew word *âdâm*, which is the word used for both "man" and the name "Adam" in these passages, is stated as such by Strong's Concordance in its Hebrew definitions.

Thus, although this specific Hebrew word is used throughout the Old Testament, it does not necessarily refer to the male portion of our species alone. In fact, there are a few instances where it obviously refers to *either* gender. This is where the English practice of using the word "man" or the generic terms "him, his," when referring generically to our species, (i.e. when gender is not specified) came from.

On the other hand, the Hebrew words *îysh* (male, husband) and *ishshâh* (female, wife) used in the Bible are very gender specific. These words make their first appearance in Chapter 2 of Genesis when God takes the "female" out of the "male" and builds it into a separate human being (i.e. "Adam, man") who was then "bone of his bone and flesh of his flesh." However, it was to the entire species of mankind that *'Elohiym* (Strong's# 430, the actual name for God used in this passage) endowed with the authority to rule and subdue this creation, and all that is within:

> "Then God said, 'Let us make man in our image, in our likeness, and let them rule over the fish of the sea and the birds of the air, over the livestock, over all the earth, and over all the creatures that move along the ground.' So God created man in his own image, in the image of God he created him; male and female he created them. God blessed them and said to them, 'Be fruitful and increase in number; fill the earth and subdue it. Rule over the fish of the sea and the birds of the air and over every living creature that moves on the ground."
> (Genesis 1:26-38, NIV)

Consequently, women have been delegated the power and authority to subdue God's creation as kings, just as their male counterparts have. Just like the Lord's "male servants" who have dedicated their lives to the service of God throughout the scriptures, God's "handmaidens" have likewise given themselves to the KING OF KINGS in service as warriors advancing His Kingdom. In order to see that, all we need to do is take a brief view of several of God's anointed "handmaidens" who exhibited the warfare nature of kings as the "men servants" of God did—and, in some instances, exhibited even more…

RULING WOMEN

> "Deborah, a prophetess, the wife of Lappidoth, was leading Israel at that time. She held court under the Palm of Deborah between Ramah and Bethel in the hill country of Ephraim, and the Israelites came to her to have their disputes decided. She sent for Barak son of Abinoam from Kedesh in Naphtali and said to him, 'The LORD , the God of Israel, commands you: "Go, take with you ten thousand men of Naphtali and Zebulun and lead the way to Mount Tabor. I will lure Sisera, the commander of Jabin's army, with his chariots and his troops to the Kishon River and give him into your hands."'
>
> "Barak said to her, 'If you go with me, I will go; but if you don't go with me, I won't go.'
>
> " 'Very well,' Deborah said, 'I will go with you. But because of the way you are going about this, the honor will not be yours, for the LORD will hand Sisera over to a woman.' So Deborah went with Barak to Kedesh, where he summoned Zebulun and Naphtali. Ten thousand men followed him, and Deborah also went with him."
>
> (Judges 4:4-10, NIV)

Without question, men during biblical times had a difficult time with the idea of being "outdone" by the women of that era. Even today, many "male" men find themselves being bettered by the "female" members of our species—and just cannot handle that fact when it happens.

I, for one, do not consider it diminishing my masculinity in any way to be beaten in a business deal by a woman. It only proves to me that I need to hone my skills in order to avoid a similar loss in the future—regardless of the gender of the others involved. However, in this story, Barak was failing in his responsibilities as head of Israel's army—especially within the social climate of the world at that time. Consequently, God ordained that for his near-dereliction of duty and obvious cowardice, Barak's male "pride" would be the price he would have to pay in the midst of that patriarchal society.

"Now Heber the Kenite had left the other Kenites, the descendants of Hobab, Moses' brother-in-law, and pitched his tent by the great tree in Zaanannim near Kedesh.

"When they told Sisera that Barak son of Abinoam had gone up to Mount Tabor, Sisera gathered together his nine hundred iron chariots and all the men with him, from Harosheth Haggoyim to the Kishon River.

"Then Deborah said to Barak, 'Go! This is the day the LORD has given Sisera into your hands. Has not the LORD gone ahead of you?' So Barak went down Mount Tabor, followed by ten thousand men. At Barak's advance, the LORD routed Sisera and all his chariots and army by the sword, and Sisera abandoned his chariot and fled on foot. But Barak pursued the chariots and army as far as Harosheth Haggoyim. All the troops of Sisera fell by the sword; not a man was left.

"Sisera, however, fled on foot to the tent of Jael, the wife of Heber the Kenite, because there were friendly relations between Jabin king of Hazor and the clan of Heber the Kenite. Jael went out to meet Sisera and said to him, 'Come, my Lord, come right in. Don't be afraid.' So he entered her tent, and she put a covering over him. 'I'm thirsty,' he said. 'Please give me some water.' She opened a skin of milk, gave him a drink, and covered him up. 'Stand in the doorway of the tent,' he told her. 'If someone comes by and asks you, "Is anyone here?" say "No."'

"But Jael, Heber's wife, picked up a tent peg and a hammer and went quietly to him while he lay fast asleep, exhausted. She drove the peg through his temple into the ground, and he died. Barak came by in pursuit of Sisera, and Jael went out to meet him.

> 'Come,' she said, 'I will show you the man you're looking for.' So he went in with her, and there lay Sisera with the tent peg through his temple-dead."
>
> (Judges 4:11-22, NIV)

Deborah was "leading Israel at that time" because she walked in both a *kingly* anointing as the "judge" of Israel, and, in the light of how I am teaching it to you, a *priestly* anointing as a prophetess of God as well. She is an early example of that Davidic anointing of both king and priest that was to later manifest in the man who would be its namesake—but as we see here, it was previously manifested in a *woman.*

She was the "go-to" person for Barak, the supreme commander of Israel's army at that time. Without question, she was the most powerful leader among the people of YHWH, and like Joshua before her, was used as God's mouthpiece to convey His victory plans for the coming battle. She was prophet *and* judge of Israel—therefore, she was both a priest and king in the light of all that we have discussed from the Bible up until this point.

It amazes me when I hear supposedly "learned" men tout such ignorance as to say, "No woman can preach or teach" or "...pastor a church." Apparently, these "educated" men never read the fourth chapter of the Book of Judges.

My wife Ann manifests a powerful anointing to teach God's word—she amazes me! She does things in the pulpit that I simply cannot do myself. Her manner of ministry is far more organized and methodical than the "whirlwind" style I am typically known for. To tell me she is not anointed because she is female will get you the same reaction from me as telling me that I am not anointed because I graduated from Yale. What difference does that make? When I check my Bible, it says that the gifts and callings of God are because of His grace, wisdom and a part of His predetermined plan—not our gender, skin color, or educational background. Such uninformed ideologies are nothing but man-made (better, "*male*-made") religious doctrines:

> "Ye hypocrites, well did Esaias prophesy of you, saying, 'This people draweth nigh unto me with their mouth, and honoureth me with their lips; but their heart is far from me. But in vain they do worship me, teaching for doctrines the commandments of men.'"
>
> (Matthew 15:7-9)

Any such teaching denies the reality of the New Testament and ignores the host of Old Testament examples. Those who teach such things build doctrines on a few "pet" scriptures in their lack of knowledge. God's handmaidens need to be released into their kingly and priestly callings for the benefit of the entire Body of Christ—just like the men-servants of the Lord need to be. Truthfully, unless they are, we will all suffer for the lack of their gifts and talents manifesting in the Body.

Moreover, Deborah is not the only example of a female "king." Did you notice the warrior spirit in Jael, the wife of Heber the Kenite? That woman stuck a general's head to the dirt with a tent peg! "Take a nap, sweet general. I'll take care of you." Three winks and the man's head became a part of the carpet! That is a warrior's anointing—the anointing of kings (Old-Testament style, of course)!

Barak lost the glory because he refused to take his rightful responsibility before God as the commanding general of God's forces. He begged Deborah, "Please go with me!" after she had already delegated to him the authority and responsibility to go and destroy the enemies of Israel. So, God had a *female king*—a "woman warrior" in the midst of a patriarchal society—standing by to get the job done and receive the reward for her prompt obedience and sheer courage.

Even today, I have seen women rise up and take ground for God's Kingdom that no man would dare tread. Listen, do not tell me that women cannot handle it—I know better. Some of them are tougher than most men I know!

Undoubtedly, many of them are also smarter than their male counterparts. Consider for a moment Abigail, the wife of Nabal in 1 Samuel 25. It says of her that she was, "an intelligent and beautiful woman" and that her husband was a "fool." In fact, that was the literal meaning of the man's name!

When Nabal treated David with contempt, he almost got himself and his entire household killed. The only reason that the entire family was spared was because Abigail had the prudence to intervene—once she found out what had happened. In fact, if it were not that so many men have married bona fide "Abigails," there would likely be more men destroyed every day for lack of good sense.

Women are smart. They are prayerful. They are often quicker to hear and obey the promptings of the Holy Spirit than many men are—although, there are plenty of exceptions, of course. And again, they have the capability to be fierce warriors when they set their minds to do so:

> "And Abimelech came unto the tower, and fought against it, and went hard unto the door of the tower to burn it with fire. And a certain woman cast a piece of a millstone upon Abimelech's head, and all to break his skull. Then he called hastily unto the young man his armourbearer, and said unto him, 'Draw thy sword, and slay me, that men say not of me, A women slew him.' And his young man thrust him through, and he died."
> (Judges 9:52-54)

Breaking heads with millstones, or pinning them to the ground with tent pegs—these warrior-women were not playing games. Add to this fact the context that these women, like Abigail, were also faithful keepers of their homes, and you can begin to see the Proverbs 31 woman in a new light…

WOMEN OF DISTINCTION

"A wife of noble character who can find? She is worth far more than rubies. Her husband has full confidence in her and lacks nothing of value. She brings him good, not harm, all the days of her life. She selects wool and flax and works with eager hands. She is like the merchant ships, bringing her food from afar. She gets up while it is still dark; she provides food for her family and portions for her servant girls. She considers a field and buys it; out of her earnings she plants a vineyard. She sets about her work vigorously; her arms are strong for her tasks. She sees that her trading is profitable, and her lamp does not go out at night. In her hand she holds the distaff and grasps the spindle with her fingers. She opens her arms to the poor and extends her hands to the needy. When it snows, she has no fear for her household; for all of them are clothed in scarlet. She makes coverings for her bed; she is clothed in fine linen and purple. Her husband is respected at the city gate, where he takes his seat among the elders of the land. She makes linen garments and sells them, and supplies the merchants with sashes. She is clothed with strength and dignity; she can laugh at the days to come. She speaks with wisdom, and faithful instruction is on her tongue. She watches over the affairs of her household and does not eat the bread of idleness. Her children arise and call her blessed; her husband also, and he praises her: 'Many women do noble things, but you surpass them all.' Charm is deceptive, and beauty is fleeting; but a woman who fears the LORD is to be praised. Give her the reward she has earned, and let her works bring her praise at the city gate."

(Proverbs 31:10-31, NIV)

Check this lady out: her husband "has full confidence in her and lacks nothing of value." What does that mean in today's vernacular? First, it means that a man secure in his own calling and anointing will not feel threatened by the calling and anointing of his wife. He knows his place within God's Kingdom, and is comfortable with his wife's as well. There is no *competition* between the spouses—only *cooperation* as they pursue God's calling on their family together.

Second, it means that she does not diminish the family's assets—she constantly adds to them. She does not clean out the family's bank account shopping at the mall—she fills it up through her own "kingly" business ventures:

- She has her own textile manufacturing business that employs numerous other women, and wholesales the goods to the retail merchants (vs. 13, 15, 18, 19, and 24).
- She invests the profits from her textile business into real estate and then plants a vineyard for a future wine manufacturing business (v. 16).
- She has a "warrior" mentality that rises early and goes to bed late in an effort to make sure her multiple enterprises are functioning smoothly (vs. 15, 18).
- And she works to position her husband as a leader in local governmental affairs among the men of reputation in her city (vs. 11-12, 23, 28-29).

All this, while keeping her household running smoothly, family fed and clothed, the employees properly paid, and feeding the poor as a benevolence ministry to boot! What man can compete with that? None that I know.

THE PROTOTYPE

The Proverbs 31 woman is a biblical "prototype" often cited by both men and women as the "pinnacle example" of womanhood. However, we rarely hear mentioned the fact that she is also one who walks in a king's anointing. She certainly knows her biblical place in God's divine order of the family—and does not mind her husband's being the head of the household. She even goes so far as to honor him above herself, and see that he is promoted as a man of distinction in her city. However, she also knows how to wield the weapons of economic conquest and take ground for the Kingdom—and even literal real estate for her family!

As we have shared throughout this book, the key thing to determine is where your dominant anointing lies—regardless of your gender. Thus, some women are called to supporting roles to their husband's calling, in addition to managing the affairs of their homes. There is certainly a level of "warfare" that accompanies such a calling, even when it is "behind the scenes," supporting him in his role.

Other women are also called to powerful professional, ministerial, political, judicial, and business leadership positions within society. Still other women are called to something somewhere in between these two examples. Regardless, if a woman is married and desires to be a Proverbs 31 example of womanhood, then she will not try to usurp the calling of her husband, nor be in competition with him. She will be very comfortable in her God-ordained role, whatever it may be, as he should be in his.

Furthermore, she will not abandon her calling in her role as a wife and mother in order to pursue her other vocational callings. To do so would endanger her marriage and family structure—just like it would if her husband failed in his marital and family roles as well.

Let me digress for a moment from our main topic and point out here that God calls families to a *shared* calling—regardless of the individual callings of each member. Thus, it is imperative that both the husband and wife share in each other's callings together so that they do not find themselves living separate lives. Cultivating one's own ministry or profession within the context of marital unity and mutual appreciation breeds love, and it cultivates bonds that hold strong during times of adversity. Failure to do so gives place to the enemy of their souls—and of their marriage—and is one of the contributing factors of so many Christian marriages ending in divorce, or worse, adultery.

Likewise, Christian parents need to appreciate the plan of God for each of their children, and seek to cultivate a family-calling consciousness while also helping their children to each discover their own God-given gifts, talents and anointings. God Almighty did not only call Abraham—He also called Isaac, Jacob, and his twelve sons. Thus, families who realize that their individual callings are within the context of a shared family-calling, are far more likely to weather storms and keep their family relationships intact—as has been proven time and again by those families who have cultivated such a consciousness.

Now, let me return again to the discussion of women's kingly callings specifically and reiterate that some women are just as qualified to be "leaders in the gate" as some men are. Certainly, one of the callings of female warrior-kings categorically is to take political and judicial positions within governments, and business leadership positions within industries. In fact, we need them there to ensure things are done right and with equity, because of their unique perspectives versus those of most men.

However, that is not the point here. The key issue we are pointing out from this passage of Scripture is that the "Proverbs 31 woman" is a king in her own right. Furthermore, in addition to being an economic conqueror, she is a tremendous manager of domestic help and affairs, and a selfless and sacrificial promoter of her husband in his calling—as he should be in promoting her in hers.

What is God's promise to such a godly woman for her kingly service, selfless efforts and personal sacrifice?

> "Give her the reward she has earned, and let her works bring her praise at the city gate."
> (Proverbs 31:31, NIV)

She is financially blessed beyond measure, exceptionally honored by her husband and children (vs. 28-30), and earns a place of distinction among the city leaders as well. All kings get to eat of the spoils they win on behalf of the Kingdom—even the women-warrior kings.

The "Proverbs 31 woman" has conquered the enemy, stuck his head to the dirt with a tent peg, and taken the spoils for her King Yahshua—all while loving her Lord, husband (if she is married), and family. Thus, the KING OF KINGS makes sure she enjoys the fruit of her efforts as well.

NEW TESTAMENT EXAMPLES

I am sure that there will be those who will say, "Yes, but—all those examples you have given thus far are from the Old Testament. Are there any New Testament examples of female 'vocational kings' in the financial arena?" I am so glad you asked...

> "One of those who listened to us was a woman named Lydia, from the city of Thyatira, a dealer in fabrics dyed in purple. She was [already] a worshipper of God, and the Lord opened her heart to pay attention to what was said by Paul. And when she was baptized along with her household, she earnestly entreated us, saying, 'If in your opinion I am one really convinced [that Jesus is the Messiah and the Author of salvation] and that I will be faithful to the Lord, come to my house and stay.' And she induced us [to do it]."
>
> (Acts 16:14-15, AMP)

Lydia was in the textile business as well. In fact, she epitomizes the example of the Proverbs 31 woman with another outstanding distinction: *She appears to have been a single mother.*

Notice that she invited them home to "her" house, that she was baptized along with "her" household—and that the only source of income listed for her family was the purple apparel business *she* owned. Whether a widow, divorced, or whatever...this girl had some cash. She also apparently knew how to get things done in the practicalities of life while still having a tremendous desire to promote God's agenda as well. Look at how she insisted on taking good care of the men of God who opened her understanding to the Gospel!

This female warrior for the King had been trained in the art of economic warfare before she even met the One Who had called her to a higher purpose—much like I had been in the Wall Street arena. And like me, she did not have to "drop everything" and become some beggarly burden on the resources of the church simply because she got saved. Some of the silly notions Christians have had about people of wealth are not only ridiculous, but they are also extremely counter-productive to the advancement of the Kingdom.

If Paul had been religiously brainwashed like so many are today, he might have said, "Now that you are saved, dear, take off all that jewelry, quit your business, raise your children and find yourself a good husband to take care of. Then maybe God will be pleased with you." However, what does the Bible say about such things?

> "Everyone should remain after God calls him in the station or condition of life in which the summons found him."
> (1 Corinthians 7:20, AMP)

The scripture already indicated that God had been wooing her to Himself since she had become a "worshipper of YHWH" rather than the pagan deities common during that day. He had even positioned her to meet Paul and Silas when they showed up in town with the good news. Her household became the "headquarters" for their ministry in that city (until they were thrown in prison), and her business was the economic catalyst for their missionary work in that region. Yes, God even wants to use wealthy people to help spread the Gospel of Jesus Christ.

Furthermore, God wants to use His anointed women in these last days to preach His Word as His *priests*, and to take territory for the Kingdom as His female warrior-*kings*. Some, He wants to use as both—as He did with Deborah. Whether in government, business, sports…or even the ministry, God makes no distinction between genders—no more than He does by race or educational background. In fact, He is even more likely to choose those who do not "measure up" according to the common "wisdom" of the day or unbiblical cultural expectations:

> "For [simply] consider your own call, brethren; not many [of you were considered to be] wise according to human estimates and standards, not many influential and powerful, not many of high and noble birth. [No] for God selected (deliberately chose) what in the world is foolish to put the wise to shame, and what the world calls weak to put the strong to shame. And God also selected (deliberately chose) what in the world is lowborn and insignificant and branded and treated with contempt, even the things that are nothing, that He might depose and bring to nothing the things that are, so that no mortal man should [have pretense for glorying and] boast in the presence of God."
> (1 Corinthians 1:26-29, AMP)

NO CAKEWALK

Nonetheless, as we end this chapter let me bring this back to the harsh realities of what combat for the Kingdom is like. Now that we have established the fact that many women are called to conquer for their king just like many men, we need to clarify for those women who are not already battle-scarred what they can expect once the sound of combat fills their ears. Thus, before you go running out the door to "conquer the world" for the Kingdom, you need to come to grips with the actual adversity that awaits your war cry.

First, keep in mind that there are groups all over the country that are excluding the women from their programs and "inner circles." The harsh reality of the situation is that in the mainstream of business and commerce, it can still be a "man's world" out there—particularly in the upper echelons of many segments of our economy. In many circles, men who wield the power have intentionally built barriers to women who desire to share the scepter.

The reason for this oft "unspoken" segregation of the genders is not simply because of male chauvinism, though. Can I get really blunt with you as a provocateur for a moment without your getting mad and running away from this book? The real reason for much (but not all) of the exclusion is because of the over-sensitivity so common with many women…and because of their insistence on having conversations with a handkerchief next to their eye.

Some of the types of things I have heard women say in business deals are: "Oh, they did not treat me right in that business meeting! I cannot believe those men were as crude and uncaring as that!" Or, "I think that they should be more polite when talking to me. They shouldn't use that tone of voice." Or even, "I just cannot believe they use language like that around a lady!" Or how about this one: "They should have been fairer with me and given me the deal!"

Listen, you are in the real world now—and when competition is high, people's faces are getting bloodied by the politics and business deals, and unsaved men are scrapping to get a piece of the pie, things get messy:

> "For every battle of the warrior is with confused noise, and garments rolled in blood; but this shall be with burning and fuel of fire."
>
> (Isaiah 9:5)

To burst out into tears in the middle of the business meeting during the proverbial "combat" is not what *kings* do. It is ridiculous to have those types of crybaby discourses over and over again. We need to grow past such behavior. If you are going to be a warrior for Christ, then you will have to stick Satan's head to the floor with a hammer and tent peg—and that makes a mess, girl!

This is not about "frou frou" games being played in little social clubs. *This is combat*—and things can get very cutthroat when money is involved. If you are going to be successful in your calling, you need to get your emotions off your sleeve and be prepared to hit someone with a proverbial "millstone" right between the eyes. Women of this caliber make it to the higher echelons of business, politics, and commerce—because they have proven themselves and "earned" the right to be there in the eyes of others. But make no mistake about it, only those of this caliber make it to these lofty ranks.

Sisters, I want you on the team. Some of you are actually tougher than me! Listen, I have been "beat up" in business deals by a lot of women in my day. So, let me emphasize that I am not saying you are any "less" than a man—on the contrary. I know how tough you women can be...because my wife is tough! She will not take any rubbish off of anybody if she has made up her mind "this is the way it is, and God says it is mine!" There are a few guys wandering the streets of New York with proverbial "millstones" stuck in their foreheads because of her—let me tell you!

I know some of you women out there can be strong and aggressive. If you are one of these women already, then you can simply add your "amen" to this portion of the chapter concerning the others, and move on. Nevertheless, many women are not...and I also want to include among the successful kings of the Kingdom the women who still need some growing in this particular area. We all need them to rise to the level of conquest to which they are called.

Let me also point out the fact that some men are every bit as handkerchief-oriented as many of the women I have mentioned. No offense is intended, but to put it bluntly, some guys even hold their pinky up when they drink tea!

Male or female, we have got to toughen up when problems come our way, and people get ugly. We need to realize that every situation is solvable. The answers are already here.

No, it is not all your fault when things go haywire. Nonetheless, you are somewhat to blame for the mess if you—regardless of your gender—have a *wimpy* attitude that just lets people walk all over you in your business deals! Everybody gets to play in this game of doing business, but once you are in the game—it becomes *war*.

Listen, if you are a woman called to vocational "priestly" ministry as one of God's five-fold ministers, you will need to walk away from the "naysayers" and get on with your life—even if it means changing churches. Use the critics and religious bigots as stepping stones to your future by allowing their opposition to toughen you up for the race God has set before you. If the critic is in your own home, then love him, and keep on doing what God has told you to do—while faithfully maintaining the home-bound responsibilities, as our Proverbs 31 woman did. He'll come along with the program eventually (1 Peter 3:1-4).

Similarly, if you are a woman called to the warfare as a king, God wants you activated into your call. He wants you to be a Jael—sticking the devil's head to the sand with the biggest tent peg you can find. He may want you to be another Lydia—taking economic territory and financing the spread of the Gospel in the process. He may even want you to become a Deborah—leading a nation in high-levels of government, even while speaking "the word of the Lord" with prophetic power to the people. Whatever your call—priest or king or both—God wants you successful, as do I.

If you want help in achieving these things in your life, I invite you to be a part of the ProVision Network team. There is godly counsel, comprised of both men and women, waiting to help you navigate the challenges and face them with wisdom and courage. You can be victorious—because you already are: Victory Himself lives on the inside of you, the woman warrior.

PART V

PRACTICAL WISDOM

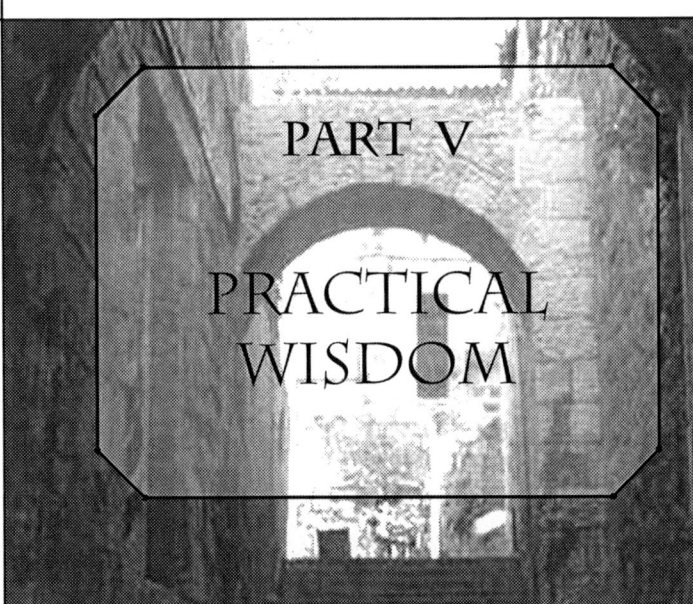

"Until what's in your head is actually lived out, that knowledge is wasted and useless, and you will never enjoy the fruit of it. You must be willing to step out, seize opportunities, and search for ways to put your knowledge and dreams into action."

—Yahshua—

Jesus—The Way, The Truth, And The Life.

"I came that they may have and enjoy life, and have it in abundance (to the full, till it overflows)."

(John 10:10b, Amplified)

THE IMPORTANCE OF TRANSPARENCY

Chapter Twenty-Two

The pastoral staff of a church is trained primarily to promote the spiritual and mental well-being of a congregation. They will intercede and pray the prayer of agreement with people, and some of them are also skilled at relationship management in the area of children and marriage, etc. They know how to counsel people on a spiritual level, but when it comes to giving practical legal or business advice, or such emergency financial issues as foreclosure, most pastors are not trained to help anyone—even from the Scriptures.

As a result, the people are prayed for, the devil is "rebuked," and they "stand in faith" for their deliverance, but they have nowhere to go to get the professional advice they need about whatever "works" they need to do to have total victory:

> "And one of you says to him, Good-bye! Keep [yourself] warm and well fed, without giving him the necessities for the body, what good does that do? So also faith, if it does not have works (deeds and actions of obedience to back it up), by itself is destitute of power (inoperative, dead)."
> (James 2:16-17, AMP)

After the "be warmed, be filled" prayer is

done, the people walk away just as ignorant as when they first came in for counseling. They are deprived of the comprehension necessary to walk out that faith. They are on their own without a map.

When we all come together in a service, the praise and worship leader and the pastor exhort us to be upbeat and excited. Then if someone in the congregation is crying over some hard situation that he or she is going through, the minister tells him that he should not be crying but he should be "in faith." I don't know about you, but I have found that some people are in situations where they *need* to be crying!

Transparency is not something often seen in church.

Somebody asks you how you are doing. You say, "Oh, I am blessed." Someone else inquires, "How's everything at home?" You respond, "Oh, it's great." Then you sneak through the back door into the pastor's office crying hysterically saying, "I'm losing my house! My wife says she's going to leave me!" Do not wait until things get that bad before you get help. Get help at the first sign of trouble—especially if you have no clue as to what to do!

"Are you getting down on pastors?" one might ask.

No, I am not. (I *am* one, remember?) What I am emphasizing is that the pastoral gift alone is not sufficient to meet the needs of the flock of God.

We pastors do our jobs well, and with great sincerity (most of us). However, unless we have specific training in these areas (business, investments, law, real estate, accounting, etc...), we will be bereft of the ability to minister to people in the practical advice they need to overcome their challenges:

The beautiful thing is that everything each of us needs is already contained within the Body of Christ—through its individual members.

That is the way the Lord designed the Body to work: The various "parts" helping the other "parts." The problem is that the church has been adapting to the world's system, and we have become extremely disconnected. We do not know each other, and we have been kind of trained to not talk to each other about anything. If someone asks a struggling Christian, "How are you doing?" The person responds, "Oh, I'm blessed."

Poppycock! What is going on in your life? If your nineteen-year-old son, who used to be a straight-A student, is going to nightclubs getting drunk out of his mind, something is wrong! You cannot just say, "Oh I'm blessed. I'm just standing here confessing my son is coming home!" No, no, no! There is a *problem* there that needs to be *addressed*. We need to help you get your boy back before he puts a gun in his mouth! We need to be able to freely communicate with each other. The struggles we have are actually gifts that make us grow—as long as there is a solution to them. They are NOT gifts if they are just going to leave us hanging.

Everybody on the team in God's great game gets to play—not just the big evangelist or the well-known prophet. Furthermore, everybody in the Body is *supposed* to play. So, stir it up! Come bring your good stuff and your bad stuff. Then we can start getting things fixed little by little by communicating with each other about our needs and desires. God will speak to you about how you can help other people, and to others about how they can help you—so that we *all* can win.

STAYING CONNECTED

How can we, the Body of Christ, compete with the world if we are not utilizing our greatest asset—us? But it must be "us" cleaned up, "us" acting right, "us" not easily offended, and "us" speaking well of each other.

Guess what? I am not perfect. That should not come as a shock to you, nor should you expect me to be. Sometimes we need to make sure we have reasonable expectations of each other—and not be easily offended or "turned off" by things that are alien to our own experience. Let me illustrate:

One time when I was speaking in one of our ProVision Network meetings in Texas, I said a particular word that is okay to say in New York—but, unbeknownst to me, is considered a curse word in Texas. I lost about 20 people, who disconnected from me—from part of the Body—because I used a New York colloquialism. Sometimes we get a little too churchy for our own good. What are you going to do if your divine connection speaks Spanish or Vietnamese?

We have to come to a place where we are willing to let God surprise us, wonderfully, and stretch us to a place where something really cool and different could happen in the form of divine connections. Your whole life could change just by meeting one person who introduces you to an inconceivable vista of opportunity.

Here is another example: My wife does not like me going to the particular golf club that I frequent because they drink beer there. Now, the problem with that thinking is that if I stopped going everywhere that beer was served, I could not go skiing anymore either because they serve beer there. I would not be able to go to most restaurants because they serve alcohol. I could no longer go to a ball game because they sell beer too! (That would also mean that we could not eat at *most* of her favorite restaurants because they serve even more than just beer—but, we'll just not talk about that right now.) The point is: Although we are not of the world, we are still in it, and we cannot expect everything here to be a model of Heaven as long as there are worldly people still on Earth. Likewise, we cannot expect *relationships* here on this planet to always be so *heavenly* either.

God will connect you with people who do not necessarily have a personality that is naturally compatible with yours. It has taken me ten years to win the trust of certain ministers in the Texas area because my New York personality was not easy for them to get used to. As I said before, "I am not 'fixin'' to do anything!" I am either doing it or I am not. I have a blunt, candid, typical-New-Yorker-type of personality that rubs some people the wrong way. If they do something that bugs me, they are going to know right away. But if I do something that irritates them, I may not know about it for years (if ever)! We do not have time for that! If I am bothering someone, I need to know about it now.

Here is the scriptural truth: you do not get to "quit" me because I messed up and said a word that offended you. And I don't get to "quit" you if I catch you drinking a beer. We are part of the Body of Christ. There are people in the Body over in Germany who drink beer every day! I am not condoning drinking here, but I am saying that none of these issues of imperfection gives us permission to quit each other.

In some countries, it is actually considered a *sin* to drink coffee! Do you want them cutting you off for drinking a latte? We are too quick to throw someone out for whatever reason—cut them off—instead of having a conversation and getting things straightened out.

The hardest thing in our culture in the church is how to grow up the new gifts in an old wine skin—in which there is only room for about four big gifts (evangelist, pastor, teacher, and maybe a prophet—depending on your denominational paradigm). God did not create anything *small*. The only reason things stay small is because we do not water them, we do not encourage them and give them room to grow, and we give them no light. The message I am preaching is "light for all, not just for some," because we cannot go to the place of dominion with only six players on the field when we need sixty million.

Another thing that I have noticed, in all my contact with different people, is that the squeaky wheels squeak early on, and they want all my attention—and all the attention of *others*. We have to work through that because the cream *does* eventually rise to the top. For a long time, especially with new people who come to my meetings, I am just stirring the barrel. I am seeing who is going to stick around and how people act when they do not get everything according to their time schedule. Once the cream starts rising to the top, deals start happening. People start getting great things going. Sometimes people start off sinking right to the bottom, but if they stick around, they rise to the top.

—Yahshua—

Jesus—The Way, The Truth, and The Life.

"I came that they may have and enjoy life, and have it in abundance (to the full, till it overflows)."

(John 10:10b, Amplified)

CAPACITY

Chapter Twenty-Three

I once heard someone say, "What you starve dies; what you feed grows; and what you continue to feed is never really satisfied—you only increase its *capacity*." What an accurate statement that is! Think about it! The more a person "puts his flesh under" in a matter, whether it's ungodly television or chocolate cake, the easier it becomes to resist those things. The Word says in James 4:7 that we are to submit to God and resist the devil, and then the devil will flee from us.

How do we submit to God? By submitting to things that are of Him—we do those things that are pleasing in His sight. How do we resist the devil? By rejecting the things that come from the enemy. Whichever things we choose to submit to—whether those that are of God or of the enemy of our soul—are the very areas in which we can expect to see our capacity grow. It is simply how the "Law of Capacity" operates.

When we think of it that way, we can see how important it is to give the devil no place. Rather than giving him a *foothold*, he is supposed to be our *footstool*. As we submit to God by feeding on His Word, praying and fellowshipping with Him, and obeying His daily commands to us, our capacity to become more like Him and to do more for Him on the earth automatically increases.

THE LAW OF CAPACITY

Throughout the Bible, God shows us that He will fill whatever size vessel we make available to

Him. In fact, in Psalm 23, we see that we can expect God to fill our "cups" to overflowing. He is indeed the God of overflow—the God Who is more than enough! An individual's capacity for the wisdom and anointing of God grows as those areas are continuously fed and nurtured. And the more that person embraces the calling of God on his life, the bigger the vessel that is being offered to God for filling.

Your cup will "runneth over," but how much you retain in your own life depends on the size of your cup! He is a "pressed down, shaken together, and running over" type of God! He always has more for us to press toward and receive.

GET EDUCATED

We have already mentioned how to increase our spiritual capacity—through studying the Word, praying, and fellowshipping with God (and also with other believers). Without question, God and spiritual things should be first place in our lives. Jesus told us to seek first the Kingdom of God and His righteousness, and then all the carnal things that we need would be added unto us (Matthew 6:33). However, there are also plenty of scriptures that talk about *diligence* and *labor* as being key factors in one's financial prosperity. For that reason, it is not only necessary to seek to grow spiritually, but we must also strive to improve in other areas of our being in order to reap the full blessings that God has planned for us.

One way to do that is through *education*—whether formal or informal. In order to excel in a particular endeavor, you must study as much as you can about that field. Preparation is never lost time—it is time invested into your capacity to succeed. The more you know about whatever you are planning to pursue, the more equipped you are to overcome obstacles when they arise. On the contrary, the more ignorant you are before going into a situation, the more you must eventually learn—the hard way.

GET EXPERIENCE

Have you ever noticed that whenever you go through a trial (aside from any beatings that occur against your soul), you come out of it a wiser person? If we can forget the mistakes but learn the lessons mined from them, our negative experiences can become capacity-stretching tools in our road to success.

By the same token, the pleasant events that occur in our lives are tremendous learning experiences as well. If we know what worked when we did it, then we know we can usually get success in that area again if done in a similar way. The more positive results you gain, the more road-tested strategies you have in your arsenal to use whenever they apply to future situations.

The fact of the matter is that you cannot learn everything from books or even from little greenhouse-type of testing environments. You have to get out there where the resistance is in order for your capacity to really be expanded. You need to *experience* the harsh realities of combat a few times, and get a taste of *both* defeats and victories, *if* you expect to be promoted in life. You need to take a good hit here and there, get up off the ground with your nose bleeding, and say, "That hurt, but you won't get me that way next time!" Toughness is bred in the realities of battle.

Until what's in your head is actually lived out, that knowledge is wasted and useless, and you will never enjoy the fruit of it. You must be willing to step out, seize opportunities, and search for ways to put your knowledge and dreams into *action*. As you do this, your capacity to contain more, accomplish more, and to be promoted to the next level in your life grows.

COVENANT CAPACITY

In our effort to increase our capacity in our individual lives, we must keep in mind that, as Christians, we are all members of a larger Body. We can only get so far in our capacity to do great things for the Kingdom without the other members. First Corinthians 12 says that God has set each member in the Body as it pleased Him. He has everyone lined up to do what he is supposed to do, with the purpose of the whole Body working together towards the common goal of taking this world for Jesus.

We really need to comprehend that covenant relationships are *mandatory*, not optional. We cannot pick and choose the ones we want to connect with and reject those who rub us the wrong way. In fact, the very ones you might be inclined to think that you can live without are the ones God calls "necessary." Although you might be able to function without others to a degree, you are still a part of a Body, which in your life becomes like a handicapped one. You have simply learned to live with your spiritual disability instead of realizing you can be "totally healed" and complete if you would allow God to connect you with the ones that are "necessary" for the development of your calling—and for theirs.

Working together for the furtherance of the Kingdom has nothing to do with whether or not we *like* each other. That is what *agape* love is for! We *choose* to love each other, even when we get on each other's nerves to a degree. We have to operate that way and be Kingdom-minded, rather than "my-little-world" minded if we want to stretch our capacity for the greater call. There is a whole world out there to reach with the Gospel, and we cannot do it effectively unless we do it as a team.

For instance…

- John Doe has been faithfully leading congregations about the size of 150 members for years. After years of service to His Lord, an opportunity comes for him to take the reigns of a 500-member church in another city. However, within a year of taking the oversight thereof, the church suffers a split in the leadership and loses many discouraged members as a result. Within months, the congregation dwindles down to an active membership of about 150.

- Businessman Bob has operated his store for numerous years on the corner of 5th and Main Streets. He decides to finally open another location a few miles away to service a growing customer base in that district of the city. However, he is unable to handle the added work load created when managing two stores versus one, and it is only a couple of years before the second store closes and his debt is substantial as a result of the failed business venture.

- Mary Sue always dreamed of being wealthy. Growing up in a lower-middle class suburban home, she never really was taught the fundamental basics of personal financial management or investment principles. One day, she discovers that she has inherited nearly a $1.5 million from an uncle she always adored in her family's summer visits to another state. Sadly, within fourteen months of the funds depositing to her account, she has amassed significant debt, lost much of the money to unscrupulous "friends" and investment scams, and is in danger of having both her new car and home repossessed because she can no longer make the payments on either. What she initially thought was the fulfillment of a lifetime dream, ultimately became a financial nightmare within only months of its realization.

What do all these hypothetical stories have in common? Can you see a familiar thread woven in each of the narratives? Is there some element that seems to "jump out" at you that, perhaps, seems to ring within your *own* heart as the reason for some of your own lost blessings?

God has promised all His children to fill our cups to an overflow state.

However, the size of our "cups" determines how much of that blessing we can retain and utilize—and how much just runs out onto the floor for the cat to lick up. Consider Haggai's message for a moment:

> "Now this is what the LORD Almighty says: 'Give careful thought to your ways. You have planted much, but have harvested little. You eat, but never have enough. You drink, but never have your fill. You put on clothes, but are not warm. You earn wages, only to put them in a purse with holes in it.' This is what the LORD Almighty says: 'Give careful thought to your ways.'"
>
> (Haggai 1:5-7, NIV)

The pastor in the previous story did not have the *capacity* to oversee a flock of over 150 members. That is why he only ever attained that level in his previous churches—and is why the larger ministry quickly dwindled to the level of his capacity. Pastors often think their problem is with their people, programs, or even the location of their ministries. It never occurs to them that the reason their churches do not grow beyond what seems to be a "ceiling" on their achievements as ministers is that they never find the key issues that keep the back door of the church swinging as fast as the front. They have reached a plateau that they cannot seem to advance beyond—and the combination of their own personal capacity limitations as leaders, and those of their ministry organization as a whole, are in reality what is restraining them. They have bags with holes in them, and have not yet considered their own ways.

Similarly, Businessman Bob had an excellent capacity to manage a single store. His customers were happy and business was booming. However, it did not occur to Bob that he might need *additional skills* and *personal growth* to handle multiple locations. He never considered taking a specialized business course, bringing in a partner, or even hiring a consultant. Violating the *Law of Capacity*, he quickly discovered that two are indeed harder to manage than one. Again, the result was that he found himself returning to his actual level of capacity—and even suffering some loss because of the expenses incurred in the failed effort.

And pitiful Mary Sue...a situation all too common with people of all ages, genders and races. Opportunity came knocking on her door, and with it came all the "leeches" and con artists who wanted a piece of her pie. Unequipped to handle the newfound wealth she possessed, she fell victim to her own ignorance—and those who preyed upon it. Like most people who win lotteries around the world, her own capacity limitations reduced her to a point below her previous level of achievement. One cannot help but think of the Scripture, "An inheritance quickly gained at the beginning will not be blessed at the end" (Proverbs 20:21, NIV).

It is a good thing to realize, however, that the only thing preventing you from "soaring the heavens" of God's grace and blessing is your own personal capacity. Why is that good news? Because through diligence, it is extremely easy to expand your own capacity for increase. And once your vessel for blessing is enlarged, you can be sure that God's best is on its way to you—not just because it is His will, but because you know that you have done *your* part for it to become a reality in your life.

—Yahshua—

Jesus—The Way, The Truth, and The Life.

"I came that they may have and enjoy life, and have it in abundance (to the full, till it overflows)."

(John 10:10b, Amplified)

ZEAL WITHOUT KNOWLEDGE

There is something that I need to impress upon you that goes completely contrary to the world's way of thinking. Often it is said that, "What you don't know can't hurt you." But in reality, what you do not know can *kill* you...

> "My people are destroyed for lack of knowledge..."
> (Hosea 4:6a)

In a way, there is something else that is even more dangerous than being completely uninformed about a particular subject. For some people, a little bit of knowledge is the catalyst for premature action in a particular issue. Such zealots do not realize how *little* they actually know:

Chapter Twenty-Four

> "Also, that the soul be without knowledge, it is not good; and he that hasteth with his feet sinneth."
> (Proverbs 19:2)

> "Willingness and stupidity don't go well together. If you are too eager, you will miss the road."
> (Proverbs 19:2, CEV)

> "It is not good to have zeal without knowledge, nor to be hasty and miss the way."
> (Proverbs 19:2, NIV)

Sometimes Christians have a tendency to take something from the scriptures concerning their finances and try to run with it without first laying the proper foundation, which involves more than *spiritual* wisdom. We need to know what to do with money in a practical sense. For example, if we want to get involved in real estate, we need to get our hands on as much information as we can in that field to help us in our success. Otherwise, we will end up learning the hard way things that we could have prevented if we had simply read some books and received some sound financial advice from those who have already been there.

Let me tell you a story. There was a young couple from Louisiana who came to our church. While they were with us, they began to prosper. He was a musician in the city, and God was really blessing them (he played for Lion King, for example). As God prospered them, in time, they bought a house.

As more time passed, they began hearing the message on "debt cancellation" as it has been taught by numerous Word-based ministers. The teaching they heard was sound, Bible-based, and well taught by very credible teachers—no problem there. Despite this sound teaching, however, this couple was lacking in their necessary comprehension of some "hands on" knowledge of financial issues—especially the dynamics of real estate.

They bought the house back around 1996. At that time, they paid something in the figure of about $175,000 for it—which in our part of the country means it was a fairly small home. It was a little three-bedroom home (with hardly any yard), and each bedroom was tiny. However, it was sufficient for their needs at the time, and they had been happy with it until...

They kept hearing, "get out of debt," from these various ministers. Yet, they were not hearing that message with hearts full of wisdom—and heads filled with adequate knowledge. Their mental "filters" and limited paradigms about finances were distorting the message they heard into something that it was not. They were truly being taught the Word of God, but they heard it in a twisted way. Nevertheless, they added up their credit card bills, mortgage, and all their other debts—and took off like a rocket to act on what they had "heard."

The real estate market was rallying out here on the East Coast at the time. So after they figured out how much they owed, and "knowing" that God wanted them out of debt, they decided to sell their house. Instead of consulting a REALTOR® or some other form of real estate professional, they decided that they would "save" themselves the commission and sell it themselves. They put a "For Sale By Owner" sign out front, ran an add in the paper, and they "successfully" sold it on their own—and for an amount that basically got them out of debt, plus put about $10-12,000 in their pockets. They came to me with great exuberance and proclaimed the praise report, "We're out of debt! We sold our house in one day!"

I said, "Praise the Lord! What did you sell it for?"

They said, "We sold our house for $245,000!"

Shocked, I responded, "You sold your house for two hundred... what?!"

Taken aback by my sudden lack of enthusiasm, they said, "Well, what do you mean? We're out of debt! We're going to move back to Louisiana and buy another house that's even bigger than the other one...and it's only $85,000!"

I replied, "Oh, praise God. Well, we're really going to miss you. And while I am at it, I really think you missed God because you sold your house $150,000 too cheap. You wonder why you sold it in one day."

They would have paid a typical real estate commission of about $24,000 and profited another $126,000 over what they actually made if they had augmented their ignorance by hiring a good professional to help them. If they had come to the leadership at the church, we could have even helped them to find a better way to eliminate their consumer debt and position themselves financially for even greater increase—without having to leave the church God had called them to attend.

Too many of us are trying to make financial decisions without good counsel. I do not pretend to know everything, but I know people who know a lot of stuff. Everything I have I am willing to make available to you—every contact I have on Wall Street and every person I have around the ProVision Network. Everywhere I go I am on a hunt for the financial answer that you need. But guess what? We have got to have a relationship. I am not going to do it for you if you are not a part of the team.

Unreciprocated love is sad; it is tough. When people come to me asking a "million" financial questions hoping I'll have the answers they need, there is only so far I can go in helping them if they have not entered into covenant with me—and the team I have assembled. They ask me, "What can I do?" but they cannot bring themselves to attend a ProVision Network chapter meeting—much less join the network.

Right now, I already have hundreds of people, between the ProVision

Network and my church, who have made the covenant commitment to be a part of the larger vision—in order to see their own "kingdoms" and successes become a reality. Soon, this number will be counted in the thousands, and I am already obligated to *them*.

I cannot take the time to fix the problems of thousands of other people who will not make a similar commitment. They can read my books and listen to my tapes; even attend my services and PVN chapter meetings without any further obligation required—but, they cannot call me on the phone asking, "Can you tell me how to fix my finances?" That level is only for the unselfishly committed—and there are levels higher yet for those who have been proven.

Covenant is reciprocal. Members of the ProVision Network and Faith Exchange Fellowship realize this. That is why I am dedicated to serve them with the resources I have—and not waste them on people who are looking for the "quick fix" rather than long-term success. Those with the wisdom to look beyond their circumstances toward the greater vision of God's destiny for their lives realize that they cannot accomplish it alone. They need relationships...they need fellowship...and they need someone who refuses to let them stay insignificant in the Kingdom of God.

You do not get to stay small, not in God's eyes, nor mine. When I go to God on behalf of the people I am about to minister to in a service or PVN meeting, He shows me their potential. He shows me a billion-dollar flow potential. But if you want that kind of increase to become a reality in your own life, you are going to have to get serious.

DUE DILIGENCE

As I close this chapter, let me introduce you more formally to a term that I have already used quite often in this book. You must understand the concept of—and your responsibility to perform—*due diligence.*

Often, people will say something to the effect of, "I did not know what I was getting myself into," or "Those people told me one thing, and it turned out to be something completely different!" Perhaps you have even heard yourself saying, "I really trusted that person, and I am shocked that he/she led me astray." Let me fill you in on a very important truth that can be best summed up in the old axiom, "Things are not always as they appear."

The basic rule of financial wisdom is this: If you do not understand something, study it and research it...until you *do*! At a minimum, hire professionals, seek the advice of the appropriate "kings" who have borne good fruit in that area of expertise before you "jump" into something and lose your shirt. Even then, you would do well to have read a book or two on the subject to be sure you even understand the advice they are giving you—and that you can even hold an intelligent conversation about the subject to ask your question in the first place. Furthermore, seek the counsel of "two or three witnesses" before making a large decision (Deuteronomy 19:15; 2 Corinthians 13:1). Otherwise, how would you even know if their advice is good?

Let me delve into another area along these lines: I find it amazing that Christians can somehow be surprised to find out that not everybody in the world is honest. "Gullibility" is one of chief reasons most believers fall into all sorts of dangerous pitfalls—they just do not take the time to check things out for themselves.

Furthermore, not every honest person is a good source of information on the topic he may be communicating to you about. It is possible that someone has beguiled him—and he is just passing the deceit on to you. Even a good man can be deceived—especially in areas he is himself ignorant of.

No matter who the source of information is, no matter what promises are made...it is *your* responsibility to look into things for your own protection and information. This is what I call "due diligence." It is the diligent pursuit of corroborating information from independent sources. It is "checking things out" earnestly...and from verifiable resources. "Due diligence" is making sure that everything is on the "up and up"—regardless of what names or personalities are involved in the deal.

When it comes to business or investments (even relationships!), the one thing that will keep you from being "taken for a ride" most consistently is not *prayer*—it is doing your investigative research first! It is doing your *due diligence.* Many a believer has been swindled out of considerable amounts of money in scams they "prayed" about, but never looked into properly.

Many a believer has married someone he or she thought was the "perfect" mate, only to find out that the person belonged in a psycho ward somewhere. The hard fact, my brother and sister, is that your own emotions, excitement, and ideas can convince you something is "God" when it is really just selfishness, covetousness, and the flesh.

YHWH intends for you to use the God-given brain and intelligence He gave you to check things out thoroughly *first*—then pray about the ones that do not obviously violate biblical precepts of integrity, legality, and consecration.

What do I mean by that? Well, if someone offers you an opportunity to buy stock in a brand new "restaurant" he plans to open, and your "due diligence" uncovers the fact that it is actually a topless bar—you do NOT have to pray to see if God is the One Who brought you that opportunity. And if you are a little bit "slow on the uptake," let me help you: THAT IS NOT GOD! You do not have to waste any time or oxygen praying that one out.

Let me use another example that is based on an actual case that my co-author, Rich Vermillion, is aware of: If you are a Christian woman believing God for a godly mate, and a fellow moves to your area and joins the church—check him out thoroughly before you go get engaged to the guy. Insist on meeting his family, talking to his "old" friends, finding out where he works—even running a background check on the guy for forty bucks over the Internet. If you discover that he is wanted in seven states for polygamy and stealing the life's savings of multitudes of gullible Christian women—run away! He is not the one for you! I don't care how good looking he is, how sweet he talks to you, how much scripture he quotes, or how desperate you are for a husband—run away!

You might laugh, but as I said, this example above was based on an actual person—and those he actually deceived. "Don Juan" took a whole bunch of vulnerable women down a path they had no idea they were going to travel. *Due diligence* keeps your finances, emotions, and life intact. *Due diligence* is the key to making sure your investments are sound.

"Yeah, but it was a minister who told me about this investment deal," someone might say. If there is ANY reason in the world to check it out before getting involved, THAT is the one thing that would send up "red flags" for me! Most ministers—unless they have extensive business or investment backgrounds, like myself—are terrible sources of information about the quality of an investment or business opportunity. You do not ask a priest for kingly advice. He may, or may not, be "up to speed" concerning the legality of the deal…much less as to whether or not it is a good investment for you specifically.

There are only four reasons a person might not do his proper due diligence before investing his time, money, and/or reputation into a business or investment, or make any serious decision that will affect his life significantly: Laziness, hastiness, greed and/or gullibility—or a combination thereof. The person to whom the responsibility is "due" to ensure that you have all the accurate facts over which to pray and base an intelligent decision is...YOU.

Do not take the word of someone else who says, "I already checked this thing out, and it is legit!" Any honest person, with at least a basic understanding of financial responsibility, will also tell you, "But you check into it for yourself...give it some prayer...and then see what the Lord would have you do."

How about this one: "She's my third cousin's best friend...you should take her out." However, the reality might be that she is taking Prozac®, Ritalin®, and seven other prescriptions in an effort to keep her out of a rubber room in the local sanitarium. *Check things out first!*

While I am at it, let me extend my advice concerning this somewhat more. Allow me, for just a moment, to expand the concept of doing your necessary "due diligence" by addressing some issues that are all-too-common in the Church—which I will do in the next chapter with some additional "object lessons" to illustrate...

Notes:

REALTOR® is a registered trademark of THE NATIONAL ASSOCIATION OF REALTORS®.

Prozac® is a registered trademark of Eli Lilly and Company.

Ritalin® is a registered trademark of Novartis Pharmaceuticals Corporation.

—Yahshua—

Jesus—The Way, The Truth, and The Life.

"I came that they may have and enjoy life, and have it in abundance (to the full, till it overflows)."

(John 10:10b, Amplified)

NAIVETÉ

Lest we neglect some very important issues that must be addressed, let us continue our theme of "Zeal Without Knowledge" as we tackle some very disturbing tendencies in the Body of Christ. If we want to rise to higher levels of financial increase in the Church through the activation of kings—and the spoils they bring into the houses of God—then we will have to eliminate some of the foolishness. We need to properly discern which are the *legitimate* business and investment opportunities, and which are not.

We have a considerable number of people in the ProVision Network who are actively involved in some forms of legitimate multi-level marketing (MLM) businesses—also called "network" or "matrix" marketing. From health products, to detergents, to makeup, to retail shopping catalogs—you name it! These sound MLM companies are often very good channels for some to produce significant incomes—and for most, to simply add a few dollars to their monthly budgets. Regardless of the actual earnings any person achieves through their MLM businesses, they are typically phenomenal training grounds for people to develop skills in business, marketing, sales and customer relations—qualities that can benefit them beyond their network marketing enterprise.

I am one hundred percent in favor of network MLM businesses. Furthermore, Wall Street is very favorable for them as well since several such companies have stock traded on either the New

Chapter Twenty-Five

York Stock Exchange or NASDAQ. As an industry, multi-level marketing firms have a general history of success, and a reputation among investors for being potentially profitable—as with any other established industry. In short, as a form of business, channel for product and service distribution, and a method for personal income enhancement and wealth building—MLM business opportunities are potentially good vehicles for any Christian to consider when seeking God for avenues of financial increase.

Nevertheless, let me also note emphatically that I do not categorically endorse multi-level marketing for every believer—you need to seek the Lord as to what He would have you do to develop your kingly mantel. Nor do I specifically infer to endorse any specific multi-level firm in this book, regardless of how successful its marketing plan or its products and services might be.

Similarly, as a former Wall Street commodities and futures trader, I am all for various forms of "traditional" investments such as stocks, bonds, mutual funds, real estate and other similar investment channels. Extreme fortunes have been made in every one of these markets by those who knew what they were doing—and heeded wise counsel when it was given. Conversely, others have "lost their shirts" by trying to "dabble" in investments that they did not fully understand.

With these facts in mind, let me remind you of this old traditional proverb: "Not everything that glitters is gold."

CHURCH-TARGETED "OPPORTUNITIES"

Because of the ready-built network of people that comprises any local church, it is not surprising that believers involved in various types of investments or business opportunities would want to market them there. Since they are Christians, their social circle primarily revolves around their local church and other Christian groups, and naturally, they would want to share their "blessing" with their brothers and sisters in the Lord.

Furthermore, there is nothing categorically wrong for them to do so—I want to make that point clear. However, because of the inherent nature of the local church, *caution* needs to be exercised, and leadership must be appropriately wary of any group that seeks to involve a significant portion of the church's membership. Let me first address the issue of multi-level marketing and its variants…

The reason MLM businesses do so well is that the entire structure of a multi-level organization is based (knowingly or not) on biblical principles. Consider the structure of the Church: Jesus "sponsored" twelve, and then

Naiveté

they expanded the membership to another seventy-two. These grew to one hundred twenty on the Day of Pentecost, and then exploded with growth to include another three thousand that same day. A few days later, another two thousand were added as well. Within a few years, the individual members of the Body of Christ had expanded that number through evangelism into the hundreds of thousands.

Today, there are over a billion born-again believers on the planet—not counting those who have gone before us up to Heaven! One can actually say that the local church, and even the Body of Christ as a whole, is in fact a "multi-level" organization—with eternal rewards for those who diligently expand it for Him.

With that said, let me point out another old axiom that Rich, my co-author, was taught in his old Amway days: "Never mix multi-levels." The biblical principle that expression is based upon is found in the book of James:

> "A double minded man is unstable in all his ways."
> (James 1:8)

> "...purify your hearts, you doubleminded."
> (James 4:8b, NIV)

The basic principle is this: if you try to intermingle one multi-level structure with another—everybody involved becomes confused, and the entire structure becomes unstable. More than one person has developed a large and profitable multi-level organization, only to watch it collapse as he attempted to introduce an entirely different multi-level opportunity to the membership below him. The people became confused as to where to direct their loyalty and attention—and the once-profitable organization simply collapsed.

Similarly, there have been numerous pastors and other ministers who have attempted to bypass God's divine order of kingly provision to the priestly vision—and attempted to introduce some multi-level business opportunity to their congregation. Because they were people of prayer, they assumed that they had all the knowledge they needed to succeed in such endeavors. And because they saw these opportunities as answers to their prayers, they thought that their continued prayers and faith alone were enough for God to bring the increase.

Sometimes if a "king" had been given the permission to evaluate it first, he could have advised against it or suggested that it be done in a different way. However, such advice from a non-preacher has often been seen as an intrusion based on doubt and distrust in the minister's ability to hear from God. The result has been not the financial "harvest" that was expected—but rather loss of members, loss of revenue...and loss of reputation in the Christian community.

GOOD INTENTIONS, BAD DECISIONS

A few years back, there was a new multi-level company founded by people who were purported to be Christians. They seemed to have a sound product and marketing plan, and they made it their chief aim to attempt to develop their network through any ministry they could. They even named the MLM enterprise with a Christian-like name, while presenting a convincing face to the Christian community that this was an opportunity from Heaven itself.

Some very reputable ministers with good intentions and large visions "signed on" to the program and offered the business "opportunity" to their support base—before taking the time to do the appropriate "due diligence." Without really researching the company or the management team, they began to present the program widely. As it turned out, these men may have been Christians (or not...that is not my call), but they were *terrible* businessmen. As a result of their poor management, things started going awry with the company, and the situation started turning bad very quickly.

I was personally called by one of those who were involved on the ministerial level and asked to help bring this situation to a right conclusion. I spent many days in an airplane traveling from New York to other states—working to clean up the mess these honorable, but misinformed ministers had made for themselves, their ministries, and those who had trusted their judgment.

Let me emphasize for a moment from this story a very important point: do not EVER get involved in a business or investment "opportunity" because certain ministers, athletes, media personalities, or businessmen have been said to be involved. First of all, that claim may not even be *true*—ask to see it in writing from a verifiable source. Second, even if it is true, that does *not* mean that the person even knew what he/she was getting into—or had done the proper research beforehand. You need to verify each and every claim, and do your own homework.

Research appropriate resources to ensure that the company or investment is, first of all, legitimate (i.e. *legal*). Then check into the company to make sure it is soundly managed and a profitable venture.

Naiveté

Request counsel from bona fide "kings" who know something about business and investment affairs. Otherwise, you might be in for the same type of financial "ride" that many trusting believers found themselves in with the debacle that I am describing to you.

People trusted the names and reputations of these fine ministers—not realizing that a five-fold ministry *priest* should not typically be considered a sound source of counsel when it comes to *kingly* affairs such as business and investments. These men, good intentions notwithstanding, simply did not have the background to properly discern and research the situation. Nor did it even occur to them to contact anyone who did have some independent knowledge about these things—that is, until everything started falling apart.

Working with an attorney in Washington, D.C., contacting various agencies in various states, and doing a whole lot of work that would take too many pages to describe here, I managed to get the entire company shut down—and minimize the loss and damage these ministries might have incurred. Miraculously, I was also able to do it before the media got wind about it and tarnished the reputations of these fine ministries. However, several people still lost money…and many were emotionally wounded that such respectable spiritual leaders had led them astray.

"Well, Dan, my particular multi-level business has been around for years, and that would never happen in my church!" someone might protest.

Listen my brother and sister, if God has called you to be involved in a particular multi-level program—that is your affair. However, when you try to be overly zealous in acquiring new recruits from your own church—especially if you are the minister—then you have stepped across the line. God takes these things very seriously, and He is not interested in seeing His sheep hurt over some business or investment deal. Even sound "opportunities" have a way of failing to make money for some people—even causing loss of money.

When believers become involved in businesses and investments that they do not truly understand, they are generally apt to lose money—and blame the one that "got them into it" to start with. When people feel that trust was broken by someone they relied on, they suffer, the other party suffers, and the consequences could be quite detrimental, to say the least:

> "But whoso shall offend one of these little ones which believe in me, it were better for him that a

millstone were hanged about his neck, and that he were drowned in the depth of the sea."
(Matthew 18:6)

Sure, you can share a legitimate business or investment opportunity with a few people in your church to consider. However, if you are a minister or church elder, extreme caution should be used to avoid abusing a leadership position in the local church for personal or financial gain. And it should *never* be done in a ministry setting from the "platform" of leadership. Remember: Do not mix multi-levels...because a double-minded man (and ministry) is unstable in all his ways.

If you walk in a five-fold priestly office, the best way to finance your ministry is simply to make sure the kings in your congregation are properly ministered to and activated into their kingly callings. Then the financial resources will come in *appropriately*—just as God planned. Any attempt to find a "shortcut" to God's divine order of financial increase for His Church will eventually result in harm, loss...and even judgment. The "good intentions" of your heart do not compensate for a lack of conformity to God's Word.

Furthermore, whether you are a leader or not, any people you present an "opportunity" to should be encouraged to seek independent resources and counsel during the investigation—not simply to "pray about it" without doing their due diligence first. Many a gullible believer has felt "led" to get involved in something that he did not understand—and suffered later because of his naiveté. Even if it is the Lord's direction for you to follow, He would want you to know what you are getting involved in first. Remember:

"Also, that the soul be without knowledge, it is not good; and he that hasteth with his feet sinneth."
(Proverbs 19:2)

PYRAMIDS AND "GIFTING" SCHEMES

There is another form of multi-level "opportunity" that often does not even purport itself to be a multi-level system—and may actually deny it. However, the very nature of these organizations cause them to fall under the legal guidelines set up by the Federal Government of the United States of America, and their violation of the precepts of those laws cause them to be *completely illegal*.

Naiveté

You need to investigate any and every "opportunity" that comes your way by first visiting the web site of the governmental agency that oversees most businesses and marketing systems: The Federal Trade Commission (FTC). Their web site is simply www.ftc.gov, and there you can do a variety of keyword searches to find articles that will inform you of various legal—and illegal—business and marketing practices.

One such type of system that is inherently illegal is the so-called "gifting" programs and "clubs" that often target gullible Christians and churches. Many of these groups actually use scripture to attempt to justify their practices—and they nearly always *claim* to be legal under IRS laws and guidelines. The deception here is that it is not the job of the IRS to govern anything but tax law issues—and how much the IRS allows individuals to "gift" another person before being taxed is completely irrelevant to the legality of the practice itself.

While it is true that the Congress of the United States saw fit to allow people to distribute their own financial assets to their family and friends without being taxed, it never intended for groups to organize informal "gifting" clubs in an effort to generate income. While some even go so far as to have you sign a "waiver" or "disclaimer" form to feign legality, the fact is that the FTC, Congress, most state legislatures, and the court systems on the federal level (and in many states) have declared them *illegal*. Listen, if the *lawmakers* said it is illegal, then all the claims of legitimacy made by any group is null and void—and sheer deception—regardless of how "trusted" the person who shared the "opportunity" with you seemed.

All it takes is for one person to intentionally deceive someone into getting involved in something illegitimate, then everyone that second person affects—and those after him—are all spreading a lie. Deception is still deception, regardless of how much the presenter thinks it is true.

"Gifting" clubs violate the basic laws of exchange—which laws I have elaborated for you already in this book. Without exchange of goods and services, any organized effort to generate money is in violation of the basic laws of economics worldwide—and therefore federal and state laws as well.

In addition to the FTC web site, the web sites of multitudes of consumer protection groups, various State Attorney Generals' offices, and the Better Business Bureau (www.bbb.com) contain specific information about so-called "gifting" programs. Names of these dubious enterprises change like the seasons. However, several names used by such scams are listed in an article entitled "Gifting Clubs are Pyramid Schemes!" at www.bbb.

229

com. The ones cited in that article are: The Airplane, The Pit Stop, The Original Dinner Club, Women's Gifting, Jacob's Ladder, Elite Activities, and Friends Helping Friends.

Rich Vermillion, my co-author (who did much of the research for this chapter) remembered watching the local news back in his home state of Virginia one evening as members of the local "Friends Helping Friends" were hauled off to jail. Names of the leaders were publicly announced on television, and stiff fines and prison sentences were given by the courts for their illegal activities.

These things are no joke! You need to get away from anything that even *looks* like it may be similar to these schemes. The reality is that only the ignorant, the gullible, the covetous, and the foolish become involved in things like these. Stay away from them.

INVESTMENT SCAMS

I guess you could call this chapter "The Good, the Bad...and the Illegal" since we are talking about discerning the true from the false, the good from the bad, and the legitimate from the illegal. There are many "opportunities" out there—and it is *your* responsibility to be proactive and investigate them fully. Keep in mind also that just because an "opportunity" is legal does not qualify it as a good investment overall—or at least a good one for you.

Some very legal businesses, investments, and opportunities have gone down the drain due to mismanagement or economic conditions beyond their control. Once you have determined that a venture is legitimate, you need to go the "extra mile" to make sure it is a sound investment of your time, money, and reputation—regardless of what its promoters claim, or who recommends it.

Furthermore, I would be remiss if I closed out this chapter without first addressing the issue of "investments" that are often offered to believers—and especially those that specifically target them. Now, as with MLM businesses, there are legitimate investment opportunities that may come your way through a brother or sister in the Lord—even a minister (although, I stress caution here). An example of a legitimate church-oriented investment that is often seen in the Body of Christ is a *church bond program*.

When properly managed by a reputable company—familiar with federal, state, and local laws governing such investment products—such programs are valuable vehicles for congregations to build a new building, add to the existing structure, or whatever God has told them to do. Nevertheless, as was already emphasized before, you are responsible to do your research, seek informed and impartial counsel, and, of course, pray about any and every investment or "deal" that comes down the pike.

In addition to state and local governmental oversight, nearly all investments are governed by federal laws—most of which are administered by the Securities and Exchange Commission (SEC). Their web site can be found at **www.sec.gov**, and should be searched as one of many resources you use to evaluate any investment opportunity that comes your way. There are strict laws, rules and regulations that govern most investment products and vehicles—and again, it is your responsibility to be sure you are properly educated and informed.

BAD INVESTMENT

Let me conclude this chapter with another story from Rich's ministerial experience regarding how investment "opportunities" circulating through the church can go bad. Here is the story in his own words:

"Several elders, deacons, and members of a large church on the East Coast where I formerly served as an Associate Pastor became involved in an 'investment' scheme that had spread from another church in the area. This 'company' targeted the leaders of churches all along the East Coast in order to involve the largest possible number of church members—and to spread rapidly to the leaders of other churches that they knew. Capitalizing on the 'good intentions' and gullibility of these ministers and church leaders, this bogus company spread their 'investment' opportunity rapidly throughout the Body of Christ—on the backs of these leaders' reputations.

"The 'investment opportunity' was supposedly managed by a 'Christian' company that claimed to multiply its investors' money through off-shore investments. There was no prospectus given to investors (they claimed that their 'secret' strategy would be undermined if competitors knew about it), but they offered 3% per month of simple interest on every thousand dollars invested—totaling a whopping 36% per year ROI (return on investment).

"As people 'invested' their money into this scam, they started receiving checks on a monthly basis—just like promised. One person I am aware of invested so much of his savings into this scheme that his monthly 3% checks were large enough to embolden him to buy a huge house—one he could not normally afford. Sadly, the 'investors' like him were unaware that the culprits behind this scam were paying out these large monthly checks from the new monies 'invested' by new people who had heard about the 'opportunity' through one of the swindle's current victims.

"Suddenly, the 'dividends' stopped as the 'off-shore' investors took their money overseas—and left a considerable number of church leaders 'holding the bag' for their illegal activities. When the checks stopped, the law enforcement phones started ringing. Key promoters of the 'investment' scam—most of whom were completely ignorant and well meaning—were questioned or arrested. Within weeks, pastors, elders, deacons, and highly involved church members all along the East Coast were finding themselves having to post bond to keep from spending the night in jail.

"The entire life's savings of many people were completely lost, as was considerable money by many others. The man who bought the overly expensive house went into foreclosure on his home…and several investment properties he owned as well. He ended up avoiding a complete financial disaster only by the grace of God helping him to liquidate his properties—at a considerable loss, I might add. He and his wife wound up living in an apartment, having sold his entire real estate portfolio.

"The congregations of numerous churches were decimated by the financial loss many suffered. Emotionally and economically wounded members fled from their pews in droves, and the Gospel was publicly slandered by the extensive media coverage this fiasco received. If only they had sought godly and knowledgeable counsel, this could have all been avoided."

Let Rich's story about this catastrophe be an example for you to learn from. Do your research, and make sure you have learned all that you can about any investment 'opportunity' or company that asks of your time, money, or reputation. In particular, when it comes to any investment or business—make sure the facts are in writing, and that you verify them thoroughly.

Most investments, including stocks, bonds, mutual funds, money market accounts—and even "off-shore" investment opportunities—are required by federal law to provide all potential investors with a prospectus. This document must meet stringent federal standards, and be filed with the SEC to be valid and legal. ANY investment being offered that transcends state lines within the U.S. or which is multi-national MUST have this document on file with the SEC, as well as many other types of legal filings. Nearly all U.S. states also have stringent legal standards and documentation requirements.

Do your homework! Wake up to the reality that this great big world out there is not going to just drop a million-dollar nest egg in your lap "if you only invest a little of your own money." If they want your money, make sure the claims are realistic, legitimate, and completely documented with the appropriate governing authorities. In closing, I want to remind you of Paul's exhortation about God's calling on governmental authorities to administer justice, and to protect the interests of society. God actually calls them His "ministers"—sent by Him to do this very thing.

> "Everyone must submit himself to the governing authorities, for there is no authority except that which God has established. The authorities that exist have been established by God. Consequently, he who rebels against the authority is rebelling against what God has instituted, and those who do so will bring judgment on themselves. For rulers hold no terror for those who do right, but for those who do wrong. Do you want to be free from fear of the one in authority? Then do what is right and he will commend you. For he is God's servant to do you good. But if you do wrong, be afraid, for he does not bear the sword for nothing. He is God's servant, an agent of wrath to bring punishment on the wrongdoer. Therefore, it is necessary to submit to the authorities, not only because of possible punishment but also because of conscience. This is also why you pay taxes, for the authorities are God's servants, who give their full time to governing. Give everyone what you owe him: If you owe taxes, pay taxes; if revenue, then revenue; if respect, then respect; if honor, then honor. Let no debt remain outstanding, except the continuing debt to love one another, for he who loves his fellowman has fulfilled the law. The commandments, "Do not commit adultery," "Do not murder," "Do not steal," "Do not covet," and whatever other commandment there may be, are summed up in this one rule: "Love your neighbor as yourself." Love does no harm to its neighbor. Therefore love is the fulfillment of the law."
>
> (Romans 13:1-10, NIV)

Apart from a totalitarian government which prohibits the preaching of the Gospel and practice of God's higher laws—as written in His Word—the following biblical truth holds absolute: Anyone who discourages scrutiny of their business practices, marketing program, or investment procedures is definitely NOT someone with whom you want to do business. Remember, we are children of the *light*, not of darkness (Ephesians 5:8; 1 Thessalonians 5:5). Therefore, anything that does not wish to be exposed to "light" can be construed to NOT be an "opportunity from God."

PVN AND MLM

Let me conclude this chapter on a more positive note and share with you—and especially with those who are involved in some form of *legitimate* network-marketing venture—what the ProVision Network's policy is regarding your activities in our meetings. Then we'll close this chapter out with a suggestion from one of our most successful network-marketing professionals within PVN, Steven Thompson.

First, the leadership of the ProVision Network is happy to have had many people from various MLM and direct-marketing organizations join our network and share in our resources. However, we require that anyone engaged in network marketing be faithful to engage other PVN members only regarding their own products and services, and not try to turn our meetings into recruiting ventures for their MLM businesses. In other words, learn your products and services, and feel free to market them to other PVN members at our events and online. If you find some new customers through PVN that express an interest in learning more about the "opportunity" side of your business, then you can also share that aspect of your MLM venture.

However, if all you know is the "opportunity" side of your business, then you need to learn your *products* and *services* if you want to freely network through PVN events and resources. We do not condone nor allow anyone to simply attempt to recruit new "downline" by using PVN as a vehicle for such activities. Regardless of your excitement about your own particular MLM business, our other members do not appreciate being targeted for recruitment by other PVN members—but they may be excited about your products and services if you offer them.

Thus, respect the purpose of PVN by limiting your activities to sales-type networking only, when attending a ProVision event. God can provide you new "downline" through your faithful diligence elsewhere. However, to dishonor PVN and its members—or your local church and its members, for that matter—by treating its meetings and resources as "downline recruitment opportunities" will undermine your success by cutting off the blessings of God. It might also result in other unsavory consequences. Thus, share with us your products and services! We want to hear about them. However, only share your business model with those who request more information from you about that aspect of your venture.

Now, one final success tip from our beloved friend and most successful network marketer, Steven Thompson. Earning seven figures annually from his own network-marketing venture, Steven has impressed me and the other PVN leaders with his sincerity to help others, and his respect for our PVN policy regarding network marketing businesses. Thus, he has even been a featured speaker at more than one PVN event, sharing his own proven success principles with people of other MLM businesses—without even mentioning the name of his own. Since Steven is a real friend and respected contributor to the membership of PVN, Rich and I thought it would be beneficial to share one nugget he specifically recommended for this chapter.

One of the most common mistakes that Steven has witnessed regarding Christians engaged in network marketing is that of "wearing their faith on their sleeves" at their networking events. In other words, business meetings designed for the expansion of your network marketing business are not intended to be evangelistic opportunities—much like PVN meetings are not intended to be recruiting events. Sure, the Lord commanded us to all "go into the world and preach the Gospel." However, as we have discussed throughout this book in various places, your *actions* speak much louder than your words.

For the most part, you need to focus your conversation at your network marketing business events on the matter at hand. Then, as you show yourself faithful and successful in your own MLM business, you will have a larger and larger "platform" from which to share bits and pieces of your testimony with others. Continue to give God the credit for your success as your organization grows, and those who may not know the Lord will begin to get the idea that you have had supernatural assistance in your achievements. Eventually, many of them will want the same advantage themselves, and will begin to inquire. Then, give them the answer they truly need—Jesus.

Rich Vermillion was saved through the Word and testimonies sown into him through his former involvement with a particular network marketing company. However, it was the love and light shown to him by others more successful than himself that caused him to pursue the same joy he saw in them. Their glorying in their Lord was simply "salted" in a savory manner within their MLM success testimonies. Although they did not hide their Christianity at all, they cautiously refrained from *forcing* it upon others. Similarly, let your light shine as you pursue your own network marketing success—just stop beating your prospects, downline, and "cross-line" over the head with your Bible as you do.

Learn to discern when it is time to talk *business*, and when it is time to talk *faith*. Sometimes both can occur simultaneously, but be spirit-led and not simply religious. The first blesses people, and the latter turns them off to you, your business—and sometimes even the Gospel itself.

So just relax in that area, and pray for God to open the doors for you to share Jesus with people. When *He* opens the doors it is anointed. Trust Him to order your steps, and show you when your opportunity to evangelize has come.

יהוה

—Yahshua—

Jesus—The Way, The Truth, and The Life.

"I came that they may have and enjoy life, and have it in abundance (to the full, till it overflows)."

(John 10:10b, Amplified)

THE SAFETY OF GODLY COUNSEL

Chapter Twenty-Six

People need advice and proper consultation at the very beginning of starting their business. We struggle a lot with people coming to us when they are just about to go to jail. Then they get angry with us because we cannot jump in there and save them in one day. What really is frustrating is that we asked them to come and create a relationship with us from the very beginning.

We asked them to share some things with us so that we could see what they were planning to do—and help them to do it successfully according to biblical principles and sound business practices. However, they did not want to communicate the information with us at the first. Why? For fear that we might get *paid*. God forbid you get paid for keeping somebody out of jail!

I have done something to deal with that fear and hopefully allow me to minister into the lives of more people from the *onset* of their business ventures—rather than at the beginning of their court proceedings. What I have done is to make it a rule in my own life and ministry that I do not take any of the "deals" I come across in my ProVision Network meetings.

I open these opportunities up to all the people in the ProVision Network—and they get to "cherry pick" and take the ones they want. I know the basic church person's fears—"What's in it for Dan? What's his angle?" Consequently, I purposely do not take these deals myself so that I can stay objective and fair, because there are times when arbitration needs to take place.

Let me share with you a story involving some wrong thinking at the onset of a business—good and noble thinking, in terms of the way we are taught in many churches, but problematic all the same. Some new technology had been developed and a corporation was started to get it manufactured and marketed. The company had been formed, and the leadership of the company did not get the proper practical financial consultation they needed ahead of time. Because of their ignorance in how to run the finances from a business perspective, they made costly decisions, thinking they were approaching things from a scriptural standpoint.

They had decided that they would tithe upon the investment capital that they had received from investors—before they got any actual profit. They tithed on the investment dollars, which is not income—neither is it biblical:

> "Thou shalt truly tithe all the increase of thy seed, that the field bringeth forth year by year...At the end of three years thou shalt bring forth all the tithe of thine increase the same year, and shalt lay it up within thy gates..."
>
> (Deuteronomy 14:22, 28)

The question often arises, "What portion of my business finances do I tithe on?" Or, "I just sold my house...what do I tithe on?" My answer is simple: You tithe on the true net "increase"—not the gross revenue or receipts. For example: When I ran my investment firm on Wall Street, I would spend about $400,000 in employee salaries, commissions, fees, rent for my office space, leases on office equipment, etc., for every $1,000,000 I made each year. What did I tithe off of? The million? No. Do the math:

$1,000,000 minus $400,000=$600,000. So my tithe was $60,000 on that $1,000,000.

Another example: Let's say you bought your house ten years ago for $150,000 and recently sold it for $250,000. What is your tithe? $10,000? Probably not.

"Well, the gross profit is $100,000 from the sale, and since a 'tithe' is ten percent, why would it not be $10,000?" you might ask. Glad you inquired! My guess is that you probably spent a few thousand dollars fixing it up during those ten years to help increase its worth. You probably had to do a few repairs along the way as well to maintain its value. If between

The Safety of Godly Counsel

upgrades and repairs you spent about $40,000, then your net "increase" from the sale of that home is $60,000—and your tithe is only $6,000.

"That does not sound like the way most pastors teach it, Brother Dan!"

Well, that is the way I teach it to my congregation in New York, because it is true—and basic math. It might not sound like the "normal" way tithing is taught, but it does sound like love. It sounds like a pastor who is more interested in your financial health than one who is more interested in getting more money for his church.

I do not want you to cripple yourself financially by attempting to live by a false expectation of what the scriptures teach you. Tithing is a powerful tool for economic increase—if you do it correctly. Tithing excessively, thinking you are doing the will of God, can harm you financially.

Now, if the Lord *directs* you to give more than the actual tithe to your local church, another ministry—or even another person—that is an entirely different thing. I have had the Lord tell me to empty my bank accounts into the Gospel...and had Him fill those bank accounts back up with even more! Offerings are another thing entirely. What I am talking about is properly tithing—being obedient to the Scriptures with a biblical application of the tithing principle...and with accurate math.

In the case of the technology company I am using for illustration, they were not properly tithing since they had not yet received an "increase" in their operation yet. They had not yet turned a *profit*—and technically, that money they "tithed" off of was not even theirs to do that with. That money belonged to the investors, and it was intended to fund the company and bring that technology to market.

In effect, they broke trust with the people who invested in them, despite any religious "good intentions" they might have had in doing so. They took the "seed" these people intended for them to put in the ground to create a "harvest increase" (which is what should have been tithed off of), and gave it away—thereby reducing the potential harvest significantly. However, that was not all they did wrong...

Then they decided to "tithe" the shares of the corporation. (Again, the shares of the corporation have nothing to do with any "increase" or profit.) When they decided to carry this out, they sent this "tithe" of shares to about thirty-one states, eighteen of which they were not registered in as a corporation. By so doing, they broke state "Blue Sky Laws" all over the place. (In addition to the Securities and Exchange Commission's oversight, each state of the U.S. has its own securities regulations.)

"Blue Sky Laws" are the laws instituted in all fifty states which govern such issues—and carry very stiff fines for violation. These misguided believers failed to seek appropriate kingly counsel, and thus created for themselves a legal and financial quagmire that vastly exceeded any "benefit" their supposed "seed" would have produced for them—even if God did honor it. However, He could not honor it because they had violated all biblical principles of integrity and covenant by breaching the trust of the investors, and breaking the laws of the land:

> "For rulers hold no terror for those who do right, but for those who do wrong. Do you want to be free from fear of the one in authority? Then do what is right and he will commend you. For he is God's servant to do you good. But if you do wrong, be afraid, for he does not bear the sword for nothing. He is God's servant, an agent of wrath to bring punishment on the wrongdoer. Therefore, it is necessary to submit to the authorities, not only because of possible punishment but also because of conscience."
>
> (Romans 13:3-5, NIV)

In addition to breaking the law in numerous states and giving away investment capital, they had severely diluted the stocks by doing what, in their minds, was the right thing to do. This had the effect of undermining their shareholder's investments even further.

They finally came to us for help. When we started checking into the mess that they had made, and looked into what it would take to fix everything, it was going to be a $185,000 legal bill—just to file in all those states and to stop all the litigation from all the "Blue Sky Laws" they had violated. And when we told the main guy that all this legal work was necessary and simply something that he had to do…he did not want to do it. He became obstinate and resisted our involvement. He literally fought us all the way.

Furthermore, we had also made it a requirement that he let us put someone on his management team as a part of his board before we would help him get out of his dilemma. We did this so that we could ensure that we would be getting all the information we needed and not just the pieces he wanted to tell us. I did not want him to tell us he was doing "four things" when he was actually doing "sixty-four things"! That was my management team's way of ensuring we had done our "due diligence" in securing accurate information in a timely manner, before we committed to becoming personally involved.

Well, guess what? He refused. He did not want to have anyone "keeping tabs on him," even if it kept him out of prison and saved his company! He did not have a submissive heart that accepts correction—and that is probably why he did not seek godly counsel from anointed "kings" before he made such unwise decisions. Perhaps, he had never read the book of Proverbs:

> "Where no counsel is, the people fall: but in the multitude of counsellors there is safety."
>
> (Proverbs 11:14)

> "Without counsel purposes are disappointed: but in the multitude of counsellors they are established."
>
> (Proverbs 15:22)

> "For by wise counsel thou shalt make thy war: and in multitude of counsellors there is safety."
>
> (Proverbs 24:26)

The war is yours…God told you to wage it. The counsel makes sure you do it correctly so that you can safely win. Out of the mouth of two or three witnesses, every word is established. If God thought enough of this issue to say it to us three times, in three ways…in the same chapter, then we all need to take heed. Let other people speak into your life, even if you have to chase them down (or pay them!) to get them to do it.

On that last note, let me close this chapter with one last thought: Don't be so cheap—it will cost you more in the long run if you do not invest in good, sound counsel.

Let that sink in for a moment….

Even just the small monthly fee to be a member of the ProVision Network can save you untold amounts of money and heartbreak—if you will heed the multitudes of counselors available through this channel to assist you. That is why I have been "connecting the dots," so that you can get the teaching, contacts and sound counsel you need.

יהוה

—Yahshua—

Jesus—The Way, The Truth, and The Life.

"I came that they may have and enjoy life, and have it in abundance (to the full, till it overflows)."

(John 10:10b, Amplified)

HAS ANYBODY SEEN MY MONEY?

Chapter Twenty-Seven

My calling is to be a bridge-builder, or a peacemaker, and put every part of the Body together and find the divine connections for everybody. Before you find your God-ordained connections, or your golden opportunity, you must prepare and position yourself to be able to seize that opportunity when it comes.

Part of such preparing and positioning involves doing your homework and getting yourself out of debt. You need to be free from credit-card burden and get your credit score improved. You need to learn a little bit about interest rates, investing, and entrepreneurialism—and become someone who thinks like a problem-solver and not like an employee only. Even if you are working for someone else, you should learn how to think on your own and create opportunities.

We are headed for the Promised Land, and when we have victories time and time again, we must have a desire to go and help the ones who are not yet in the Promised Land. There is a lot of teaching out there that implies that the goal of prosperity is to get a Cadillac. I have heard preachers out there say, "Fake it 'til you make it." They live in a land of false prosperity which is based on maxed-out credit cards, leased luxury cars, and foolish spending—all of which is done to impress everybody.

I love meeting a guy who comes into a meeting wearing jeans, a flannel shirt, and a twelve-year-old Timex watch. I start talking to him and find out he has been retired since the age of 49. He has been developing passive income and has a million dollars put away for each of his six kids. He still drives a Buick LeSabre. He and his wife are so in love because they do not have any money pressures whatsoever. He never made more than $100,000 per year in his entire life, but he never spent a dime on interest payments. He never stretched into a lease for a Jaguar or bought a latte. He never tried to impress you with an Armani suit that he had on layaway for six years.

From the start, he refused to pay rent. He bought a home and had a mortgage, but he paid it off as fast as he could. Then he leveraged out of that house and moved into a larger house. He turned his first house into a rental property. This guy retired from the company he was working for by age 45—and was not even an entrepreneur. His mind-set about money was that it was going to work for him; he was not working for the money. He also did not care about impressing other people. He was more interested in becoming free financially.

On the other hand, I have been in boardrooms with people dressed to the hilt in $4,000 suits, wearing $10,000 cuff links, and having ties that cost more than some of my employees make in a week. They go out to dinner and order $800 bottles of wine. Their kids do not talk to them; they are in debt up to their eyeballs; they are paying $1,200 per month on a lease for a car; and they are paying $9,000 per month rent in Manhattan.

They are making money, but it goes out the window as fast as they are making it. You might try to impress me by stretching out your arm so that I can get a good look at your diamond-studded Rolex. But I will tell you what impresses me—*common sense!*

Here are a few practical financial tips. Own your home and stop renting. Start a diary and list everything that you spend every day. You must begin to pay yourself (and if you do not know what that means, you need to find out). Put some money aside into tax-deferred shelters, such as IRA's or pension plans. You must begin to save money. If that means that you downsize wherever it is that you are living, then so be it. You should be paying no more than 30% of your net income on housing.

Own your cars instead of leasing them. Keep them for a long time and take care of them because they are expensive and valuable to you. If you maintain a car well, it lasts a long time. Even be aware of how much you are paying for gas. Gas these days is expensive! If gas costs twice as much in the city, then wait until you drive out of that area and buy it somewhere else.

Has Anybody Seen My Money?

Another thing you must do if you want to get ahead financially is to stop spending money on silly things. You must take the simple little advice that I give, which includes sitting down every Sunday night and planning out what you are going to spend for that week. Do not reactively manage your money.

If you sit down on Sunday night and think through all your spending for the week, then when unexpected things come up, you are at least aware of the fact that you overspent. It at least becomes a decision you make, instead of money automatically disappearing. When you do that one thing, you will be more *aware* of how many nickel-and-dime purchases you make that are really putting you into a jam. You will begin to take responsibility for why you are where you are. Most of us do not look at our financial life as directly as we need to.

Find out what your credit score is—and how easy it is to improve it. There may be some things that are holding your credit score down and could keep you from buying a property that could make you a hundred grand. You have to be ready for such opportunities when they come across your path. You cannot seize an opportunity without money in your pocket.

Get with somebody and assess any kind of credit that you have, including your mortgage, a car loan, equipment loans, and credit card debt. You need to know what your options are because it makes no sense to be paying more interest than you should.

You must face your enemy, who is yourself—meaning your habits and the way you look at things. You need to start thinking about what it is costing you to be that way. Some people go out to eat because it brings them emotional relief from the fact that their credit cards are maxed-out. They live in numb land. They think everything is bumping along okay because their mortgage payment was made and they are only a few days late on their car payment. They go to the coffee shop and do not have any cash, so they buy a latte on their credit card.

Everything we do is a seed and has an effect down the road. Yes, we want to be in that place in which we are not thinking about every little penny we spend and in which we can live luxuriously. But the way we get there is by having the mind-set of, "We will do that when we get there." When you are living from week to week, from paycheck to paycheck, lavish does not make sense!

You may think you know how to budget. You may think it is as simple as listing out your liabilities on one side and your income on the other. But the amount you spend on housing, insurance, food, clothes, education, etc., and the amount you should be saving should all be budgeted according to what percentage of your income should be applied to each area.

Budgeting should also include moving you towards a five-year plan. You should look ahead and ask yourself where you will be in five years. Ask yourself, "Where am I going to be in five years? How much am I going to be making? Am I going to get into that place called 'passive income' in five years? How do I increase my income and control my outgo?" These are all part of budgeting and are things you may not have thought of.

We need to learn the basics of budgeting—for example, 10% tithe, 30% housing, and certain percentages for food, clothing, utilities, insurance, etc. But after we have mastered that, we need to take our finances to another level and move from a budget mentality and into an opportunity mind-set. When your mind is on budgeting, it is problem-oriented and focused on circumstances. It is pain-oriented so it makes a person want to talk. But when that person moves into the realm of looking for opportunities, he becomes more interested in listening to others concerning their needs.

Another thing you need to do to make sure your financial life is in order is to have a will, no matter how young you are. You need to make sure that it is always in place. I know that many of us are believing that we are going to go up in the rapture, but that is actually a good reason to have a will because more than likely, not everybody in your family is going up.

There is also something called "estate planning," which involves protecting your inheritance so that it goes to your children and so that they pay the least amount of taxes possible. Also, you can find out how to make sure your money can be left to a church or another organization instead of paying the government.

Furthermore, you should have all of your insurance policies checked to make sure that no silly little mistake that you make in your life ends up putting you back ten years in your financial plan. You should have your financial plan checked by professionals.

You also need to make sure that you are getting regular physicals. If you cannot afford it because you do not have insurance, then you need to speak up about that so that someone can help you. The littlest thing could set you back financially. My wife recently had an operation that would have cost us $20,000, but we had insurance that covered it. But someone who cannot afford insurance certainly cannot afford a $20,000 hospital bill. So what often happens is that the person does not get the operation, the situation worsens, and more complications take place—all because the person has no medical insurance.

What am I saying here?

Expand your thinking to look at your life from the "bigger picture" of how each part of it affects others—and what you can do to move beyond where you are now to where you need to be. One effective way you can do that is to find people who are already there who will mentor you in different areas in which you need to come up. When you are wise and duplicate wise men and women who are teaching you, then you are going to get a wise man's results.

—Yahshua—

Jesus—The Way, The Truth, and The Life.

"I came that they may have and enjoy life, and have it in abundance (to the full, till it overflows)."

(John 10:10b, Amplified)

"IT ISN'T DONE"

In 1904, there was an incredible revival in the country of Wales (part of the British Isles in Europe). The power of God was manifest to such a powerful extent that people were saved by the droves in Christian gatherings and churches—to the degree that the rugby matches were shut down for lack of interest! The modern American equivalent would be like the Super Bowl being cancelled because of revival! The people were so turned on to God that they just couldn't care less about non-spiritual activities like sporting events. That is something for us to shoot for! Hallelujah!

During this time period, there were these two brothers who were living there in Wales. One brother went to church one morning and the other decided to play hooky. But they met later to get a bun and cup of coffee after church. The brother who had skipped church said to the one who had attended, "Is the sermon done?" And the other brother said, "Oh, it's been preached, but it certainly isn't done."

What did he mean by that? Just because the pastor has stopped ministering the message doesn't mean that the message is supposed to stop ministering to us! We are to be changed by the Word of God that is ministered from the pulpit, and carry that change with us from that moment on—everywhere we go.

Well, the message of total, whole-life prosperity has been preached by many faithful ministers throughout the world. The message that, "God is love, and He is not interested in having His children broke, starving, and lacking in this world's goods" has been revealed from Heaven and taught to the Body of Christ through many vessels.

Now we have got to get to work.

Have you ever been to a carnival? Maybe you've seen the movie, *Carousel*. In that movie, there was a "barker" calling people in by saying things like, "Oh, come see the thousand-pound lady! Come see the world's largest merry-go-round!" Really, what that person does is call people to the amusement park away from their normal activities. He is getting their minds off of the cares of the world. That was his purpose.

But what has happened to some of us is that we are waiting for our ship to come in. Our mind-set is that of, "Well, next week things will be better;" or, "Maybe in two weeks or two months…" We are standing around waiting—waiting for somebody to make our life all better. If you are one of those people, you need to know that *you* are the one who is going to make your life a success!

No one is going to do it for you. Jesus has already done that, and you will know it if you *Shabbath* first. You need to go to Jesus and discover, or re-discover, what it is that you are supposed to be doing. You must reestablish inside of yourself—at the deepest core of who you really are—that you are more than adequate; that you have what it takes to obey what God has called you to do.

There are some practical things that you must do financially. You must have an understanding of the nuts and bolts of laying a strong foundation for financial prosperity, such as budgeting, credit repair, and taking the necessary steps in improving your financial plan from your mortgage to various investments, etc. You must do the practical things to prosper—but will you? Some people are not ready to get their financial life in order because it just does not fit into their kids' little league schedule. Such blasé thinking kills your chances of being truly successful in God.

People are dying all over the world. People are being converted to Islam. People are falling into Mormonism. People are falling into denominational, non-Holy Ghost, no-hope Christianity. All because we will not budget, fix our credit, stop impulse buying, and start getting serious about the Kingdom—and our place in it.

You are a *king*! You are a *royal priesthood!* And with that privilege comes a great responsibility. You will fail and make mistakes, but you are not allowed to quit. We cannot just give in church, then go home, and wait to receive. We must walk in the kingly anointing that God has placed on us and have dominion. And the way we get there is to proactively give and serve on the six levels of prosperity—spiritually, physically, mentally, emotionally, socially, and financially. We need to get our houses in order!

We need to get around people who are doing what we want to do and respect them. You already know everything *you* know! Learn what someone else might have to share. Many times people come and get in the presence of my experts—my investment bankers, my lawyers, my accountants, my artists, and the other guys who are in my different business groups—and they sit there and do all the talking.

Here are some guys who have produced huge things, and they say, "Dan, when are these people going to get it? We really don't need this guy who doesn't have a job telling us what we are supposed to be doing." Half the people in the Body of Christ are yelling at me and saying, "How come you don't let me meet So-And-So?" I say, "Man, you don't even treat me right! How are you going to treat him?"

You know, when the student is ready…the master appears.

I teach this revelation all over the country, and sometimes my wife will say to me, "Why are you traveling around the country? They don't get it." For the most part, I am at the individual chapter meetings more than the people that live there are.

I am a warrior. I know that the Body of Christ has to get out of debt. I know that there is a trillion-dollar flow for the believers to have. I see it every day. I fight it every day. My car was parked six spaces from where the bomb went off in 1993 in the terrorists' first attempt at destroying the World Trade Center. My church went up in flames in 2001 when they attempted it again—and succeeded! I just tried to buy a building on Wall Street and the Muslims bought it right out from under me. This is no joke! People are being beheaded and cut up in different parts of the world because we are lazy with our finances and with our health, and with our spiritual lives.

Those of us who have been hearing the covenant message of prosperity for several years have no excuse. We are going to be responsible for much of the progress that is absent in the Body today. There are a lot of good things happening in the church, but we need a strategic plan to transform this earth into the Lord Jesus' footstool:

> "But when this priest had offered for all time one sacrifice for sins, he sat down at the right hand of

God. Since that time he waits for his enemies to be made his footstool..."
> (Hebrews 10:12-13, NIV)

Our current President, George W. Bush, believes in God. But there are not enough of us who operate in the dominion principles and who stand up and say, "This is right, and that is wrong." And the only way we are going to be listened to is when we do what Jesus told us to, which is to "occupy until He comes" (Luke 19:13).

Although I am not just teaching you how to budget or repair your credit, you need to do both of those things (and more)—now. You need to make sure you have the absolute best product for the mortgage on your home if you have one, and do not be ashamed about having a mortgage. You need to do your homework and pay attention to your insurance policies, investments, bank accounts, etc. Why? Because we are not allowed to continue to be financially lazy and ignorant.

As a provocateur, I am here to say to you, "Get it together! Now!" This message must be preached. You must get your financial house in order. You must budget and get your credit repaired. You must get your house completely financed the way it should be, so you are free to seize financial opportunities when they arise. This is not only about giving checks to your church—it is about buying up buildings in your town. It is about your beginning to own everything around you.

God has already made you "the head and not the tail, above only and not beneath" in Christ Jesus, but the key to having it become a reality in your life is that you *obey* Him—not just *confess* it is yours (Deuteronomy 28:13). You are not going to confess yourself into this kind of prosperity. Rather, you are already in it!

My message to you is, "Don't get left out!" Do not get left behind. This "fixin' to get ready" thing has got to stop. You have to get ready now! You need to *dalet*—humble yourself to receive the Word of the Lord that is coming to you today. Remember what Jesus asked about John?

> "And as they departed, Jesus began to say unto the multitudes concerning John, What went ye out into the wilderness to see? A reed shaken with the wind?"
> (Matthew 11:7)

Do you want to listen to somebody that is just going to tell you what

Conclusion

you want to hear? Did you pick up this book expecting me to stroke your ego and tell you that you are already doing everything just right in your life and finances? Would you rather have someone just come to your local church and tell you, "Oh, praise the Lord, you are going to the greatest church in America! You are perfect just the way you are"? You *are* perfect in God's eyes as a *seed* (remember the acorn), but now you have to develop it.

The Word of God is not composed exclusively of the "motivational" passages we all love. "Greater is He Who is in you…," "You are more than a conqueror…," "You are a royal priesthood,"—yes, these are all in there. However, do not forget that the Word of God is for reproof and correction also:

> "All scripture is given by inspiration of God, and is profitable for doctrine, for reproof, for correction, for instruction in righteousness: That the man of God may be perfect, thoroughly furnished unto all good works."
> (2 Timothy 3: 16-17)

It comes back to that word "freedom" we discussed in Chapter 20—to be free from obligation and purged from iniquities and bad habits. That takes work.

To get there, it also means you will need to learn how to take loving rebuke. You take instruction from someone who has "been there, and done that" before you—and do it all with a good attitude that says, "I need this to become better." Getting there also takes fellowship, relationship, and transparency.

Finally, if you are diligent to do these things, and whatever specific instructions the Lord directs you to do along with them, then you will see the "divine provision" of God come alive in your life. You will accelerate towards your destiny. Sometimes just when we think we have mastered something or finished our training, we have really just begun. Nevertheless, the good news is that:

> "And I am convinced and sure of this very thing, that He Who began a good work in you will continue until the day of Jesus Christ [right up to the time of His return], developing [that good work] and perfecting and bringing it to full completion in you."
> (Philippians 1:6, AMP)

I trust that the Lord has spoken to you throughout these pages. If He has, then Rich and I have done our work, and our purpose in this book has been fully accomplished. Be sure, however, that you act on what God has spoken to your heart. Remember, faith without obedient action (works) is dead (James 2:17). So, get proactive with what He has revealed to you by His Spirit.

May God's "divine provision" be yours as you lovingly pursue Him… and obediently pursue your destiny in Him. Peace, happiness, wholeness, and prosperity be to you. Or in Hebrew…

שלום

—Shalom—

RESOURCES:

BargainChristianBooks.com

An outstanding online Christian bookstore and more! This phenomenal site offers over 150,000 books, gift items, homeschool supplies, music, software and more—with most items 20% or more off the suggested retail price everyday. Even more exciting is the huge selection of family-friendly and Christian videos!

BargainChristianBooks.com also has services links to additional resources and products through other Christian providers. Without question, this site truly offers believers excellent value when seeking "bargains" or doing their shopping online. Visit them today!

ProVisionNetwork.org

A growing international network of Christian business owners and professionals that is advancing the Kingdom! Founded by Wall Street millionaire and Christian pastor, Dan Stratton, this organization seeks to network those who have business and professional callings with each other to help propagate the gospel by increasing the financial resources of Christ's Church.

Their web site includes Dan's phenomenal biography, details about the network, and links to many Christian resources and businesses. Whether you are a minister, professional, business owner or consumer—there are plenty of things on this site to bless you. Check them out today!

ThriftyGetaway.com

Airline tickets, hotels, car rental, vacation and cruise packages—at prices lower than most of their secular online competitors! You should consider shopping ThriftyGetaway.com before buying from any non-Christian site. Why? You are not only supporting the business of another believer, but saving money to boot!

The entrance page (which you should bookmark) even offers you an opportunity to learn how to become a freelance travel agent and save even more—plus get special perodic "agent only" travel incentives!

Be sure to visit ThriftyGetaway.com and book your future travel arrangements for less!

(Note: Be sure to remember that there is no "s" on the end of "getaway" if you want to be sure and find the Christian URL, and not one of its secular competitors.)

FEATURED NEW PARADIGM TITLE:

ISBNs:
1-933141-03-4
("paperback")
1-933141-04-2
(e-Book edition)

ABOUT THE BOOK:

The premier real estate book for Christians, Possessing Your Promised Land is the believer's guide to SUPERNATURAL real property acquisition. Combining the author's own extensive knowledge as a REALTOR® with his numerous miraculous testimonies, this book seeks to inform Christians and non-Christians alike in the practical considerations of buying lands and homes, while intriguing the reader with his remarkable stories of supernatural property transactions. Readers will readily find their faith encouraged to acquire properties for their own homes or investments—while gaining the practical wisdom necessary to actually see it happen. A tremendously helpful *Glossary of Real Estate Terms* is also included, along with Rodney's listing of *Scriptures for Possessing Your Promised Land.*

Paradigm Resources

From the book's faith building content, to its supportive resources, this title an extremely adept Judeo-Christian resource for those who are desiring to acquire real property.

ABOUT THE AUTHOR:

H. Rodney Johnson is a gifted writer, speaker, worship leader, and a veteran of the real estate industry for nearly twenty years. An experienced real estate broker, Rodney has been personally involved in property transfers totaling well-over a hundred million dollars. He has been the top CENTURY 21 Fine Homes and Estates™ agent in California's San Fernando Valley since 2001.

Rodney has been featured on HGTV's number one rated television program, *House Hunters,* and also serves his industry as a real estate coach to other real estate professionals around the nation. His blog site, accessible from www.rodneyjohnson.com, also provides phenomenal resources to home buyers, investors, real estate professionals and other people interested in keeping up to date with the real estate industry and related current events.

FROM THE BACK COVER:

"...Within these pages, Rodney has provided the Body of Christ an exquisite tool with which to begin the task of obeying our Lord's command in Luke 19:13 to "occupy until I come"... Herein, Rodney points the way to lay hold of significant biblical keys that will enable your taking possession of actual lands and houses. Nothing could be more practical for anyone, and no one is a more verified tutor or aide in such personal and business pursuits than Rodney...." —JACK HAYFORD

"Possessing Your Promised Land is full of hope, faith and encouragement to believe your real estate dreams really can come true...." —LISA WHELCHEL

"...Rodney uses biblical examples and characters to show us what we need to do in the 'here and now.' I encourage you to read Possessing Your Promised Land and then do what the title suggests." —MICHAEL REAGAN

Available everywhere!

You can obtain it at your favorite local bookstore—or you can order it *online* at BargainChristianBooks.com!

RECOMMENDED READING LIST

To expand your business and financial intellect beyond the foundation already laid through *Divine ProVision*, the following titles have been recommended by the authors. Although most of these titles are not geared specifically toward the Christian reader, *most* are written by Christians—and *all* of them are compatible with the Judeo-Christian priciples of morality, ethics, and faith.

This list is given in the recommended order of reading for those believers who have not yet obtained—but desire to acheive—total financial freedom quickly. However, since every person's financial situation is unique, these recommendations are not to be construed as specific financial advice from the authors or Paradigm Seed Publishers, Inc. regarding your individual situation. Prayerfully select each title as you seem directed by the Lord.

Finally, these books listed were all available at a significant discount online at **BargainChristianBooks.com** when this text was written.

Financial Peace Revisited, by Dave Ramsey

Rich Dad, Poor Dad: What The Rich Teach Their Kids about Money—That The Poor And Middle Class Do Not!, by Robert T. Kiyosaki with Sharon L. Lechter C.P.A

The Total Money Makeover: A Proven Plan for Financial Fitness, by Dave Ramsey

Becoming A Millionaire God's Way: Getting Money To You and Not From You, by Dr. C. Thomas Anderson

Rich Dad's Cashflow Quadrant (the sequel to the best-seller, *Rich Dad, Poor Dad*), by Robert T. Kiyosaki with Sharon L. Lechter C.P.A.

Selling Among Wolves: Without Joining the Pack!, by Michael Q. Pink

The Bible Incorporated, compiled by Michael Q. Pink

Who Moved My Cheese?, by Spencer Johnson M.D.

Rich Dad's Guide To Investing (book three of the best-selling *Rich Dad, Poor Dad* series), by Robert T. Kiyosaki with Sharon L. Lechter C.P.A.

Note: Be sure to also watch for more title releases by Paradigm Seed Publishers, Inc.—including subsequent additions to the *Divine ProVision* Series, as well as related titles by other powerful authors. You can visit us today at www.pspublishers.com for the latest updates.

Find these titles *and more* at...

...or at your favorite local bookstore.

Your Notes:

Your Notes:

Your Notes:

Your Notes:

Your Notes:

Your Notes:

Your Notes:

Your Notes:

Your Notes:

Your Notes:

Your Notes:

Your Notes:

Printed in the United States
75662LV00003BA/220-225